FOR HIRE: THE INTIMATE ADVENTURES OF A GIGOLO

Born in a small town in Western Australia, Luke Bradbury was brought up to enjoy the simple things in life, especially the outdoors. He decided to come to London after the death of his father. His many hobbies include Australian Rules Football, swimming, soccer and generally staying in good shape. He now lives back in Australia.

By the same author

UNDERCOVER: The Adventures of a Real Life Gigolo

LUKE BRADBURY

For Hire: The Intimate Adventures of a Gigolo

With Catherine von Ruhland

AVON

AVON
A division of HarperCollins*Publishers*
77–85 Fulham Palace Road,
London W6 8JB

www.harpercollins.co.uk

This Paperback Edition 2012

1

First published in Great Britain by
HarperCollins*Publishers* 2009

A catalogue record for this book is
available from the British Library

ISBN-13: 978-0-00751-385-7

Printed and bound in Great Britain by
Clays Ltd, St Ives plc

MIX
Paper from
responsible sources
FSC
www.fsc.org FSC C007454

A special thank you to Keshini Naidoo and the rest of the team at AVON/HarperCollins and to Diane Banks.

To Catherine, thank you for another great book
and for capturing my story perfectly through
hard work and many late nights.

Along for the ride

Don't move a fucking muscle. Julie's cold fingers pad over my hard dick which is cradled in the palm of her other hand. I hold my breath. Julie's focus is just as taut, her attention fixed on the wet plaster she is spreading over my entire cock. I watch her from above the hardening cast that runs all the way down from my shoulders to just above my knees.

Julie's top teeth bite into her lower lip with the concentration. Her fingernails. That bite. The cast's brittle white outer shell. It is *me* that is putty in *her* hands.

She could do whatever she wants to me.

I breathe out. She catches my eye.

'Not much longer,' she smiles, and the lines crinkle around her eyes.

She takes a step back to observe her handiwork.

'Looking good,' she mumbles, 'looking good.'

Julie picks up her mug of tea from the paint-splattered trestle table and takes a sip. I lick my lips. My own mug sits tantalizingly out of reach.

'It shouldn't take too long to set, and then we'll have you out of there. Free at last,' she winks.

While we wait, I try to imagine what I must look like from Julie's point of view. A fit young guy caught in suspended animation in the middle of her studio, and on the way to giving her a new coat hanger. Or whatever she plans to do with my sculpture.

I was Julie's muse, her model, her material all in one. It was my dick that had got me this far. But standing here now, I had a hunch that maybe sometimes it was taking me *too* far. Because the only reason I was here was because of my prime-quality cock, legs and torso. I could be *anyone*.

I now knew what it felt like to be treated like a lump of meat. My hands might have been free, which meant that I could help Julie a little with her work, but I had to be careful, as the very movement of my underarm muscles threatened to do serious damage to Julie's cast.

I'd shake my head at what my escort work got me caught up in – If I didn't fear that moving my neck and chest muscles might ruin Julie's artwork.

I'm not sure what I'd expected when Julie had called earlier in the week and asked me to help her out; I was just happy to be able to do so. When she'd told me she'd need to cover me in plaster for her artwork, it had taken me right back to the beginning of this game when I'd needed photos for the agency websites and paired up with a photography student who wanted snaps for his portfolio. We'd been doing each other a favour.

Even though Julie was paying me, I still liked the idea of being an artist's muse for the afternoon. And who knows? I might end up on someone's wall.

As long as none of my clients recognizes me!

In my mind's eye, I could see the metal length of me – from breastplate down to my thighs and, jutting from the midst of it, a shiny golden cock – featuring in a Sunday supplement or a famous gallery. And someone pointing out, 'I know him. He was a good lay.' Well, of course, *that* went without saying.

Yup, it was Dick who was more of interest to Julie than Muggins here. I couldn't help wondering if I was the one being dragged along for the ride.

I didn't know much about art, but this situation certainly *felt* surreal. Me standing here, butt-naked except for the cold damp paste that Julie had been slathering over me. I'd had enough trouble finding Julie's cottage. My scooter had stuttered up a dirt-track country road in Kent to reach here and it felt like the back of beyond. I'd barely seen another house once I'd turned off the motorway slip road. She'd taken me along a garden path to a renovated barn filled with her artist's stuff. Yeah, this was all happening in the middle of nowhere. It meant we were free to do whatever we liked. And no one would know anything about it. But then again, I'd laid myself wide open to *anything* happening. And that thought sent a shiver of vulnerability down my stiff spine.

Julie set down her mug, and took a walk around her masterpiece. I relaxed a little too, beneath my solid second skin. From where I was standing I couldn't help feeling pretty impressed by the shape my cock was in. I'd feared that I wouldn't be able to remain erect while the plaster set. But Julie had made sure that was sorted by leaving my dick until last. Her hands sweeping the whiteness over my chest and then up my legs had certainly fired me up.

Julie was back in front of me, looking me up and down, assessing me. She clapped her hands, then rubbed her palms together like she was satisfied with how things were going. She was ready for the next stage.

I still had to remain stock-still. She looked me straight in the eyes, her fingertips clipped over the upper edge of the cast at my collarbone. 'Right, Luke, this is the moment of truth. It's time to get you out of these dry clothes.'

Julie winced as she worked as if the plaster was being pulled away from *her* skin. The trouble was that the skin was mine, and as the cast was drawn away from my body it was dragging my body hairs with it.

I whistled with pain through my teeth, and then exhaled. There was a responding glint of concern in Julie's eyes.

'Careful,' she whispered, as if she was directing herself as much as me. 'Not long now.'

I rolled each released shoulder, enjoying the freedom my arms now felt. Julie drew the cast away from my diaphragm and a hairline crack suddenly appeared across the concave smoothness, splitting the plaster apart. The chest-piece slipped to the floor and shattered into lumps like chalk.

'Shit, shit, shit,' rattled Julie. She was still gripping tight to the lower casing. I froze and said nothing.

After all, *everything* was in her hands.

Julie bowed her head, wondering what to do next. She then looked up at me.

'It's salvageable. I hope.'

She bit her lip, as though she was trying to stop herself quivering. It wasn't working.

It wasn't exactly as if she had much alternative – unless she wanted to begin all over again. Standing here for another few hours certainly wasn't my idea of a good time.

Then Julie rallied, as if making a new plan. 'No,' she reassured herself, her voice stronger now. 'I can make something of this.'

She picked up a scalpel and began to lever it under the remaining edges of the casing. Her other hand was round the cock-shield as if she was using it as a handle to steady herself. The cast came away from my lower half without any trouble at all.

She settled it down on the floor in front of her knees. Her whole face beamed.

'Go and get yourself a shower, Luke, while I finish off here.'

I slung my clothes back on and headed back to the house. The golden light in its windows promised warmth against the late afternoon's growing darkness.

My entire body savoured the rush of hot water. My limbs relaxed and shifted in pleasure like they had just woken up. I closed my eyes and stood directly beneath the shower nozzle and raised my head to let the water pour over me.

I opened them again at the sudden opening of the curtain. Julie stepped into the cubicle, as naked as I was. This was more like it. I didn't know if it was her plan all along – whether this was exactly why she'd ordered me in the first place. For the art, and then the show afterwards. I couldn't care less, to be frank. I was only happy to oblige.

Julie's hands once more glided all over my body, her touch mixing with the streams of water. I pulled her to me, wrapped my arms around her and kissed her. She slipped beyond my grasp.

Julie looked longingly at my hardened cock. *Again.* Her eyes flickered up to meet mine at the very same moment that her hands encircled my dick.

'I'm going down,' she cackled, dropping to her knees and drawing my prick between her dripping wet lips. Her tongue flickered to greet me.

The rush of water seemed to get louder around us. Who cared where my cock had dragged me to this time? The pleasure was all mine.

A New Beginning

Eva, her husband Lars, and I came at exactly the same time.

God, I am so on top of my game.

My eyes met Eva's beneath me. Hers shone with raw bliss.

She flicked a look across at Lars, sitting low down in his armchair, still collecting himself. Eva wanted *him* to have the pleasure of her pleasure. Apart from the sex, I wasn't needed at all.

Fine by me, love.

Eva's arm reached out to stroke her husband's leg. I didn't have to turn to look at Lars. From the look of love his wife was giving him, I knew his scheme had worked for him as much as for Eva.

Because Lars had hired me as her birthday surprise. On top of the suite at the Dorchester Hotel he'd booked especially. Eva had had no idea I'd be turning up as her extra treat.

The surprise had made things a bit awkward to begin

with. I'd been hired before by this pair when they came up to London from Cornwall. But since Eva hadn't been expecting me, I couldn't help wondering as I travelled upstairs whether she'd be in the mood. Suppose she was looking forward to a night alone with Lars? Though I was sure I'd be fine once she'd clocked me and realized what was coming to her.

Fortunately, as soon as I'd stepped into the suite, I could tell that we were all on the same page. Lars had made sure of that.

'Ta-da!' he'd announced, raising his glass of champagne to his wife: 'My present to you, darling. Luke. For you to unwrap.'

I'd bowed as dashingly as I could. 'Happy Birthday, Eva,' I'd beamed.

She'd made a point of looking me up and down, the smile creeping up her face topped by the sheer lust blazing from her eyes.

'Just what I've always wanted,' she'd laughed.

Eva released herself from my hold, slipped out of the bed and crept on to her husband's lap. Lars enfolded her in a bear hug and buried his face in her coppered brown hair.

Eva was a slight woman in her mid-thirties, with a sleek figure and cute neat ass that just begged a guy to run his hands over its contours. Lars was a few years older than his wife, and far taller than me. I'd presumed that I was doing well as a six-footer. Yet he was lean and must have been close to seven foot, and a brunette like Eva. When we'd first met a month or so ago, I'd been surprised to learn these two were Norwegians. With my blondish hair, I looked more Scandinavian than either of them.

I didn't want to look as if I was gawping at them entwined in each other, so I stared out of our sixth-floor window towards the shadowy treetops of Hyde Park, shaking in the wind. An image of the Dorchester's phallic tower flickered through my mind. I smirked to myself. Lars was sure making a statement when he'd booked this place for our rendezvous.

I'd done the job I'd been hired for – to be hors d'oeuvre to Lars's main course. I collected my clothes, nodded my 'She's all yours' at him over her shoulder, and got a grin and a 'Thanks, mate' in return. Creeping into the sitting room to dress, I let myself out.

I took the lift down to the ground floor, satisfied that I'd left a couple of clients pleased with my service. *Happy Birthday to you, doll!*

I checked my watch as I hotfooted it across the lobby. It had just turned midnight and I needed to get home. There were people milling around the reception area but I took no notice. I'd pick my scooter up from round the side of the hotel and head back to my bed. I'd had a run of late nights this past week and needed to catch up on the zeds.

I stepped out of the main doors behind a glamorous-looking couple who were being snapped by a barrage of paparazzi. As I turned left out of the hotel, I took a quick look back. I instantly recognized the two of them. She was Shelley Yates, an American movie starlet who I'd read in yesterday's paper was in town for the release of her new film. And on her arm was Guy Raynor, an English pop star who was last year's cool thing and sure needed the publicity *now*. You couldn't tell if the pairing up meant anything to either of them, but they were milking the attention for all they were worth.

Good luck to 'em.

But I was too damn tired to desire such sparkle at this time of night. I walked away from the cameras, down the side road, stepped onto my scooter and was away from there.

As far as I was concerned, Sunday was meant for lounging around, maybe watching the football on the box in the afternoon. I'd benefited from my lie-in and was in the mood for not doing very much at all.

The Girls seemed to have the same idea – I could hear them pottering around as I pulled on my jeans and a T-shirt and cut across the hall to make myself some brunch.

Carrie was sitting at the kitchen table, the dregs of her own breakfast strewn around her. She'd pushed her plate and the jars of jam and marmalade out of her way and was engrossed in her Sunday redtop.

I started to prepare my own breakfast, putting bread in the grill and cracking a couple of eggs into the pan. Carrie looked up from her paper as I hovered beside the oven.

'You had another night on the tiles? I didn't hear you come in last night.'

I was unsure whether this was Carrie's way of finding out my business. Since I'd moved in earlier in the month, I'd managed to fob my three new flatmates off about what I actually got up to, but I was very aware that that was going to be more difficult to get away with the longer I lived here. But for now, I was prepared to put that aside and only cross *that* awkward bridge when I came to it.

'Oh, I can assure you I came in last night!' I grinned.

'Clubbing, were you?'

'Oh, I had a night of it, y'know,' I lied.

I decided to shift her focus away from me. 'What about yourself, Carrie? Were you and the girls out larging it?'

'You bet,' she moaned, clutching her head in mock pain.

'The others are still paying for it, I'm afraid, so no bashing any pots and pans when you're putting together your fry-up, thanks.'

'No worries,' I replied, focused on the two eggs crisping round the edges just the way I liked them.

I sat down opposite Carrie with my breakfast and poured myself a mug of tea.

'Anything happening in the world today?'

I was more interested in the back page, but I knew that the girls never read that far. Carrie flapped the front pages back and forward.

'No *X Factor* scandal today, I'm afraid,' she mused.

'God, I don't know what the world's coming to!' I spluttered. 'What, have they got a blank front page or something?'

She flipped a wry grin across at me: 'Might as well be, eh?'

None of us took the paper seriously. It was light relief of a Sunday. Hangover reading. But then again, the tabloids did help me keep in touch with who was in and who was out in celeb land – and that couldn't but help me in my work. Especially some of the circles I found myself in. If only to massage some famous person's ego by not looking blank when they told me what TV show they'd been on or pop group they were in. Not that I could let on to my new flatmates about *that*.

I let Carrie get on with reading and laid into my fry-up. God, there was something about a good English breakfast that set the world to rights whatever was in the news.

Carrie got up from her seat. 'I need to shake the girls up. We're off shopping this afternoon. You want to read the paper?'

'Thanks,' I mumbled through my full mouth.

She left me to finish off my breakfast alone.

I pushed my empty plate away and dragged the paper across the table towards me. I turned the pages without looking too closely at anything. My mind wasn't ready for any proper news. I wasn't up to looking at much more than the pictures, to be honest.

I stopped at the celeb pages. They snapped people coming out of the same nightclubs and restaurants that a good number of my clients hung out at. I focused on the photos, though I wasn't taking a lot in. My head was still throbbing. And then a picture of a young woman and a guy managed to get my attention through the haze of my half-asleep brain.

Those two last night! Shelley Yates and Guy Raynor.

That brought me to my senses quick-smart. I took a closer look. They were standing in front of the Dorchester. For a second, I was back leaving the foyer through the glass door to be met by the paparazzi shield.

Oh fuck. No.

The thought hit me before I saw the truth in the photo. If they were being shot just as I was coming out, then chances are the paps had caught me too.

Panicking slightly, I smoothed out the page to take a closer look. *Right first time.* There was me at the back of the photo, heading out of the doors to my scooter round the corner. Only from where anyone else was sitting reading the paper at this time of the day, it appeared that I was part of Shelley and Guy's entourage.

A wave of cold fear swept over me. Suppose someone out there who knew me – one of my clients, say, who definitely knew what I might be doing coming out of a top hotel around midnight – saw this picture, put two and two together and made five? And then all they needed to do was phone up the same paper and let them know about The Celeb Couple's Appointment with The Hooker.

Oh God.

It wouldn't take too many steps for the path to lead to my door. And my cover to be well and truly blown. And, God knows, in those sorts of stories it was always the escort or call girl who came off worst.

I closed my eyes for a second, half hoping that the picture would have disappeared when I opened them again. But it hadn't, and Kirstie was breezing into the kitchen.

'Morning, Luke,' her voice rang out, crashing into my dread.

I rallied, turned over the page, and greeted her with a sunny, 'And a good morning to you too!', silently praying that she hadn't spotted my unease when she entered the room.

I sipped at my tea and tried to read the rest of the paper as she busied herself around me. My mind was elsewhere. Even the sports pages didn't do it for me. All I could think of was the photograph and me hovering in the background, just asking to be identified.

Kirstie sat down with her bowl of cereal. She ate a spoonful, and reached across for the paper.

'You finished with this?' she asked, her mouth full of cornflakes.

'Yup,' I replied, 'not that there's anything worth reading this morning.'

I felt sick with nerves. There was nothing I could do. The morning paper always did the rounds of the flat of a Sunday. It wasn't my paper to snatch away and hide in my room – its absence would have been noticed. And if I'd simply removed the celeb spread, that would have been noticed too. It was the page we *all* turned to.

That hit me. Carrie must have seen the pages before I'd even entered the kitchen. Had she seen me? *Surely not.* If she had done, she'd have mentioned it to me, wouldn't she?

My mind was a mixture of horror and worry. The shock of seeing myself in the paper. The fear of my cover being blown. The trouble that would cause. The Girls recognizing my picture. The questions they would

14

ask. *What if, what if . . . ?* All I could hope was that Carrie hadn't seen the photo, and Kirstie wouldn't. If any of the Girls did pick me out, then all I had to do was lie.

They had no idea of my business, so all I had to do was say I was there because I was visiting someone from home. A distant relative, or someone like that.

I would have to think on my feet, but sitting here, fearing the worst, was no help to me. I stood up from the table.

'I've got to sort myself out for the day,' I smiled. 'I'll leave you in peace.'

I left the room only hoping that all the damage that picture *could* do would remain in my imagination.

Gray

Early March

Gray had his hand around his pint and was staring intently at the picture in the paper. He looked across at me and screwed up his eyes as if he was really taking me in, looked back down again and shook his head a couple of times. Then he picked up his beer and took a couple of gulps. Gray was playing for time, keeping me in suspense, in that way he had.

'Come on,' I laughed. 'Give it to me. What do you think?'

'It's definitely you, all right,' he teased, setting his glass back down on the table.

I rolled my eyes in mock exasperation. 'I knew *that*! But do you think I'm likely to be found out?

That was the crux of why I'd called him up. The paparazzi shot had got under my skin, and the only person I knew who'd help me make sense of it was Gray. As the manager of my 'Satisfaction with Luke' website, he knew *exactly* what I was about. There was no having to explain myself with *him*.

He half whistled out of the side of his mouth. 'That's a hard one. It's a possibility, of course.'

'Isn't everything?' I countered, as I picked up my beer glass to take another swig.

'True. My point is, there's a strong chance nothing'll happen.'

'And if it does?'

'Cross that bridge when you come to it, mate. And never admit guilt or shame. That's what the bastards want, y'know.'

He set down his glass hard on the table, signalling that that was the end of it.

Gray wasn't telling me anything I hadn't expected, or already thought about myself. But it helped to have him reflect it back to me. And to have *someone* listen to my worries.

Let's face it, it wasn't as if I could talk to my flatmates about my escort work. They were the very people I feared would find me out. It was just too early days for them to know my business and, anyhow, why should they need to? As long as I paid my bills on time and was friendly enough, surely that was all that mattered?

It was as if Gray was reading my thoughts. 'Have the Girls seen this? They know about what you do, right?'

I nervously ran my fingernail against the table edge, filing a groove. Certainly it *did* concern me that the wider world might find me out. Because should I ever get mixed up in some scandal or other, there wouldn't be too many steps between my identity being made known here in Britain and it being picked up by the

17

expat Aussie press and beamed home for my friends and family to read. That's not what I wanted *at all.*

But my more immediate worry was that Carrie and the others might find out. And where would that leave me?

'They don't know?' gasped Gray, his pint held in mid-air on the way to his mouth. 'What the fuck do they think you're doing?'

'Oh come on, Gray. Why the hell would I *want* to tell them about the escort work? I'm getting paid for sex, for God's sake!'

He had a broad grin across his face. 'Exactly! So what's your problem?'

I laughed along with him. Both of us knew exactly what I was getting at. It might have been fine for us guys to make light of the way I made my living. After all, it was most blokes' dream. But there were plenty of other people who just didn't get it. God, in this country, most people still believed prostitution was illegal.

But it wasn't just that. The idea of someone they knew being involved went way beyond most people's imaginings, and I couldn't be sure how my three female flatmates would respond to having a hooker in their midst. I didn't want to risk things, especially so early in my tenancy. I'd only just got here. I'd hate to have all the hassle of moving out again any time too soon.

Gray was frowning, as if he'd just thought of something. 'What *do* you tell them, then? Y'know, about the countless phone calls. And especially the overnighters?'

I gave him a massive grin in return. 'I'm an Aussie

guy in London, Gray. What else would I be doing?' I raised my glass to him and we chinked like a high-five.

Not that I put it so bluntly to the Girls, of course. They raised an eyebrow at how often my BlackBerry went off, but I just shrugged it off by hinting at my amazing popularity with their compatriots out there. I'm not sure they completely believed me.

Or whether Gray was convinced, come to that.

'And they're OK with that?'

'Seem to be,' I shrugged.

He gave a low whistle through his teeth: '*And* you're shacked up with those three too. It's women all the way with you, isn't it? God, I wish I was in your shoes, Luke!'

I set my half-full pint down on the table: 'I bet you do!'

It was funny how the guys I knew made such a big deal of me being the only bloke in my flat. I mean, it wasn't as if I didn't have sex on tap. What difference would three more babes make to me? When I'd just moved in, just before my Aussie mates had left for home, they'd been the same as Gray. Not believing my fucking luck. None of them seemed to get that I didn't see Carrie, Kirstie or Laura like that. They were just *mates*. Good fun to have around, but anything beyond that wasn't top of my agenda.

Not that I completely ruled out a drunken fumble some time with one or other of them – a wild night that we'd look embarrassed about in the cold, hungover light of the next morning. *Never say never*. It wasn't that I was planning anything of the sort. It was just . . . Three of them, one of me; a statistical probability at some point in the future. *Surely.*

But I could see where Gray was coming from. The Girls'd be certain to get curious about what I got up to some day soon. And end up asking questions I needed to have answers to.

I'd been on good terms with enough women to find out that they were open about their own relationships and sex lives amongst themselves. If I wasn't too careful I could see myself getting caught in the crossfire – being forced to open up about my own relationship status.

But as Gray had said, *Cross that bridge when you come to it.*

I let out a heavy sigh. 'God, it was so much easier when Mark and co were still in London.'

Gray got my drift immediately. 'You miss 'em?'

'They were me mates, y'know? Mark, Simon, even Rob knew what I got up to. I didn't have to pretend with them . . .'

For a moment, Gray looked affronted: 'You don't have to pretend with me, *mate.*'

I put my palms up to face him. 'I know, I know,' I smiled, to show I hadn't meant to diss our friendship, 'but you know what I mean. They were Aussies. They knew where I came from.'

'Yeah, I know.'

I placed my hands flat down on the table again and thought back to almost two years ago when I'd just come to London and moved in with Mark. I'd got to know the others through him and they'd turned out to be such a major part of my life in the UK. For one thing, it was our mutual lack of funds that had got me started in this escorting game in the first place. And when I wasn't working at that or, in the early days, any other job I could find, then we were generally in each other's pockets.

They had helped keep me grounded through the perils and pitfalls of my hookering. The guys had helped to remind me of where I came from and stopped me getting up myself, or losing myself in the wealth of my clients. I'd seen it happen to many of the other escorts. They forgot that they were only short-term guests in the rich world. The only thing they had to show for it was the expensive designer gear they'd bought into.

It had been tempting to return to Australia when my friends had, but because I'd arrived in the UK after them, I still had some time to run on my visa. And I was making good money from the escort work.

But it wasn't just that. They had been bolstering up their CVs in a way that my work just couldn't. I had gaps where they had jobs. And their work experience actually counted for something. I could hardly boast of my escort skills as something that I could put to good use in any other field. All the more reason for me to make as much money as I possibly could while I was here, then. So, my friends had ended up less tied to the UK and more ready to return home. I simply couldn't. Not yet, anyhow.

I gave Gray a rueful smile. He was right. I was lucky to have someone still here who understood me. But I couldn't help reflecting that my mates' absence really emphasized how much I had to make things work as an escort – whether or not I kept my lifestyle close to my chest.

Still, it didn't mean that I couldn't help wondering if I'd made the right choice. It was difficult to gauge whether the money was really worth remaining here for. I could have been on my way *home* to Australia right now with the rest of the gang, beginning the rest of my life, with a new job, which might pay less than I'd grown used to but that on paper would actually count for something.

But I hadn't, had I? I was sitting here with Gray. The Last Mate Standing.

I got up. 'You'd like another?'

Gray nodded up at me: 'Same again, thanks.'

I ordered our pints, and as the barman poured them I observed Gray sitting alone. He looked as out on a limb as I was beginning to feel. But it meant I was damn glad we got on so well. I had a sneaking suspicion he got a lot out of our friendship too. As a website designer, a lot of the time he was chained to his laptop, so he liked me telling him about my experiences. It was a window into a pretty alternative world to his.

For me, it wasn't just that Gray was doing a great job managing my site. Such a great job, in fact, that he was practically my PA these days. I knew that I'd be nowhere near as successful an escort if it hadn't been for him helping to get my presence on the Net where it mattered. Whenever anyone Googled 'London Male Escort' I was there, at the top of the page.

He never seemed fazed either by tales of my exploits.

Which proved a fucking good thing when I needed to offload stuff. I don't know how long you could keep going at this game without sharing details with someone of what the job involved. Or, conversely, being able to have a friendly conversation *without* having to mention what I'd really been doing with my life.

When I was starting out, my client Jenny had been like that for me. We'd met up for a half-hour coffee break every Friday. That seemed such a long time ago. She'd been my very first client, but I had no idea where she was or what she was getting up to these days.

I paid for the drinks and picked them up and made my way to our table. I couldn't help wondering if Gray even realized how much he was helping me out, on so many levels.

'I tell you what,' I remarked as I handed him his pint and sat down.

'What?' he replied, taking a deep gulp of the beer.

'I'm not saying it's likely to happen, but if ever I can't make a session and my clients are fine about me sending them an alternative, you'll be the first person I'll call on.'

Gray sat there, mouth open, utterly amazed. It struck me that it had never crossed his mind. That he'd been happy enough beavering away on the sidelines, setting up my goals. That that was where his strengths lay, and he got kicks enough just from hearing about what I'd got up to.

'You'd do that?'

He looked worried – a far cry from how cool he was when dealing with the concrete stuff of his web design.

23

He reminded me of how nervous I'd been before I'd had my first call-out.

Wouldn't most guys be? It was one thing to be an escort in your head. Quite another to go out for the first time not knowing who you were going to meet. And fearful that you might not be able to perform when the crunch came. How humiliating would that be? How much easier *not* to offer your services. Remain the back-room boy.

I back-pedalled to put him at his ease again. 'I was only joking,' I laughed.

He gave me a quizzical look, but his shoulders visibly relaxed. 'Thought so!' he lied. His paw was tight round his pint, like he was steadying himself.

'But should a regular client ever be open to the idea of using a replacement, I'll definitely mention your name,' I winked.

He chuckled, now aware of my joshing. 'Thanks for that, *mate*.' We both sank our pints.

There. I'd set him thinking about being an escort. What was the betting that, down the line, he'd find himself thinking that actually he wouldn't mind giving it a go after all? And that he'd be kicking himself too for having missed his chance. Which would mean I could do him that favour after all, should the opportunity arise. And that time, he'd be ready to accept.

I put down my empty glass and wiped my mouth on the back of my hand.

Gray tapped his fingers on the table, relaxed now. 'That reminds me. I got a call before I came out. Remember Pearl Agency?'

That put a smile on my face: 'Oh yes, my friend!'

Didn't I just? I'd been the only guy in their stable of hot babes, but they'd dropped my pic from their home page because it unnerved some of their male clients. The last thing they wanted to see was me among all those girls.

'Seems you're still in demand from those high rollers of theirs. There's some big-shot guy who wants to hire you.'

'You're supposed to say that I don't do gay stuff,' I groaned.

Gray rolled his eyes but there was a glint there too. 'He's straight, stupid. Apparently there'll be a couple of Pearl's girls along for the ride too.'

'What, we're putting on a show for him? That sounds *much* better!'

Gray shook his head and chuckled: 'God, Luke, you have one hell of a jammy life!'

I said nothing and simply gave him a salute, grinning.

'Oh, and this shows how major this client is. Apparently you'll know him the moment you walk through the door,' reported Gray. 'That's what the Pearl girl said, anyhow. And you're under strict instructions not to let on to anyone who he is either.'

It was my turn to look mock-affronted. 'Of course.' I'd learnt a thing or two about client confidentiality by now.

We sat in silence for a few seconds.

'No, but who do you think he is?' I quizzed.

Gray laughed. 'I *knew* you were going to say that. I can't help you, I'm afraid. I'm as in the dark as you are.'

I whistled through my teeth. 'God, if he's as famous as they're making out, then that cuts down the list quite considerably.'

Gray drained the dregs of his beer. 'You think so?' he asked.

I nodded. 'Must be. I mean, there are celebs and there are Celebs with a capital C. This guy could be a major footballer or pop star or something.'

Gray was looking directly and deadpan at me. 'You make sure you get a signed photo for me then, eh?

Aidan

The woman from Pearl Agency had been right – I recognized Aidan before we'd even been introduced. His name flashed through my mind the instant I saw him. He wasn't just any celeb either. He was *huge*.

Play it real cool, Luke.

He was standing on the other side of the lounge room, his full attention fixed on the two gorgeous leggy babes who hung off his arms. The assistant who'd opened the door to me made a swift exit, so I was left standing on the threshold.

Aidan calmly turned his head towards me and, tilting it to one side, flicked me an approving gaze. He dropped his arms so the girls slipped away from him and then he made a beeline across the marble floor. When he reached me, he held out his hand for me to shake.

'At last. You must be Luke. I've been expecting you. I'm Aidan.' His grip was firm. 'But you knew that, didn't you?' he winked.

'Of course I do,' I laughed. 'Doesn't everyone?'

Aidan was a London lad in his late twenties, known for his relaxed manner. It was this charm that had helped him on the road to his current celebrity status. People easily warmed to him, especially women. He was known for working his way through them. He was rarely out of the papers, being pictured coming out of some West End club with his latest conquest hanging off his arm.

'Flattery will get you anywhere,' he grinned, while shaking his head in mock disdain.

'Has so far.'

I liked how easily we'd hit it off. Not in any deep way, but with friendly banter; neither of us taking ourselves too seriously. Maybe that was the point. Both of us could see past the bullshit. It was something I'd seen work with the actress Charley and her husband David. If you showed that you weren't overawed, but rather made light of their fame in a way that most people they met didn't, it got you places. Mind you, I'd also sussed that such familiarity only worked with the big stars who were secure enough to take it. It was the minor celebs you generally had to handle with kid gloves.

Aidan stretched out an arm to beckon the girls. 'Now you're here, we've got the full complement. Sherry, Haley, come and meet Luke,' he invited.

This was the moment I'd been waiting for. The agency said that I'd be joined by a couple of girls. Presumably our job would be to put on a sex show to entertain Aidan.

Sherry and Haley's svelte, hot bodies swept across the floor towards me.

All the better to see you.

They were both blondes, and my height too – as if

we'd been selected because we all matched. I hugged and kissed each of them.

'*Very* pleased to meet you,' I smiled.

'You too,' they chorused. Like a double act.

'Let me take that,' drawled Aidan seductively. And he placed his hand in Sherry's and drew her up close to him in one fell swoop and planted a long, hard kiss on her lips.

I took the hint. This wasn't going to be a display for Aidan, after all – he was actually going to get down and dirty with us. I recalled the double-couple sesh I'd had at the wealthy Ralph's Thameside house last summer. This would likely turn out the same way – the guys starting off with one girl and then swapping her, only the other guy this time would be the client rather than a fellow escort.

I was OK with that. Aidan was paying his money so he was calling the tune. If he wanted to get caught up in a four-way session, then so be it.

Let the games begin!

I took Haley's hand. 'Step right this way, love,' I directed.

She was happy to oblige. As we kissed, her hands started to tug at my clothes as if she was desperate for me to be naked.

I helped her unbutton my shirt, slipping out of my jacket even as the shirt was falling to the floor. And now it was my turn to help her disrobe. I slipped the straps of her dress off her shoulders and unzipped her all the way down. The dress fell away from her.

Haley turned back towards me even as I was

unclipping her bra. By the time she was face on, the cups had slipped from her breasts into the palms of her hands. She tossed the bra across the room.

'There,' she breathed in deep satisfaction. 'I'm ready for my close-up,' she winked.

I wasn't much aware of what Sherry and Aidan were getting up to. I sensed their presence next to me and Haley, but my focus was on her. That was what I was here for. Haley's tits had my full, undivided attention.

I cupped them in my hands and bowed my head to cover each in kisses. Haley's breasts rose to meet me as she arched her back in delight. Her hands gripped my sides tightly and the pressure of her fingers set me hardening too.

I whipped open my belt, and forced my trousers off. At the very same moment, Haley's hands had left my sides and she'd slipped them between my legs. Her fingers curled around my dick, and she dropped to her knees.

God, I knew *exactly* where she was going with this. Her hot lips drove down my dick with a practised ease and I pushed down on her shoulders as my whole body shuddered with pleasure.

When I collected my thoughts and had returned to my senses, I caught Aidan's eye. He was perched on the arm of one of the armchairs and Sherry was wrapped around him like a second skin.

I had the distinct impression that he'd been watching me through the entire incident, though I couldn't be sure. I hadn't known what the fuck was going on around me while Haley had been going down on me, that was for sure.

'You enjoying yourself, Luke?' Aidan threw at me over Sherry's head. There was a huge smile on his face. The misgivings that had flitted through my mind dissolved.

'You bet!' I grinned back.

I got what he was on about. Though he had hired the three of us, because I was the only guy, Aidan couldn't help seeing me as on 'his' side. That is, we were brothers in arms, enjoying these girls on tap.

Not that Sherry and Haley weren't up for putting on a show for the two of us. That was something I'd soon learnt about the female escorts I met on the jobs we'd been booked for together. They never seemed averse to a spot of girl-on-girl action when the mood took them. They clearly knew it set straight guys' pulses racing too.

They were sure fucking right about that! Haley released herself from me and tripped across the room into Sherry's open arms. Aidan leaned back in his chair to let them get on with it. As the girls sank their tongues into each other, Aidan and I looked on in admiration.

The two of them were offering us a preview of what they'd be giving us as the night hotted up. They were damn well heating *me* up. I couldn't wait to have Haley back. And then move on to Sherry. The night was gearing up for a sizzling sexual merry-go-round! God, there was no other place in the world I'd rather be at this moment.

It was as if Aidan and I hit on the idea at the same time. Just watching the girls writhing together set us both homing in on a girl each – as if they were a great sandwich filling, with us guys as the bread. I ran my hands over Haley's back and down and round to her breasts so her tits were cupped in my hands, even as she was licking Sherry's throat. Sherry's head was stretched back and turned towards Aidan behind her, kissing him hot and hard, his tongue halfway down her throat.

I, meanwhile, had my mind on far deeper things. I pulled away to cover myself, then in the next minute brought my whole body back up against Haley's behind. Even as she was sucking Sherry's tits, she was bending so her ass stuck out towards me, as if inviting me in. I entered her, doggy fashion, my hands fondling her cute breasts at the very same time as I was drawing her to me.

In our girl sandwich, it seemed that now Sherry and I were the bread. Haley was getting it from behind from me but she was also licking out her friend. And Aidan was standing, locked tight behind Sherry, his arms wrapped around her to stop her from falling. He was nuzzling her neck, almost tenderly.

I looked up and saw Aidan staring at me, a definite look of longing in his eyes.

What the fuck?

I dropped my gaze instinctively and immediately went back to sweeping away Haley's hair from the back of her neck, my same hand reaching forward to savour Sherry's firm tits. But I found it hard to give my full attention to the girls. I could feel the hairs bristling on my neck.

I thought Gray said there was to be no gay stuff. What? We got the wrong end of the fucking stick?

One second, my whole body felt as if it was shrinking at the thought that Aidan might want more from me than I was ever about to give. The very next I was in flight or fight mode, my muscles tightening, preparing themselves to give him a good kicking should the situation demand it. But at the same moment, I just knew how dangerous beating up a world-famous star would be.

I certainly didn't want to go *there* if I could help it.

I drew away from the girls without realizing quite what I was doing. The shift of Haley as she and Sherry regrouped before me brought me to my senses.

Get over it, Luke. You're imagining the worst.

Aidan now had an arm around Sherry's waist, and she in turn held Haley's hand. Aidan reached out and ran the tips of his fingers down my chest. My muscles tautened as he did.

'You'd do that for me, wouldn't you,' he declared.

He obviously felt he didn't even have to ask. I could *taste* entitlement in the flat way he said it. The dread was sickly and metallic in my mouth. I swallowed down the nausea. He was the big shot in the room paying for our presence, and whatever he desired he presumed he could get.

Not that easily, mate.

The two girls looked on, their heads both slightly tilted to one side, as if they were wondering why I was hesitating.

I switched into my best professional mode to stand my ground. 'I'm afraid it seems there's been some mistake,' I stated.

Aidan raised an eyebrow. So I made damn sure not to make it *his* mistake.

33

'Perhaps Pearl didn't make it clear that while men might hire me, it's for services to women only?'

A flush of embarrassment swept across Aidan's face, accompanied by what looked like disappointment. And in that moment I realized that his feelings went a whole lot deeper than *that*. The sure-fire hit with the girls had just outed himself. It showed in his eyes and his willingness to watch me fuck Sherry and Haley.

He was staring at me, poker-faced, keeping things locked in. I could only read it as him demanding from me that I keep his secrets. I realized that *that* was what he was paying me for.

'Look, Aidan. I've had a good time tonight.'

I was telling him that there was no reason for me to spill the beans to anyone. That I had no axe to grind. He remained silent.

'The girls were here before I arrived. You were clearly having a good time with them, weren't you?'

I shot a glance at Sherry and Haley, imploring them to grasp what I was getting at. For them to give him a *real* good time for the remainder of the session.

I touched his arm to show there were no hard feelings. That I wouldn't hold his pass at me against him. 'You've got a reputation to uphold, haven't you?' I winked.

I bowed, stepped backwards, picking up my clothes en route, and turned and headed out of there. Leaving them to it.

Karen

Late March

Why did I even pick up the phone?

I was on my scooter, on my way to Karen's house, and though we were heading into spring, there was still a chill in the air. It wasn't even as if I needed the money these days. Business was going so well that I could pick and choose. I should have let my 'Berry ring until it switched to voicemail.

Just my luck.

But I *had* answered the call, and now I was on my way to Balham. I stopped outside a block of flats. The place didn't look a million miles away from the ex-council housing that the Girls and I lived in, though our place was in a leafier part of London. As they say, location was everything. This block and indeed the whole estate had a shabby air about it. Rubbish dotted the grass verges, and various tags were scrawled over the brickwork.

I braced myself and rang the bell. The buzzer sounded and I pushed open the heavy-duty fire door and headed down the corridor to Karen's flat. She was standing on the threshold.

Mutton dressed as lamb.

I knew it was unfair of me, but before Karen had even opened her mouth I'd made up my mind about what she'd be like. She was the sort of older woman that me and my mates back in Aus would have sniggered over for trying too hard to cheat time.

Not that Karen was ancient. She was in her forties but dressed like someone half her age, in a skimpy black vest, crotch-length miniskirt, fishnet stockings and four-inch heels. It all left nothing to the imagination and it didn't do her any favours either. She clearly hoped to make an impression on the guys she met.

Well, yeah love, but not quite the impression you wanted . . .

But the irony was that it clearly wasn't working. After all, she'd had to resort to hiring me, hadn't she?

When Karen did open her mouth to invite me in, she all but crowed. 'Luke, do come in,' she leered, looking me up and down with a keen eye.

'Thanks,' I replied, wondering how things might pan out tonight.

Karen leant against the open front door to let me pass, but leaving so little room that I couldn't help but brush against her. Or she against me.

OK, I'll let you have that one for free.

I stepped straight into the lounge room. Karen's place was sort of what I'd expected. That is, nothing special.

'Do sit down, and I'll get you a drink. You'd like a

beer or something?' she said as she disappeared into the kitchen.

'Thanks. That'd be nice,' I said loudly and sank down into an overstuffed armchair that threatened to swallow me up. There was a matching sofa that seemed to take up half the room, then a huge telly and digibox on a black tubular metal stand in one corner, but that was it.

I heard the fridge door slam shut, and a second or two later Karen was back in the room with a couple of cans of Budweiser, handing me one of them. As I upped the ring pull and licked off the excess beer from the can's top, she dropped onto the sofa with a loud 'Ahh' of relief.

Fiddling with the can and giving it my full concentration ate up a few minutes until we got down to business. I took a gulp from the can, and looked over at Karen.

'It's the first time I've been this far south, I think,' I smiled, as if I had just ventured out on some exotic adventure to uncharted lands.

I looked around the room again, desperate for something to talk about. There was a photo of what looked like a younger Karen holding hands with a small boy.

'You have a son?' I fished, nodding at the picture.

'Callum? Yes. You might get to see him. He's not as small as that. Obviously.'

Obviously.

'He lives with you?'

'Yes, it's probably about time I kicked him out, but I like having him around. I'd miss him around the flat. He's around your age.'

I did a quick calculation. She must have been in her

early twenties when she'd had him. Pretty young. I certainly wouldn't want a toddler around my feet any time soon.

'Oh, there's no need to worry about Callum butting in on anything. He's round at his girlfriend's tonight,' Karen blurted out.

That was a relief, though it hadn't really crossed my mind.

'But I'm sure you'll get to meet him at some point,' she smiled.

That sounded promising. Karen had booked me for an overnight this time, but it sounded as if she'd already made up her mind that she'd call me again some time. Maybe it wasn't such a bad thing that I'd come out so late tonight after all. Karen might turn out to be a lucrative regular if I played my cards right.

'When you do meet Callum, you won't tell him why you're here, will you?' she blurted out.

'Of course I will!' I joked.

'You'll tell him you're my boyfriend, won't you?' she stressed.

Blimey! She'd already sorted out her story before it had even got started. Of course, I could act the role of 'boyfriend', no sweat – but whether I would be able to convince Callum that I'd chosen to get together with his mum in the first place was a different matter.

'No problem, Karen. I will.'

I pulled myself up and out of the armchair, moving closer to Karen as I took another gulp from my can.

I gave a sideways glance at the white flesh of her thigh above the top of her stocking. I reached out my hand and stroked it with my thumb. She shifted her leg towards the pressure, and I answered that by slipping my fingers beneath the fishnet itself and giving her a strong brush with my hand.

Karen swivelled her whole body to face me, her miniskirt riding up even higher with the movement. I chose not to look too closely just yet and focused on her face. It wasn't as if she was bad looking. Just over-egged.

I released my hand from her stockings and gave her whole thigh a sweep with it. She shivered.

'You'd like to show me the bedroom, Karen?'

She nodded furiously and jumped up from the sofa. Gagging for it.

Karen gripped my hand and pulled me up alongside her. 'Follow me,' she gasped, though it wasn't as if I had any say in the matter. Not that I really cared. I knew what I was getting into the moment she opened the door to me. Money for sex. Nothing more.

Karen's bedroom was as basically furnished as her lounge, with a double bed in the middle of it, a cheap white chipboard wardrobe and a small chest of drawers. Another framed picture of her and Callum stood on the side table by her bed.

'Would you like a massage to start with, Karen?' I asked to get things started.

I unbuttoned my own shirt and caught her fumbling with her top. 'Would you like some help with that?'

The thought sped across my mind that Karen might have just set me up with her own practised routine. 'Step One: get him to get your clothes off.' Not that that bothered me too much. As far as I was concerned, it was whichever way I could get from A to B; I would give her a decent bout of sex to satisfy her, yet at the same time curtail it as soon as I wanted by going off to sleep. I'd already planned on escaping early the next morning, before Karen herself had got out of bed. I simply didn't fancy Karen, so didn't feel up to giving her anything more than she was paying me for. What she would be getting was my standard overnight package.

Once we were in bed, I sorted out the protection as I nestled against Karen's huge tits, and then dived right in. She held me tight, grunting and shrieking her way through the session.

Sex with Karen wasn't as bad as I feared. Though neither was it going to be one of those nights I was going to list among my most memorable. Those, like my session with Sasha and Chloe, and the Aussie model, Mae, were what helped me guarantee Karen a top-class escort session tonight.

I gave her a good time, that's for sure. After all, if she was about to turn into a regular, it was important that I did. It's just that I kept myself at a distance. And I was damn glad that her son hadn't made an appearance.

I climbed off Karen and lay beside her to catch my breath, gave her one last kiss, then held her hand and did the post-orgasm guy thing of dropping off to sleep as fast as I possibly could. Though I at least made the effort not to act so cold that she felt she'd in any way been snubbed.

As it happened, I had a good night's sleep. I woke at around seven, as I normally did, and pulled myself away from Karen and watched her lying there still fast asleep. It hadn't been a bad night, just not a great one.

I got out of the bed and went to the bathroom to wash and get dressed. Karen had already handed me the money last night, so I poked my head around her bedroom door, and since she was still cold to the world, I wished her a silent 'Goodbye' and left.

I was having a cup of tea back at the flat later that morning when I got a call from Gray.

'Karen so enjoyed her sesh that she wants to book you for tomorrow night. You up for it?'

Bloody hell, love, give us a break.

But then again, if Karen was going to be calling me on a regular basis for regular money, why shouldn't I be?

'You bet!' I crowed. And booked Karen into my diary.

Heather

Easter time

Heather was on her third tequila shot. Not that she was counting.

I, on the other hand, was party to her total shift from the after-work businesswoman who'd hired me for a drink only a couple of hours ago, to the increasingly dishevelled – let's be honest, *pissed* – creature before me now.

It wasn't a pretty sight.

'C'mon Luke, schyou have one too,' she slurred.

I raised my beer bottle to her. 'I'm sorted, thanks,' I smiled broadly.

It was never my job to get plastered, however much a client demanded it. However much it tempted me. Because I needed to remain in control.

But God, it was tempting me *now*. From our table we had a clear view of the dance floor, and though Heather was likely too far gone to realize, I was very aware that she was the oldest here by a mile.

The point being that she was over twice my age.

Whichever way you looked at it, we appeared a very odd couple indeed.

It hadn't been an issue when we'd first clapped eyes on each other at the bar where we'd arranged to meet. Both of us had been in relaxed professional mode. She'd clearly accessorized her business suit for the evening, and I'd gone for my smart gear, so we'd sort of complemented each other.

It was supposed to have been a preliminary drink before she made an actual booking. A chance to suss me out. But we'd hit it off so well that we'd moved on to the neighbouring club without much thought.

A choice I was regretting now.

'I can't keep up with you, Heather,' I pointed out. 'Can you hold back a bit to let me catch up, eh?'

Not that I had any intention of doing so, but I wasn't quite sure how else to rein in her alcohol intake. If she kept up this rate, I'd soon have to scrape her off the floor where she fell.

If Heather was trying to prove how she'd still got 'it', she certainly wasn't doing herself any favours. At the start of the evening I was certainly aware of the age difference. But she wore it well and the overall effect was one of class.

God, that sure had slipped since.

Heather stopped in her tracks. She fiddled for a second with the empty shot glasses, and reached out and gripped my hand. She looked directly at me.

'I'm happy to wait for you, Luke,' she said, speaking very slowly, in that way that drunks had, trying so hard to get the right words out.

43

Then the familiar intro beats of 'I just can't get you out of my head' flooded the sound system, and Heather was instantly reanimated. 'I like this one!' she all but squealed as she jumped up.

She was still gripping my hand and didn't let go. It wasn't as if I could refuse to budge. It wasn't my place to cause any sort of scene. She tugged me on to the dance floor. Like a lamb to the slaughter.

Oh God.

I wasn't any sort of dancer at the best of times. I shuffled from one foot to the other, very aware of how out of step I was with the other guys. They were at least free to take advantage of the range of babes that filled the floor. I could smell their pity for me as I faced Heather and tried to mirror her moves and give the impression we were a real couple.

We were getting into some sort of rhythm when I spotted Rich, one of my Aussie mate Simon's old teacher pals, through the crowd. My heart sank. I could only hope he hadn't noticed me, though I realized that was just wishful thinking. I had the distinct impression that the entire fucking club was watching our strange, mismatched pairing.

I turned my attention back to Heather in front of me. There was a glazed smile across her face. She seemed lost in the music, oblivious to any attention we might be attracting. Maybe that was the better approach. Forget about everyone else and just enjoy the night out.

Yet, even in her drunken state, Heather could sense how feeble my dancing was. She grabbed hold of my wrists.

'Come on, Luke!' she jeered, pulling my arms wildly to and fro.

And then she lunged at me, wrapping her arms tight around me and swung me round with her, and I tried not to think about what was happening to me and where I was.

But over Heather's shoulder I could only watch the dance floor clearing around us. A sea of heads turned towards the two of us, eyes and mouths wide open, laughing like hyenas. Through the flickering lights I could make out pointing fingers, and mobile phones raised and aimed at Heather and me. Taking pictures of *us*. The fucking centre of attention.

Beneath my floundering feet, I was dying for the ground to open up and swallow the both of us.

The DJ clearly had the same idea as we'd all but emptied the floor. He wound down the Kylie song and phased in some Gorillaz track. The guys started refilling the floor again. I used the opportunity to drag Heather back to our table.

'No more, Heather,' I fake-laughed, taking her hand. 'I'm no dancer. You've seen that!'

We flung ourselves down in our chairs again. I had nothing more to lose – I had just died of shame. We were still getting one or two glances from some clubbers, but now we were off the dance floor, the crowd had resumed its shape as if we'd been forgotten about. At least, I hoped so.

It was strange. Feeling so humiliated was weirdly liberating. I suddenly realized that there was simply no point in giving a damn what people thought. Heather and I snogged. When we came up for air again, we turned our attention back to the dance floor. Heather leaned drunkenly against me, and my hand was on her thigh.

It was a relief just to sit like that for a few minutes. Out of the limelight. My sense of shame hadn't completely disappeared, then.

And then the empty chair beside me was being pulled back from the table. I glanced up and Rich was standing there looking at me.

Not now.

'It's Luke, isn't it? You didn't go back to Australia with Simon and the others?'

I shook my head mutely as I watched him sit down. My hand was still on Heather's thigh. She had straightened up but was still drunk.

'Hello, Rich. This is Heather,' I introduced.

He looked at her – I could see the surprise in his eyes. He'd been expecting someone younger. Heather and me didn't *match*. And that didn't fit with what Rich had seen of Simon's mates. I wasn't sure how I was going to explain what I was doing with a woman her age.

'Pleased to meet you, Heather,' he chimed.

Rich reached over to shake the limp hand she offered and, as he reached in front of me, I saw him clock my hand still on her thigh.

Don't you dare say a fucking thing, Rich.

Rich sat back in his chair, looking uncomfortable, I guessed he had questions he wanted answering. But I wasn't about to give them to him right now.

To his credit and my eternal thankfulness, he wasn't

about to raise them. He stood up and looked down at me. 'It was nice bumping into you, Luke. You'll say "hi" to Simon from me when you're next in touch?'

I nodded: 'Sure, will do.' I raised my BlackBerry in the air. 'Look, I'll text you. It'd be nice to catch up,' I told him, flicking a glance at Heather as I did.

Rich responded with a knowing smile. He knew what I was implying. That when I'd made sure Heather had got home in one piece, and I'd given myself time enough to get tonight's humiliation out of my system, I'd call. So I could let him in on what the fuck *that* was all about.

I watched Rich as he left our table and headed towards the exit. Some people had no problem with me being an escort. They could handle it. My mates had been like that. They envied me the girls on tap, and the money. The fact that I knew Rich through Simon told me that Rich could handle it too. To be honest, I was looking forward to getting it off my chest.

I turned my attention back to Heather and squeezed her hand: 'A friend of a friend,' I said.

'Hmm,' she nodded. 'He seemed nice.'

She'd grown subdued. It was time to think about calling her a cab. I winced as I recalled our dancing fiasco earlier in the evening. That was the *down* side of this business, the one that those guys who presumed I had the best job in the world didn't think about. Sometimes escort work wasn't all it was made out to be.

Melanie & Alison

Late April

It was Saturday night and I was out clubbing with my flatmates and a couple of their friends. Carrie and co had decided that I was their 'project' and they were determined to pair me up with someone. We were at least agreed on that score, though what I thought of as 'pairing up' was, I suspected, rather different to what they meant.

I hadn't yet told them that I wasn't on the market, but that for me a nightclub was purely a prime place for pulling one-night stands. Just because I was having plenty of sex for cash didn't mean I didn't give it away for free when the opportunity arose. No-strings sex suited me and my lifestyle just fine – though I wasn't sure that my flatmates would see it like that.

Fly-by-night guys with a different girl coming out of their bedroom each morning could get their own reputation. I imagined seeing disapproving looks between my flatmates as I let the latest conquest out the front door. It'd surely be ten times worse if they knew what I did for a living!

In the nightclub, I hovered by the wall while the others danced in front of me, so I still had a relatively clear view of the rest of the floor – and any available talent.

And then I spotted her through the shifting crowd on the other side of the room. I recognized her but I had to rifle through my mental Rolodex to realize who she was.

Melanie.

I was more used to seeing Melanie dressed in sexy lingerie in her bedroom than anywhere else. But here she was, in the same club as me. A completely different venue. The incongruity shocked me.

Fortunately, Melanie hadn't yet noticed me as far as I could tell. And I didn't want to point her out to Carrie in case that drew *her* attention.

I took a swig from my beer bottle and kept an eye on Melanie as I lent a casual ear to the girls' talk. They were pointing out hot guys to each other while trying not to be caught gawping. It made me think of how Mark and the gang and me liked to give any babes we spotted marks out of ten.

I'd never thought of Melanie like *that*. Sure, there were your nines like Sasha and Chloe, the delicious yet intimidating twosome from my early escorting days, or a rare ten like beautiful model, Mae, but the rest of my clients merged into 'a better than average shag'. But what surprised me about Melanie as I glanced at her through the crowd was that she was one of the *last* of my clients I'd expect to see on a night out. She was off sick from work because school teaching had taken its toll on her. She'd always struck me more as someone who'd prefer a quiet night in. And at the moment that I was realizing how mistaken I'd been about *that*, she caught sight of me too.

Our eyes met and we nodded a greeting at each other. Melanie made a step towards me from the other side of the dance floor, but stopped dead when I didn't make any move myself. I could tell that I'd spooked her a bit; that she wasn't sure whether to approach me or not.

The problem about escort work was that there was no rule book. I had to make the protocol up as I went along. I'd been fortunate that I'd never yet bumped into a client when I was out with another – I'm not sure quite what I'd do if that happened. Presumably I'd ignore the one I wasn't with, and pray that they'd do the same for me. But when I was having a night off and I spotted one of my regulars, then things were a little less cut and dried.

From experience I'd worked it out that it was best dealt with if I at least acknowledged them with eye contact and a warm smile, but had also decided that it wasn't my place to do anything more – as much for my own 'safety' or peace of mind as theirs. After all, a client could be shit scared that I might put them in a really awkward position by forcing them to explain themselves to any friends they were with. My reason for not approaching them was simply because I wanted to live my own life apart from the escorting.

I'd been seeing Melanie almost once a fortnight for

the past three or four months. And, if I was being honest, I wasn't altogether sure that I was happy being forced to acknowledge, even to myself, what our relationship was while I was on my own time.

Seeing a client when I was in a different groove of my life muddied the waters too much. The first time it happened shocked me, because I'd imagined London to be such a *large* place that it simply wouldn't be possible. God, how wrong I'd been about *that*! It stood to reason that some day I just would end up hitting the same club or major shopping street at the same time as one of my customers. Coincidence was just the law of chance. But whichever way I looked at it, I had to admit that things were so much easier when we all stuck to our demarcation lines.

If Melanie wanted to touch base with me this evening, then it had to be completely up to her. But even if she didn't, the very fact that we'd caught sight of each other meant I would have to ensure that some time later in the evening I'd text her just to say 'hello' and hint at why I hadn't gone over.

In my experience, clients seemed to like that. The next time they contacted me, they'd mention it in an understanding way – and then book another session. Which suited me just fine.

I turned back towards the Girls. They'd each made a *real* effort tonight and it was nice to see them out of their student uniform of jeans and T-shirts. I looked down at my own white shirt, jacket and jeans – smart casual – and trusted that they thought the same of me. I knew standing here with my back to the dance floor was a cop-out, but I wasn't sure how else to deal with seeing Melanie.

Just ignore her and hope she goes away.

In the very next moment, she was at my elbow.

'Luke?'

I took a deep breath, and in the next second had switched into 'escort mode'. I swivelled on my heel to look directly at her with my carefully composed smiley face, and she had a huge grin for me. We embraced and kissed in greeting.

'Fancy seeing you here!' she gasped, like it had never crossed her mind that I might have any sort of life outside her flat.

'I didn't expect that you'd be here either, Melanie. It's a small world, eh? It's lovely to see you,' I beamed in return.

I now had the full attention of my flatmates. I could sense them at my shoulder, checking out the competition, the way girls did. I could only hope that none of them would dig too deep to find out how Melanie and myself *really* knew each other. 'We met on the Internet' was a pretty useful explanation to keep in my back pocket.

Melanie scrubbed up as well as my friends. She had a good figure and was tall, with dark-brown shoulder-length hair, but she was older than them which I suspect reassured them. Early thirties sounded ancient to a young twenty-something. An age away.

Melanie turned to three girls standing behind her who had followed her across the dance floor in clear curiosity. They were around the same age and not bad looking either, and immediately struck me as quite a raucous bunch. They were dressed similarly in high heels and short shift dresses that left little to the imagination and were damn easy to remove. The message was loud and clear: 'That's what we're here for.'

'Everyone, may I introduce Luke? He's a friend of mine.'

Friend. The catch-all term. There was a chorus of 'Hi Lukes' from the other three.

'And Luke, these are my other friends: Hanna, Alison, and Jayne. They're teachers too.'

'Pleased to meet you,' I smiled back.

I realized then that I had nothing to worry about. If Melanie was fine about being seen with me, then I was OK about that too.

'And these are my flatmates, Carrie, Kirstie, and Laura.'

'Nice to meet you too,' the girls chorused to each other.

I was amazed how quickly the two parties melded into each other. I could tell it was going to be a good night. As long as Melanie didn't reveal our secret. That was the one thing that could spoil the whole evening. I pushed it to the back of my mind.

Cross that bridge when you come to it.

Watching Melanie and her mates, it struck me that the very fact that these girls were out tonight showed that they were good enough colleagues to enjoy each other's company on their nights off. That was the trouble with my work. Being a *straight* male escort made it something of a 'lone wolf' profession. And I was especially aware of that since my mates had left for Aus without me.

Having a close-knit group of friends was certainly something Melanie needed, I knew that. She'd told me she hadn't been at school since before she'd hired me, which by my calculations meant she'd had *months* off sick. She'd had depression and it'd taken a while to get back on her feet, but obviously her girlfriends hadn't forgotten her just because she wasn't at work either. That said something about both her and them. That they were a nice bunch of people.

'And what do you teach?' I said to the nearest of Melanie's companions. It wasn't something I was particularly interested in knowing, but I knew it'd set the ball rolling. Though, even as I was saying it, I was very aware that it was also a fucking bland and unimaginative question to ask a teacher.

At least she had the decency to reply. She pointed at each one of her friends in turn, ending with herself. 'Art, maths, English, English.' Alison paused: 'Like you *really* want to know,' she joked.

She had me sussed. I liked that.

'The same way you're interested in what I do for a living,' I fired back.

I noticed Melanie taking a sip of her drink like she was trying to disappear in the glass. It seemed like she was willing me to keep her secret. She hadn't realized that she had nothing to worry about on that score.

'So, what do you do?' Alison quizzed, now curious.

'Oh, y'know, this and that.' I winked. 'What most Aussies do when they visit Britain, y'know.'

It was a shame Mark and the others weren't with me now. They sure would've backed me up on *that* one. I watched Melanie relax, clearly relieved that I hadn't given any hint of *her* game.

I had a split-second realization that if I played my cards right I might have a chance of pulling Alison – but not as a client.

I could be in here.

Yet I remained mindful that I had an arrangement with Melanie and I had to be careful not to mix things up. For one thing, it might lose me work. And, frankly, *that* was the bottom line.

I had been seeing Melanie on a fortnightly, some-times even a weekly basis for months now at her place in Hendon, round the corner from the police cadet school. Any early awkwardness on her part had been replaced with bouts of friendly, familiar sex that was fluid and fun. I liked having Melanie as a regular because our sessions were uncomplicated – easy money.

Trouble was, I couldn't help now wondering what sex with Alison might be like. Not that I was about to signpost *that*. I noted she was watching me closely. She took a step away from Melanie and the others to join me. She *was* on the same wavelength, then.

'Well, who's for another drink? Would you like to help me carry them, Alison?' The oldest, most obvious techniques sometimes worked the best.

I took the orders over the sound of the thumping bass. There was laughter from our group.

'Don't Aussies tend to hunt in packs?' asked Alison at my shoulder as we queued at the bar.

I looked down at her and nodded, smiling. 'True. I did until recently, you know, but my mates went home again.'

'And left you alone in a nest of English girls, you poor soul!'

I shrugged playfully. 'Depends which way you look at it.'

'You're not missing your mates, then?'

I had to admit I was. They'd have enjoyed tonight's spectacle, I just knew. Finding themselves surrounded by a bevy of up-for-it girls.

'Actually, I am,' I said.

I thought of all the good times I'd had in London with those guys, practically from the time I'd touched down here. They'd been as good for me as I suspected that Melanie's friends had for her. A gang to catch up with and go out with.

'That must make a huge difference to you, doesn't it?' she sympathized. 'All on your tod in London.'

'I'm a pretty sociable kinda guy, I can assure you,' I winked, though I knew there was some truth in what she was saying.

'Oh, I'm sure you are, Luke,' she agreed, placing the palm of her hand against my chest.

I flicked a glance back at our friends. Melanie thankfully had her back to us and seemed to be in deep conversation with Jayne, so I reckoned I had until Alison and I returned with the drinks to make any move I was going to make that night.

I felt the pressure of Alison's hand and looked directly back at her with a grin across my face. She'd seen me look at Melanie and cocked her head.

'Is there a thing between you and Melanie that I don't know about?' she queried, and let go of me.

'What, me and Mel? I don't *think* so,' I lied. 'And, if there was, we're each going the wrong way about it, aren't we?' I chuckled.

I looked towards the bar. Our turn was rapidly approaching so I knew I didn't have long.

Apart from our greeting, Melanie and I had barely spoken a word to each other. I could see she wasn't up to giving any hint tonight to her friends that we knew each other *too* intimately, so she overcompensated for that fear by acting distant, making a point of talking to the girls. But I was suddenly aware too that it wasn't as if I'd done anything to try to close that forced gap between us. I wondered if it was that reserve between people who were supposed to be friends that Alison had noticed.

'Oh, we're friends,' – that word again – 'but that's as far as it goes. Look, she's got more to say to my flat-mates tonight than to me!' I laughed and nodded my head in their direction.

Alison pursed her lips. 'But you and Melanie are *good* friends. Anyone could see that the way you two said "hello".'

I winced inside as I stepped up against the bar and ordered the list of drinks. Alison was getting too close to the mark for comfort.

'Well, y'know, she's been ill and I've made it a bit of my business to try and cheer her up. That's made us close.'

Hadn't it just.

I placed my hand on Alison's wrist, and repeated myself, 'But that's as far as it goes.'

Hearing this, Alison smiled slightly to herself.

'Alison, I tell you what. I bet I can *prove* how much me and Melanie are just good friends,' I challenged as the barman poured out our drinks.

Alison licked her lips, then turned her face directly to me. She had pretty features, which were given strength by the assertiveness in her eyes. 'Oh, I'm always open to a gamble. And how might you do that?'

'Pass me your mobile,' I said to her as I paid for the drinks.

Alison did so, raising an eyebrow. She duly picked up three of the glasses and watched as I tapped my number into her contacts page. I slipped the phone into her shoulder bag.

'Call me,' I mouthed to her. She nodded silently, turned, and made her way through the crowd back to her friends.

I picked up the remaining glasses, and followed her back across the room.

I was sitting at a small table with my eye on the door of the bar, waiting for Alison to arrive. I'd only been here around five minutes and we'd arranged to meet at eight p.m. so she still had another quarter of an hour. I didn't mind that she wasn't here yet. It gave me time to collect my thoughts and wonder about what I was doing with her.

And then Alison herself came sweeping through the door and strode straight towards me.

'Luke!' she exclaimed.

I rose to greet her as she gave me a warm hug.

There wasn't an awful lot of romance in *that*, but then again maybe that was fitting, seeing as we didn't know each other very well yet. We'd been out a couple of times since we met at the club and I for one was happy to be taking things slowly. It meant our relationship was still casual enough for me to swat away any niggling worries about how it might affect my time spent with Melanie.

'You had a good day at school?'

'You don't really want to know that, do you?' she laughed.

She was right in one. The trouble was that I wasn't sure where to turn from there.

Because there was so much we *couldn't* talk about when it came to seeing Alison. It was difficult to even mention Melanie because of the discomfort I felt about being out meeting Alison instead. But it was also because I had to conceal so much about how I had come to know Melanie in the first place.

'You due for another night out clubbing with the girls any time soon?'

She nodded: 'Hope so. But you know how it is. Teaching takes up so much time. You're at school during the day, then after that you're at home marking books until the early hours. We're certainly due a break.'

'I like it that you go out as a gang,' I admitted. 'Teachers on the prowl!'

I chose not to mention Melanie by name, as I suspected Alison was trying to avoid doing too. I knew I felt that asking Alison out betrayed my friendship with Melanie, and I wondered if Alison might somehow feel she was cheating on her friend? But then again, why should she?

I was getting paranoid. I'd made it quite clear to Alison and in my own head that Melanie and I had nothing going on, so the three of us were each free to date whoever we chose. Yet somehow Melanie was still getting in on the act, demanding to be noticed. It made me shiver.

'"Out on the prowl"? I like how you put it,' smiled Alison. 'But sometimes I think I'd like to break out of *that* mould. I love the clubbing, but being surrounded mostly by teachers can feel a bit claustrophobic at times. I guess like you Aussies!' she teased.

That got my attention. I thought back to me and the lads out on the pull.

'Used to be,' I reminded her. 'My mates are back home. I'll be returning too pretty soon.'

Alison sucked in her lips and I realized I might have said the wrong thing. I'd just signalled that if anything was going to happen between her and me, it wasn't going to be anything long term. Not that that bothered me. But I could see it might not be what she wanted.

To be honest, due to my guilt about Melanie, I couldn't see whatever I had going with Alison lasting very long at all anyhow. Even as I was trying to concentrate on the girl in front of me, I was mentally arguing with Melanie to shut the fuck up.

I haven't let you down, for God's sake. You're only my fucking client, Melanie. I owe you NOTHING. Except to turn up on time and give you what you want for the duration. The rest of my life is entirely my business.

But the trouble was that there was a quieter voice at

the shoulder of my inner Angry Person, reasoning with me that, even so, I was still sitting here, wasn't I, and having a drink and a date with a good friend of Mel's. I couldn't shake off the feeling that I was betraying her.

The truth was that I wasn't quite sure how to play my evenings spent with Alison. With Melanie and any of my clients I was 'Escort Luke', a friendly, happy-go-lucky bloke with a perpetual smile on his face. They could never see me having an off-day.

When not working, I was able to be more myself, though even with my flatmates I could never tell the *whole* truth. But because of who she knew, Alison fell between the cracks. Which meant that I needed to come up with a *third* persona to fill that gap. Just finding something to talk about over a drink while not letting on *too* much was proving exhausting.

Alison picked up her glass of wine and drank from it, watching me as she did so, as though she was mulling something over in her head.

And then she spoke. 'Luke, how and where did you and Melanie meet? I'm curious.'

Aren't you just?

I played for time. 'You really want to know?'

She nodded, and there was a quizzical look across her face.

'It's just I can't make out how or where a teacher like her would meet an Aussie working shifts.'

I had nothing to fear after all. She'd tossed me a damn easy ball. 'It's not *that* difficult!' I laughed. 'I was a barman and she wanted a drink. Simple as that. We just hit it off. That's all.'

I stressed that the subject was effectively closed with that final 'all'. Alison took the hint.

'That makes sense. And it doesn't surprise me. Anyone could hit it off with *you*, Luke,' she teased, and reached out to squeeze my wrist.

I couldn't help wondering if she realized what she was actually saying. That as regards *my* sex life, I could indeed hit it off with *anyone*. That's what made me a damn fine escort, wasn't it? And I couldn't help wondering too if *she* was hinting that she had continued suspicions about my *real* relationship with Melanie. She presumably hadn't guessed about any money changing hands between us. But when she referred to us 'hitting it off', she seemed to be saying that me and Melanie were still somehow linked up.

She'd hit the nail on the head there. To be honest, try as I might to get Melanie out of my mind as no more than just another one of my clients, I couldn't. Perhaps because of her illness, I was very aware that I was betraying our professional relationship by getting close to a friend of hers. It shouldn't have mattered, but somehow it did. I enjoyed having Melanie as a client. I didn't want to chance losing that.

I finished off the dregs of my pint and observed Alison through the glass. Yes, I'd ask her out on another date, but I could still guess where we were heading. Nowhere fast.

Like the Princess said, there were three people in this relationship.

Tash

It wasn't as if I had a clue what Tash looked like. But I couldn't help creating a mental picture of my clients, sketching out the life they might live even before I'd seen them. It was based solely on what they'd told me over the phone.

She had introduced herself as Natasha when she'd picked up the phone, 'But everyone calls me Tash,' she'd said. She'd called me out for an eleven o'clock session on a Monday night in Luton. That struck me as odd. Most other people were in bed at this time because of work the next day. It suggested she didn't want the neighbours to know. I figured that that likely made her a thirty-something housewife whose hubby was away on business.

I was standing on the forecourt of Luton railway station waiting for a cab to take me to her place. The station was almost deserted and then a car swung off the road, the light box on the roof advertising Ace Cabs, and I relaxed. The car drew up and the driver leaned over to the passenger window.

'Where to?'

He drove me out beyond the town centre, where the housing was less crowded together. We turned off the main road and up a side street to the address Tash had given me. I was dead in the middle of Thirties suburbia, and Tash's was one of the middle houses in the row with a little tiered garden out front. The wooden gate clicked shut behind me, and I hurried up the path and rang the bell.

Minutes later the front door was opened and Tash hovered in front of me, a nervous, close-mouthed smile across her face.

She didn't look anything like I'd expected at all. Her feet were bare, which only added to the vulnerable air that wrapped itself around her. She must have been all of twenty-one. She had long straight blonde hair that looked like it had been ironed. Her slight frame was dressed in hipster jeans and a loose pale pink silk top and she had delicate, pretty features. To be frank, she was gorgeous.

So, what is it you're after?

'Luke, do come in,' Tash half-whispered in a voice that suggested that now she'd got what she'd asked for, she wasn't altogether sure she knew what to do with it.

Tash took my coat and hung it on the rack, and asked me if I'd like a drink. I followed her down the hall and into the kitchen. This was all normal stuff I did with any number of my clients, but Tash gave the clear impression from her nervy air and measured, step-by-step manner that she was biding her time, gearing herself up for the session.

'You'll come with me upstairs?' she stated, not looking me in the eye.

'Sure, Tash,' I agreed, hoping that my light mood might put her at her ease at least a little. 'Just show me the way.'

Tash handed me my tumbler, and I followed her up the stairs to the first floor.

'It's a nice house you've got here,' I commented.

'I've been here about eighteen months.'

It wasn't just small talk on my behalf – it *was* a nice place. The house looked neat and simply decorated, the walls in pale colours that matched her top. It felt just the right size for a young girl to make a home of.

'I still feel like I'm settling in,' she smiled.

'It can take a while, can't it?'

I noticed she found it easy to talk when it wasn't about what I was doing here in her home.

Tash led the way across the landing to her front bedroom. She opened the door, and for a second before she turned on the light, I could see the bed highlighted in the golden glow from the streetlamp outside. She hurried over to the bow windows to draw the curtains and shut out the world, all the while keeping her back to me.

I went and sat down on the side of her bed closest to her and waited. I ran my hands over the duvet each side of me and flattened it down. I kept my mouth shut and watched her. I knew she couldn't stand at the windows forever, her hands gripping the edge of the closed curtains.

Tash turned and I gave her my warmest smile on cue. I patted the bed beside me as though we'd known each other for years. 'Come and sit down,' I beckoned.

Tash could handle that. She walked over to me, and sat down square beside me as if we were waiting for a bus. Her hands held each other on her lap and she stared straight ahead. I could see that I was going to have to take this one *real* slow.

I leaned back slightly on my arms so I looked as relaxed and unthreatening as possible.

'You haven't been here long?' I turned to her and started the small talk rolling, even though she still wasn't meeting my eyes.

'No, I moved here for work. I'm in office admin. In the town.' Tash's shoulders dropped a little, though her voice remained stilted.

'That's quite a change, settling into a new job and a new house. Just one of them's stressful enough.'

'I know!' she nodded with her smile and, forgetting herself, turned her head and looked right at me. 'It's taken me this long to feel at home.'

That's better.

Tash's hands had slipped on to the bedspread beside her. I weighed up whether to reach for one of them, or to leave things be for a short while longer. I didn't want to frighten her back inside her shell.

'Have you got to know your neighbours, Tash?'

'Not really,' she shook her head. 'They're mostly

young families, and a few elderly couples. There doesn't seem to be anyone my age around here . . .'

She bit her lip. I stretched out my right hand and placed it over hers. I could feel it shaking slightly.

I'm not going anywhere, Tash.

'I've never had sex!' she blurted out.

Tash was back to looking wide-eyed, staring straight ahead at the curtains. Though she was biting her lip, it still trembled ever so slightly.

'That's OK, Tash,' I said in my most reassuring voice. 'A lot of girls your age haven't.'

Not as many as have – but hey.

But then, a split second later, I feared I might have put her off and scrambled to reassure her. 'But you want to, don't you?' I spoke softly.

She turned sharply towards me and spoke clearly and firmly, which I wasn't expecting at all. 'I've had boyfriends in the past. It's just that we never went the whole way.'

She was speaking as much to herself as explaining things to me. 'And I'm twenty-one, and y'know . . .' The words trailed off.

I took my hand off hers and reached up to touch Tash's straight blonde hair. I hooked a strand behind her ear and looked straight into her eyes. 'And you feel it's about time you did?'

She said nothing but nodded back.

'Well, that's why I'm here, Tash. That's why you called me, isn't it?'

'But not just the sex. You'll be careful, won't you?' she whispered.

She didn't move on the bed but I could still feel her pull herself away from me.

'I will. Don't worry,' I said, and rubbed her bare shoulder.

That went without saying. I could more or less divide my clients into two camps. Those who booked me for my time and as much hard sex as we could fit in. And those, like Tash, who needed it served up in a gentler manner. The journey getting there and the aftermath were just as important, just as much what they were paying for.

Tash looked down at the small space of pale pink duvet cover between us. She swallowed her fear and bridged the gap between us, taking my other hand in hers.

'Since I've lived here I haven't had . . . I miss . . .' she stuttered. 'It's not just not having had sex . . .'

She looked up at me with piercing blue eyes full of yearning.

'You miss just being with a man, don't you?'

Me saying it made her a little more bold. Her hand reached up my wrist and her fingers and thumb played over it, enjoying the sensation.

'They must be walking around with their eyes shut in Luton, Tash. You're a very pretty girl.'

She didn't say anything in return, but a bashful little smile flashed across her face as if she really needed to hear those words.

I placed my other hand to her neck, drawing her close to me, and kissed her gently on the lips. I pulled back slightly and whispered: 'Are you all right?'

'Yes,' she replied in the same tone and moved closer to me.

Our lips met, and hers opened slightly, and I took my cue, teasing her mouth with the tip of my tongue to open wider. She offered me no resistance.

Tash wrapped her arms around me and held on tight. I gave as good as I got, warming her up with my hug. This was where the skill came. Taking a girl like Tash from the chat to the embraces and physical intimacy. And from there to the sex itself. You could fall at the first hurdle. Or the second one, come to that.

Not that they ever have in my company.

But that was the threat hanging over me. That girls like Tash might just go on talking and talking out of sheer fright until their time was up. Which meant that it wasn't just my job to get her to go the whole way. My expertise lay in making her feel she was in safe enough hands to let her guard down early on and relax into every step of the journey.

We were still both clothed.

'Tash, if you could undress and slip under the covers, I'll do the same and join you, OK?'

We unlinked from each other, and she shifted, turning away on the bed, and with her back facing me, began to hitch her slip of a top over her head. She wore no bra.

In the minutes that followed, Tash kicked off her jeans and I headed to the corner of the room and stripped naked too. By the time I'd turned back to the bed, Tash was lying inside, waiting. I didn't jump in but pulled back the cover and slid in slowly beside her.

We lay there, saying nothing for a couple of moments.

I knew to take things carefully, so as not to frighten her off. I hitched myself up onto my elbow, giving her my full attention.

'You're fine, Tash?'

'Yes. It's getting used to this . . .' Her thin voice trailed off.

I reached across with my free hand and began to stroke her belly. It was soft and smooth under the bedclothes. She lay still and let me.

'You've got nothing to worry about. You just let me know if there's anything you feel uncomfortable with, won't you?'

She said nothing in reply. My hand widened its sweep up her body, and cradled one breast and then the other. I nibbled at her neck and her head stretched back into the pillow.

Is she going to just lie there?

She wasn't. He own arm reached up to clench my shoulder, and she pulled herself up so that our lips met again. Her fingers ruffled my hair and felt their way tenderly over my scalp and down my neck. I shifted closer to her and we were now clasped in each other's arms.

It was just a step away for my right leg to swing over both of hers, even as our embrace grew tighter. But with a practised manoeuvre, I held back for a matter of moments to sort out the protection. So, it was her first time. A guy still had to show some respect round here.

After all this time, I'd got condom-manoeuvre down to a fine art, so a girl would barely notice any gap in the flow of action. Though it wasn't as if Tash was going to, was it? That was one of the advantages of sleeping with a newbie – she had nothing to compare me with.

Not that I wouldn't compare favourably with the best of them.

I slipped my hand around Tash's hip bone to steady myself and guided myself between her legs. She winced with the pain of entrance and the new sensation, but I soothed her with the closeness of my breast against hers, and the gentle caresses of my hands.

'Are you OK?' I asked her.

'Yes, I'm just a bit sore,' she gasped.

And that was the other thing about sleeping with a virgin. It was likely to hurt to some degree. It was my job to introduce her to what it was like to make love. But I had to ensure I took her beyond the pain barrier far enough so she came back for more. Whether with me or her next boyfriend.

After all, there was a reason a woman called in an escort for her first time – it was because she wanted a decent experience. Not for her the 'walk of shame' after a tawdry night with a guy she'd picked up in a club just so she could get the moment over with. She wanted a good memory.

I knew full well that was my job. To give Tash an evening she wouldn't forget in a hurry.

Tash needed tenderness and compassion. To physically feel the warm weight of a man as much as tick off her 'To Do' list. And since I knew that the first experience of sex often hurt, then it was all the more important that I compensated with my touch, making every other part of her body feel damn special.

No, it's not just about the sex.

Our hands and our lips explored each other. Words weren't needed but I gave them to her anyway. 'You've got a beautiful body, Tash. You really have.'

Tash said nothing but she gave me a shy smile. I followed my words with action, tracing my kisses across her breasts and licking her belly. She rippled with pleasure. Her lips were on my shoulder and her hands played up and down my back as if she was searching out unexplored territory.

I looked up at her, and our lips met again. I could feel her budding confidence in her tongue's playfulness with mine. My hands ran over her torso and her breasts once again, and then I eased myself away from her.

'I trust that didn't put you off,' I declared deadpan, as I backed off the bed. Tash didn't shift at all, though the bedcovers were half pulled away from her. She lay naked before me, looking utterly contented.

'No. Not at all.'

Her voice was steady and stronger, any traces of her initial fear gone. 'I could lie here like this all night,' she mused.

I picked up my trousers from the floor and pulled them back on, along with my shirt, which I buttoned swiftly. When I turned back towards Tash on the bed, she surprised me by now standing close beside me, her own clothes back on.

'That was lovely, Luke. Exactly what I needed.' Tash rubbed my arm tenderly.

'I'm glad I could be of help.'

I kissed her forehead.

She went over to the dressing table, picked up the envelope of money and came back and put it in my hand. Some girls paid upfront, others at the end of a session. It was a risk – that they might not have the money. But I'd yet to be stung that way. What I was aware of was that nervous clients such as Tash could be intimidated by me asking for payment before we'd even got started. It could be too blunt an approach – reminding them that our time together was a financial transaction, when what they needed was tenderness.

'You were,' she said. 'Very much so.'

We returned downstairs and she called me my cab to the station. When it arrived, we kissed on the lips one last time. I stepped out of her house and into the midnight darkness. It had been a pleasure to help her out. She was gorgeous, for one thing. And whomever she had from now on, she'd never forget me for being her first.

Josephine

Mid-March

The elegant clock on the mantelpiece told me I'd already been here well over an hour – and we still hadn't got beyond the talking stage.

I ignored the voice in my head telling me I was losing my touch. I knew exactly what I was doing with Josephine. I was letting her talk herself out until she felt comfortable enough to move to the next stage.

She was telling me about her family visits to India. It was funny, because when I'd first spoken to Josephine on the phone, I'd presumed by the lilt in her voice that she might be Welsh and had been surprised when a handsome, fifty-something Asian lady had opened the door to me. She lived in a quiet street in leafy Twickenham.

As I settled into the comfy sofa, I noted the array of Indian carvings among the immaculately arranged antiques. A pair of knee-high elephants guarded the marble fireplace.

I looked across at Josephine. She was sitting far back in a striped armchair that matched the sofa, nervously holding onto her teacup and saucer. If she gripped it any tighter, I was sure the thing would shatter between her fingertips. I smiled with my eyes to reassure her.

'It's not often I come out this far.'

'I'm a solicitor at a local practice,' she disclosed, which surprised me, since she spoke in a quiet voice that didn't especially fill me with confidence – and suggested that she still had a way to go before she felt totally relaxed in my company.

'I came to the area not long after I qualified. I can remember when the houses round here were divided into bedsits. I've got this place –' she looked up to the ceiling to indicate the entire house – 'all to myself.'

Josephine looked down at her cup and then across at me with a timid smile. She was proving very hard work indeed. Her nervousness reminded me of Jenny, my first ever client, and how shy she'd been.

I was even getting to the point where I wouldn't have been surprised if Josephine had suddenly stuttered that she couldn't go through with it. Though that took enough courage in itself. Not that any of my clients had ever yet bailed out on me, thankfully, but I recognized the possibility. And until Josephine openly admitted *that*, we were at stalemate.

I certainly wasn't about to suggest that possibility, just in case it gave her the permission to follow it through. But, on the other hand, while the two of us were sitting here and the mantelpiece clock went on ticking loudly, we weren't really getting anywhere. Yet all the same, sitting on Josephine's sofa in front of her and drinking her tea, I wasn't getting any vibe that she'd rather I *wasn't* here. And sooner or later about to have sex with her. After all, she'd booked me, hadn't she?

It was time to push things forward. 'You've some lovely pieces, Josephine. Especially the Indian antiques. Have you done your whole house up in this style?'

Josephine became animated, as if I'd just put an idea into her head. Which I had. I'd given her an excuse to naturally move to the next base.

She set her cup and saucer down on the coffee table, and I handed her mine. She stood up proudly: 'I'll show you round if you like!'

'Yes, please, I'd like that.'

As we headed upstairs, Josephine pointed out the paintings and embroideries that lined the stairwell: richly coloured illustrations of Indian figures and elephants and tigers.

We crossed the landing towards the bedroom at the front of the house. 'And this is my room,' she said, finally sounding a little bolder as she put her hand on the doorknob and pushed open the door. It was similar in style to what I'd seen of the rest of the house. A double bed sat in the middle of the room.

As I followed her into the room, I was about to close the door behind me as an unspoken signal that we were now moving towards the crux of our session, and that she had nothing to worry about, when Josephine turned and slipped past me back through the door.

Where's she going?

She spoke very quietly. 'I'd like you to come with me.'

The spare room was smaller than the main room, but also contained a double bed. The only other piece of furniture that shared the room was a heavy, dark wood double-fronted wardrobe.

'Now, Luke, if I can show you something?'

Josephine opened the cupboard door, and I swear I couldn't have been more surprised if she'd been hiding a real-life tiger in there. I only hoped that the shock didn't register across my face.

Because the wardrobe contained no clothes. The only things hanging from hooks at the back of the wardrobe were a tangle of whips and paddles, and leather straps and apparatus that I wasn't even sure how to use.

My eyes felt as if they were bulging at the pressure of all that I was trying to hold in. I would have been less surprised if she'd announced that in fact she'd never yet had sex at all.

In all my escort encounters, this was the first time I'd set my eyes on anything as kinky as this. It was strange if I thought too much about it. Twenty-first-century sex in the UK was supposed to be more liberated than it had ever been, but the vast majority of the stuff requested of me remained plain old vanilla-flavoured.

Of course I was aware of the existence of this stuff. It was the section I walked past quickly whenever I happened to be in a sex shop. It *disturbed* me. This display in front of me was sure damn unnerving me now – and so was Josephine standing next to me, come to think of it. Because now she'd actually admitted to the hooker that she had the equipment to play with, there was only one direction we could be heading in.

What the fuck does she want me to do with it? Or do to me?

I turned to face Josephine, swallowed hard, and spoke with as measured a voice as I could muster. 'Is there anything you'd like me to do for you, Josephine?'

Mixed up with my fascination at what was going on in this shy lady's mind was a sense of dread at the worst she might request. Whips, paddles, bondage. At least one of us in the room could really get hurt.

Josephine bit her lip. The brash flourish with which she'd flung open the cupboard door was now hidden again behind a cloud of shyness. It was as if she'd used up her entire reserve of confidence just to let me see something of what she was really like.

Her voice quivered. 'You don't think I'm weird, do you?'

'Of course not, Josephine,' I mustered.

Whether I thought her weird wasn't the point. I was fucking *terrified*. The way she'd swept open the cupboard door with such force didn't bode well for what damage she might do with one of those sex toys.

Toys? Who was I kidding? *Weapons* more like.

I stood there, silent, not really sure what to do next – but it was Josephine who took matters into her own hands. She reached out for a black silk scarf that didn't look to me as if it could do much damage.

'I like being blindfolded, Luke. Would you do that for me?'

I took it from her hand.

'Not yet,' she instructed. 'Once we've got going.'

She nodded towards the bed. That was to be the scene of the action.

I hooked the scarf round my neck like a tailor's

measuring tape and hovered, ready for Josephine's next instruction.

'Is there anything you'd like to do to me, Luke?'

I was dumbstruck. This was so outside my comfort zone. Yes, she was right; this was all so fucking *weird*.

I played it damn cool. 'I tell you what, Josephine. You tell me what you'd like me to do. I haven't done this before,' I admitted, 'so I'm going to need some guidance.'

That cleared the air – as much for me as for her.

Josephine reached into the cupboard and took out a few long strips of black leather. There was a velvet bag hanging off a hook on the inside of the door, and she pulled it open, dipped her hand inside and I heard the chink of metal. She drew her hand out and held out her palm so I could see. There was a silver pair of what looked like bulldog clips. I had a pretty good idea what those were for, but I could only pray that she didn't want to use them on *me*. They made me wince just to look at them.

Josephine turned and placed the ties and clips on the pillow and sat on the bed's edge and looked at me as she unbuttoned her blouse. I took the hint, and began to undo my own shirt. When we were both naked, she pulled herself up the bed so her back was against the headboard. She picked up the tie, ran it through her other hand and watched as I knelt beside her.

I decided to take things into my own hands, if only to stop her using any of that stuff on me. I took the leather strap from her. 'You'd like me to tie your wrists?' I gestured to the bedpost.

'Not together. One each side of my head, please.'

I concentrated on winding the strip round and round the bedpost and her arm. This was completely new territory for me. 'I'm not tying this too tight, am I?'

Josephine didn't answer. And then she did. 'And when you've finished doing that, I'd like you to blindfold me, Luke, and then gag me too, if you would, please.'

Fuck me!

I tried not to laugh at Josephine's politeness. Never mind the paddles and straps. The weirdest thing was that this sweet, nervous lady was so different to how she appeared. And how she spoke! Maybe that was the point. Hiring me for this was a way for the gentle solicitor to let her hair down.

And then I remembered the bulldog clips. *Fuck!*

There was no getting around it. I had to find out what she wanted to do with them. If it was anything to do with me, then at least I'd have some warning. Or be able to run the hell out of there while she was still struggling with the ties.

'Josephine, the clips. What . . . ?' When it came to it, I hadn't a clue what to ask. I wasn't sure I wanted to hear the answer. What if she *did* want to use them on me?

'I could put them on my nipples, Luke, but they're just not as effective if I do it myself. I need a helping hand . . .'

I mentally breathed out a sigh of relief. They were *nipple* clamps. *Thank God!*

My cock, I could tell, was as relieved as I was.

'You'd like me to put them on for you?'

She smiled up at me from between the V of her

tied arms. 'You'd do that for me? But not just yet, all right?'

I nodded.

'The blindfold!' she exclaimed, as if she was desperate for it.

I bit my lip as I drew it from around my neck. Josephine noticed. 'Is there something bothering you, Luke?'

'It's just I'm worried I'll tie it too tight. You'll let me know if I'm hurting you, won't you?'

Her eyes were supportive and warm. 'Take it slow and gentle and you'll be fine.'

I placed the strip of black silk gently across her eyes and knotted it at the back of her head. I sat back and surveyed my handiwork.

Josephine said nothing – her demeanour calm, yet expectant. She knew exactly what she wanted. I was impressed, too, how she'd willingly let me put her in such a vulnerable position. She'd made it clear that she trusted me, even though she could no longer see me.

I stretched out and stroked the inside of her thigh and a current of bliss carried up her entire body. Her bottom lip quivered. I was tempted to slip a couple of my fingers into her wet mouth for her to suck on.

'Will you gag me now, Luke,' she instructed in a bolder voice, as if the very fact she could no longer see brought out an otherwise hidden strength. 'Tight,' she growled.

I raised the leather strip to her lips, and splayed it across Josephine's face. Silencing her. I pulled the laces taut at the nape of the neck, and when her head jerked back with the pull on the trapped strands of her jet-black hair, she rallied, shaking her head violently. I read it as her wanting me to keep my hands off, and drew away sharply.

She was an odd sight, this olive-skinned lady, strung up and naked except for a couple of parallel black strips across her face. She could have been anyone. But at the same time, it had the effect on me of drawing my attention to the rest of her. She'd looked after her figure; it was slight and lithe like a dancer's.

I swept my palm up the length of her left leg and hovered for a beat at her pussy just to get her racing, then lifted my hand and gripped the side of her waist. I dipped my face into her soft belly and licked my way upwards to her tits. Her back arched as her breasts rose to meet me. A guttural moan of pleasure sounded deep in her throat and I took it as an invite to head further north, flicking my tongue hard against her neck and up to the tip of her chin. Her entire body twisted and shook beneath me and her bound wrists coiled and pulled, as if she was trying to escape; at the very same moment she was writhing with bliss at all the enjoyment I was giving her.

I half feared that her head might blow clean off with the sheer heat and thrill of it all. I lightened my touch to let her regroup and catch her breath and gently stroked her shoulders.

And then she forced her breasts out at me like the crack of a whip. *The nipple clamps.*

I was unsure whether to even say the words. Maybe

she'd get more thrill out of *not* knowing when they were about to bite. Maybe that was part of the game.

The clamps were glinting under a corner of her pillow. I grabbed the pair of them and shook them in my fist so that they clicked together. She quickly turned her head towards the sound.

'Uh, uh,' I laughed, drawing my hand away and shaking closer to the opposite ear.

A deep frown cut across her forehead.

'Oh, come on, Josephine,' I chuckled, before bending my head to suckle a hardened nipple.

I let her wait a few more minutes. There was a groan of wanting trapped in her throat. Her head was thrown back as if she was crying out for me to use the clamps.

The trouble was that this wasn't my idea of fun at all. I knew putting the damn things on her was going to hurt me every bit as much as it was likely to pain her. Though, presumably, she at least would be getting some sort of warped pleasure out of what I was doing to her. I, on the other hand, would be spending every moment wincing through gritted teeth at the thought of how they would feel.

I ran my fingers in an ever-decreasing circle over her left breast and then, with a clip in one hand and her nipple held between the fingers of my other hand, I swallowed hard, pursed my lips and narrowed my eyes as the metal clasped tight on to her flesh. Josephine's entire body stiffened with the shock of it. God, she was getting off on it. Whereas it left me cold. It all looked so painful. I wasn't even sure I was happy helping

Josephine out. I just didn't understand how anyone could be aroused this way.

I shook my hand again so the second clip nestled between my fingers, and went in for the kill a second time. A mix of a shriek and a deep moan pierced through the gag.

Now my own hands were free, I got into my stride. I traced my fingers down between Josephine's legs to tickle her clit. Once I'd got her aroused, I ran the heel of my hand in a quickening sawing rhythm against her pussy.

Bound though she was, her body still snaked across the bed, accompanied by a low groan of delight. I heeded the signal. I slipped my hand down between her legs to ease them apart and held off for a couple of seconds to get myself covered, then thrust into her up to the hilt. I rode her fast and hard, all the while keeping my eye on the sharp little grips on her tits. I knew the damage they could do to me if I wasn't careful.

For Josephine, the blindfold and the gag left everything but sound to the imagination. She couldn't see or use words to work out where she was. Neither could she tell me to go easy on her, pace myself, or even ask me to call a halt. The rawest of feelings were at the tips of her breasts and as deep as I could thrust.

It was if that very realization encouraged me to go at her full tilt. The top half of her body was turned on – courtesy of the blindfold and the pained nipples – whereas it was my job to go hell for leather between her thighs. The very fact I could no longer fully see her made me fuck her even more furiously to force some reaction out of her. As far as I could tell, apart from her writhing, panting torso and the sweat and the guttural sighs, I had no idea of what she was really getting out of this. I couldn't see the whites of her eyes or hear any yell of deep bliss, I could only read the movement of Josephine's body. Her hips and pelvis writhed beneath me. Her head rocked back and forth. The way she was forcing herself towards me, her strength meeting mine, told me that she was as up for it as I was.

When my orgasm came, and hers almost at the same time, our chests met in the crush. Afterwards I looked down at my bruised, chafed torso. Josephine's nipple clamps had given me a souvenir of my visit.

I drew myself out from inside her, and pulled myself away, all the while watching her lying there before me, unseeing. Or seeing it all in her head. Me wondering what I'd conjured up for her.

I laid a gentle hand on her bound wrist and, with my other, flutter-stroked around her breasts and along her neck, letting my touch grow ever lighter.

She quivered until her breathing too was measured and peaceful.

'Josephine,' I whispered, 'I'm going to undo the ties, is that all right?'

She nodded her head in two slow movements of agreement.

In spite of what we had just shared, it still felt strange to be sitting in this room with this naked, bound woman. I picked at the leather laces with my finger-nails and cursed myself for tying them so tightly.

Suppose I couldn't get it undone? What then? The scissors? I could see how this whole scenario could switch from fast sex and lust to danger to sheer farce in the blink of an eye.

The laces were now undone and I unwound them. Each of her arms relaxed down on to the bedclothes. I undid the knot at the back of Josephine's neck and held the tie for a couple of minutes so she remained unaware that she was yet free. I took a deep, silent breath and peeled the ribbon off from her hair and then away from her face.

Josephine kept her eyes closed for a little while as if acclimatizing herself to the very idea of being back in the 'real' world. The unbound one, where she was quietly rattling round this house on her own, seemingly out of step with the fast-paced world beyond her door. Or maybe she was, like me, wondering how she'd look her ten-minutes-ago sex partner in the eyes after what we'd just experienced together.

I decided not to remove Josephine's gag just yet. I instead took her now free hands in mine and guided them to her breasts and the still erect glittering silver nipple clamps. Those clamps still claiming that there was some sex and arousal in the air, that their time wasn't yet up.

I let my fingers wind round hers and together we unclipped them in silence, with as much tenderness on my part as I could muster, though there was a neediness in Josephine's scrabbling at the metal.

The clamps came away in her hands. My fingers were clasped over hers, gripping them, and my mouth was open in suspense and release and I was sucking in a whole heap of fresh air. It was like I was doing exactly what I supposed Josephine might have done. Had her mouth not been tied shut.

I ran my thumbs over each of her nipples to salve them. Josephine's eyes were wide open now and she was looking directly into mine. I bent my head and gently kissed each of her breasts. I was telling her that that was as far as I went with the pain I had caused her, however much pleasure she might have got out of it.

'I'm going to remove the gag now,' I said, to warn her and give her the chance to get used to the idea.

She could have taken it off herself if she'd wanted to. But the fact that she hadn't made it clear that she was leaving the final act to me. To finish what she'd asked me to start. This was all part of her submissiveness package. It wasn't her place to release herself. She was giving that privilege to me.

I undid the leather and drew it away from her. She licked her lips and I moved in to kiss them. There was a red pressure line like a moustache across her upper lip, leading to each ear.

All that dominance had done the trick. I now saw Josephine in a completely different light. It struck me as ironic. In spite of her submissive role, by leading me upstairs to reveal this side of herself to me, the quiet solicitor had shown me that she had real balls.

Melanie

The sex with Melanie tonight was red hot. Any previous inhibitions there might once have been had fled sessions ago. Now, both of us were absolutely sure what each of us was there for.

A quick and fun fuck.

We'd ripped each other's clothes off and got down to it almost before we'd crossed the threshold of her bedroom. Britney Spears's *Greatest Hits* played in the background. I felt 'Toxic', all right. I dug right into her. Our bodies flexed easily in our sweat.

Afterwards, when we were relaxing side by side in the bed, she sat up and looked down at me so that she had the upper hand.

'Luke, have you been seeing Alison?'

She asked it boldly, right out of the blue. At least she'd had the decency not to mention it until the post-coital lull.

I was stunned but pulled myself together fast and took a deep breath. As I did, I racked my brains for something to say. I'd decided a while back that I wasn't going to say anything about Alison unless Melanie asked. But I knew that when she did ask, as she just had, I wouldn't be able to lie. I was adamant up to this point that I would tell the truth.

But as it happened, it turned out to be damn easier said than done. I opened my mouth to speak, still unsure of what exactly I was going to say. Melanie's eyes hadn't left mine. She was silently waiting for my response.

Here goes.

'Yes, I have, Melanie.'

There, I'd said it. A momentary flush of hurt washed across Melanie's face. With her other hand she gave me a punch that barely brushed me, but she still said nothing. She'd realized in that lack of momentum she had to really *wound* me that she had no emotional claim on me *at all*. She was paying me for my time, *goddamnit*.

But that didn't mean that she didn't feel betrayed by my dating Alison. I suppose there might have been an underlying jealousy that Alison had been *chosen* by me. That the two of us had immediately hit it off and some sort of fledgling relationship had evolved naturally out of that.

Whereas the only way that Melanie had been able to catch my attention was by employing me. I winced when I thought about that. That *must* have surely hurt.

And presumably Melanie hadn't been able to let on to Alison that she and I knew each other a whole lot more intimately than occasionally bumping into each other in a London nightclub. She had to keep her mouth shut on that score, so she couldn't express to Alison why she felt upset by her coupling up with me. That must have been awkward. Whichever way you looked at it, Melanie had a right to feel hard done by.

I leant towards Melanie and wrapped an arm around her shoulders and drew her to me.

'Ah, but Melanie,' I half whispered, in the most seductive voice I could manage, 'she's not the one who's just shared a fantastic sex session with me. She *never* has, you know,' I stressed.

Melanie was still trying to act cross but a satisfied smile crept up her face. There was no arguing with my words and what we had just done. That glimpse of her smile went some way towards making up my mind for me.

I spent the next night mulling over the whole so-called love triangle I'd got myself caught up in. Though it wasn't really that at all. It might have made more sense to me if it had been the usual common-or-garden 'three's a crowd' love triangle. But 'the friend, the escort, and the client' made everything all the more tangled.

I *liked* Melanie and enjoyed her company. I definitely liked Alison too, but we'd not even slept together yet, and the relationship hadn't yet reached the point where I was about to schedule that into my BlackBerry for any day soon. Ironically for a guy like myself who was supposed to be so relaxed when it came to sex, we had never reached that stage. Maybe there were just too many secrets between us.

The situation had been so much of a head-fuck for each and every one of us, whether we'd been aware of the whole truth or not. And whatever little the three of us had, love or lust-wise, it was causing problems and coming between each of us. I wasn't yet sure what I felt about Alison, or she about me, come to that. We were still testing the waters, though I knew I for one was holding back for whatever reason. It was Melanie I was more concerned about. She felt *something* for me. I could tell that from her disappointment at finding out about me and Alison. And then there was their friendship that was being threatened too.

I wasn't in the habit of breaking up others' relationships if I could help it – whether they were friendships or anything else – and I wasn't about to start now. I decided to end whatever I had with Alison for the sake of all of us. And especially out of a renewed respect for Melanie. She had enough crap in her life to contend with, without me adding to the load.

It was a fortnight since I'd broken things off with Alison and I was visiting Melanie in Hendon for our latest session. It had been a relief when she'd called to book it. Clearly she hadn't thought me enough of a shit to dump my services altogether, though she had every reason to.

It turned out that Melanie had herself been giving some thought to our tangled 'threesome'. As soon as she opened the door, she declared, 'I've dumped Alison.'

What the fuck?

I hadn't expected *that*. I hoped the shock didn't show on my face. Melanie had pre-empted anything I might have done – had I known what to do. The finality of it shook me too. The thing that had impressed me about

Melanie's mates at the nightclub, including Alison, was how they'd stuck around for her in spite of her illness. Melanie's decision flew in the face of that.

As I followed her down the hall, I tried to work out what to make of this new twist. And then it struck me: I hated to think it, let alone say it, and I certainly hoped the relief didn't show in any way across my face as Melanie handed me my whisky and soda, but her decision had made it miles easier for everyone.

The whole sorry mess brought me to my senses, that's for sure. I'd got off lightly. It could have turned out so much uglier. Trying to have any sort of relationship while I was an escort was tough enough as it is. But making a stab at any of my *clients'* friends – well, I'd damn sure learnt my lesson with the Alison scenario. I had to wonder why I'd got mixed up with her in the first place. What was I doing? Why couldn't I have had a quick shag with Alison that night and left it at that? There was something niggling at me that I didn't want to think too much about. That sex, whichever way I got it, wasn't giving me all that I wanted. Trying to have something more with Alison had proved more trouble than it was worth.

And what's more, I'd been damned lucky this time. It had worked out to my advantage, though I recognized the close call I'd had, even so. I sure didn't need anything like *that* in my life again. For now, it looked as if I had to be content with sex for its own sake.

Karen again

June

Sheila *knew* that my relationship with Karen didn't add up *one bit*. I could see it in her eyes.

She was damn right, of course. This was the fourth time that Karen had called me over, and already I was having to act the 'boyfriend' in front of her mates and her son, Callum, and *his* girlfriend too. But Karen had invited her friends, Sheila and Imogen to check out her new toy boy. At least Karen had warned me in advance that they'd be here.

I was standing in the middle of Karen's sun-filled kitchen, the proverbial centre of attention. Karen had clearly hired me to show off. And if everyone could see what Karen saw in the fit Aussie almost half her age, Sheila's fierce gaze was demanding to know what the fuck was in it for *me*.

I turned my attention to Karen, who was leaning against the fridge with Imogen, her best mate, beside her. They chuckled in unison like a double act. These women were two of a kind, equally up for it with guys

93

a fraction of their age. Imogen was friendly and open and unfazed about me being so much younger than Karen.

'You got any *mates*' – she said it in a strangled Aussie accent – 'you can introduce me to, Luke?' she trilled.

'I'm so sorry, Imogen. I did have. Plenty. But they've all flown south for the winter, I'm afraid,' I commiserated.

'And left poor Luke all by himself. It's a good job I found you, isn't it, love?' cooed Karen.

Breathing deeply, I looked directly at her and smiled like a guy in love. Inside, I winced.

I quickly changed the subject. Karen's son was looking down at his feet, holding his girlfriend Cassie's hand. She too had her head bowed and was whispering something to him. Karen had told me that he was twenty, but he looked younger than that. There was an adolescent air about him that reminded me of my younger brother Jack.

'Callum, I've heard a lot about you,' I shot at him, and his head jerked up to take a good look at me.

He grunted a 'Hi' in return.

Maybe Callum's awkwardness was just that he was a fish out of water among all these women. They were dressed to the nines, while he wore slashed jeans and a black Metallica T-shirt and black boots. His looks were nondescript. It wasn't as if he was *bad* looking, but he didn't look distinctive. Unlike his mum, who'd made up for it with slap.

I stuck out my hand to shake his. 'It's nice to meet you at last.'

Callum looked uncomfortable and I realized he

94

wasn't used to shaking *anyone's* hand. And at the same moment it struck me that he was also likely to be highly suspicious of yet *another* man in his mum's life. I was just one more guy passing through.

Why should he even give a damn?

'So, Callum, did you catch the match on Saturday? What did you make of the line-up?'

Fortunately there had been an England friendly against Poland at Wembley. Not that I cared. But it gave me something to talk about with Callum, and since I had no interest in either team, there was no chance of us coming to blows over it.

That got him interested, as I expected it to. His face lit up and he became animated. 'You really want to know what I think?' he sneered with a glint in his eyes. 'Fucking crap. The lot of them. They *gave* it away.'

It suddenly hit me forcibly that I was so much closer in age to Callum than his mum. As with a lot of obvious things, it took a while for the penny to drop.

I've got more in fucking common with him than her.

We could have been any two guys talking about the footie, the universal language of men of our age, over pints in the local pub. But instead we were standing here nursing beers in his kitchen. And the only reason *I* was here was because I was knocking off his mum. It was one hell of a mind-fuck.

It was funny. Every time I thought I'd got the hang of my job, that I'd seen it all, escorting would throw up something new – like this little setup.

Which reminded me. *Karen.* It was time to get back to business.

I swallowed my pride, turned away from Callum and gave his mother a huge beaming smile. I marched across the kitchen, took Karen's hand and sidled between her and Imogen.

Imogen gladly gave me space. The curved edge of the worktop dug into the small of my back. Imogen was enjoying her best friend's luck with the lads, though I detected an element of envy in her eyes too. Which, presumably, was what Karen was paying me for too.

'So, how did you two meet?' Sheila directed at me.

There was a wolf-like tinge to her smile, and the way she cocked her head and stared at me as she said it told me she was digging for all the *wrong* reasons. I squeezed Karen's hand to reassure her that she had nothing to worry about, that I was on her side and wasn't about to say the wrong thing.

'At the pub!' blurted out Karen.

She was about to say the wrong thing. It was my own fault. I should have got our story clean and sorted when Karen was booking this session and told me she'd have friends round this time.

'But we found each other on the Internet first, didn't we, love? We arranged to meet up in the pub once we found out how well we got on.' I smiled encouragingly at Karen and willed her to go along with the story I was peddling.

Just the phrase 'the Internet' dialled up a whole heap of possibilities. You could find *anything* on there. I hadn't really answered Sheila's question at all. And I was damn sure she realized that. I looked her straight in the eyes to let her know that whatever game she might be playing, I was an equal match and would always have the last word.

Karen had told me the last time we met how she had a thing about younger guys, so I wouldn't look out of place when I met Callum and Karen's friends – they were used to meeting her toy boys. I would just appear to be the latest one hanging off her arm.

I wasn't altogether sure how I felt about *that*. I was obviously doing my job, so whatever she wanted of me should have been just water off a duck's back. But even so, the thought of hanging off *Karen*'s arm and everyone assuming I was that into her left me cold.

And that reminded me. Just because it made me cringe didn't mean that I *didn't* have to keep playing my part to keep Karen onside. I leant against Karen to show to all the world – or at least these four in her kitchen – that I was *so* happy to be her boyfriend. Though this certainly wasn't what I'd got into sex work for. It was all so much easier when it was just me alone with a client and I was swapping a shag for good money.

Karen nestled a little closer to me, sliding her hand beneath the waistband of my jeans. I felt like her puppet. But I was hoping beyond hope that my humiliation wasn't in any way showing on my face.

I could almost hear the others, especially Callum, thinking, 'What's wrong with you? Why don't you date someone hotter and more your own age? Why *her*?' I felt as uncomfortable with the setup as they must have been about this odd couple I was one half of.

It wasn't as if Karen was unattractive, but she wasn't even the best looking of the four women in the room.

She'd told me that she'd had no trouble pulling men at least ten years younger than her. She'd even claimed to have dated someone in Callum's year – though thankfully not while either of them was still at school.

I assumed these lads had all worked out that she was easy. If you were in the mood for it, she'd give it to you on a plate. But, then again, she was clearly not so hot at that game that she didn't have to call out an escort to fill an obvious gap. Karen was trying to kid everyone that she could pull these young guys, but only I knew the truth: that the ones she didn't pay for weren't biting any more.

But why should I care? I reckoned that Karen might well be up for sex on more than a weekly basis if I played my cards right. With overnights, too, I wouldn't need to do any other work. She was desperate to keep up the pretence – as much for herself as anyone else – that I was her boyfriend, and had been happy to spend her money keeping up that illusion this far. If she had the funds, she could be the type of client every escort dreams of.

I wrapped an arm across Karen's shoulder and smiled defiantly back at Sheila. Her jaw tightened. She could think whatever the fuck she wanted. Karen and me were good for each other, and there was nothing she could say or do about it.

I'd lost count of how many sessions I'd now had with Karen. To her, they were 'dates' and she was calling me out so regularly, sometimes as many as three times a week, that they might as well have been.

I lounged back on her sofa, my hand on Karen's thigh. Callum was sitting in the armchair with Cassie on his lap and her legs swinging over the arm. We were watching *Phone Booth*, which Callum had collected from Blockbuster on his way home from the takeaway.

I picked up a slice of pizza from the box on my lap and handed it over to Karen. Instead of taking it, she lowered her head so her open mouth was beneath the drooping end of the slice. I raised my arm and the piece of pizza with it, and her head followed me. Like a fucking performing seal. I let her bite into it, and laughed with her as I did.

It *might* have been a bit of harmless fun – fore-fore-play, sort of – but, please, not in full view of her son and his girl. That only made this setup of me and Karen deeply cringeworthy for everyone. Except Karen.

She was so thick-skinned, so entranced with her 'young man', that she simply couldn't *see* – had no intention of seeing – the sheer absurdity of our fake relationship. And God, did *I* feel fake.

It shouldn't have mattered to me, I was dead aware of *that*. After all, I was only here because I was being paid to be. I'd got things down to a fine art with Karen too. I wouldn't turn up until eight or nine when my overnights officially began; we'd sit around watching a flick until late, then eventually get to bed for some quick sex before turning in for the night. And then I'd be out of there as early as possible the following morning, often before Karen had woken herself.

Because, I knew if Karen wasn't careful, she'd start believing that I *was* her real-life lover. It wouldn't be difficult for her to cross over that line. After all, wasn't that what she was already telling people like Imogen and Callum and Cassie, and hadn't they taken her and me at face value?

Only Sheila showed any suspicion. Everyone else seemed happy that Karen was so in love. Even Callum got on well with his mum's boyfriend. God, if I thought about it like that, it was *me* who was up to my neck in it, never mind Karen.

I watched Colin Farrell stuck in a tiny phone box with a sniper aiming at his head. *I know exactly how you feel, mate.*

When the film had finished, and we'd cleared up and had a final drink, Callum and his girl went off to his room. And very soon, Karen and I would be going to hers.

I suppose it must have been the same in homes the world over; different generations at it in different rooms, but it still felt very strange to me. What's more, somehow I'd managed to get myself caught up in a family setup while working in a job that signalled I was doing everything to avoid it. If that wasn't ironic, I don't know what was.

Karen poured me a whisky and ice. She knew what I had by now. She made one for herself too. Copying me, like someone in love might do.

Well, here goes.

'Thanks, love,' I said, and sat back on the sofa. I took a sip, and then Karen came and sat on my lap and turned to me with her glass and we chinked them.

'Cheers,' she murmured, as if we had to be quiet so

100

as not to disturb whatever was going on in the next room. I had a pretty good idea. Truth was, I'd have preferred a session with Callum's girlfriend.

But that could only ever be wishful thinking. As with Callum, the only reason I knew Chrissie in the first place was because I was seeing Karen. I had to remain mindful of that. But then again, it didn't hurt to use Chrissie as a helpful means of getting in the mood with her boyfriend's mum. Any tool at my disposal, frankly.

Karen was unbuttoning my shirt, and her hand slipped beneath the white cotton and began stroking my chest. Her tongue followed. That was more like it.

I had to admire the fact that Karen hadn't given up the chase. She might seem absurd at times in the way she dressed but, on the other hand, there was something life-affirming in the fact that she hadn't resigned herself to being defined by her son. She'd kept playing the field. You could say she was too old for this game, or you could raise a glass to the fact that she was still kicking the ball around.

God, if Callum could hear my footie comparisons!

I kissed Karen's neck while she pawed my chest, and slipped my hand up her short skirt. 'Shall we go to your room?' I whispered.

The last thing I wanted was the chance of Callum or Chrissie wanting a glass of water and walking in on Karen and me getting it on in the living room. That'd be the worst.

'Uh, huh,' replied Karen, her focus still on my body.

'Hey, love,' I muttered, directing her off me, 'let me get up and I'll take you there and show you what's what.

I'm going to fuck you rotten,' I said it slowly, as seductively as possible.

Karen slipped on to her feet and I stood up beside her. She straightened her skirt the same way she always did, pulling down the hem in an unconscious movement. It suggested she was trying to maintain some dignity even while she was giving it away to whichever young buck she was currently shagging.

We wrapped our arms around each other and I led her the well-trodden path to her door. I was taking her money – which meant I owed her a bloody good time of it. I prided myself on the service I gave, after all.

I kick-slammed the door behind me. *Who cares about Callum?* I looked at Karen looking at me with a huge grin across my face and we simultaneously burst out laughing. 'It's not as if we're going to *wake* them, is it?' I snorted.

'Let's show 'em how steaming things get! Let's drown them out,' Karen guffawed.

I pulled down her skirt and pushed her hard onto the bed, spread-eagling myself on top of her.

'I will if you will,' I growled into her ear.

I slid my hands under her top to pull it over her head whilst she was dragging my shirt over my shoulders. I drew away to remove the shirt completely, and she, blinded by the top, sent her arms flailing for me, searching me out.

I grabbed her arms and, pushing them out of the way above me, set myself nibbling at her belly. She chuckled and wriggled beneath me.

This is more like it.

I let go of her arms and she pulled her top over her head and flung it across the room so it landed at the door of the wardrobe. I kicked off my jeans so I was down to my boxers. Soon, both of us were in just our underwear.

'Oh, God, you've got a beautiful body,' she hissed.

'All the better for you to enjoy,' I murmured, as I slipped my hand under the wire of her bra and fondled her tits. She ran her hand up my torso as if she was sensing every bone and sinew.

'Aw, God,' she breathed out as her whole body sank deeper into the bed with the pleasure I was giving her.

I slid my hand around her torso and undid her bra and, as it fell away from her breasts, let my tongue follow my hand. I licked a trail from her back round to her cleavage, up her neck and then tunnelled into her open mouth.

While we were snogging *hard*, I scrambled out of my boxers. I was so practised these days that I could roll on a condom with my eyes closed. My dick was burning for me to get on with the show. Karen helped by pulling down her knickers, and the very next moment I shagged her. Our bodies grappled together on the bed, our tongues still entwined, our heavy panting in unison.

There was no one else here. Not in the next room, the block of flats, the estate or the city and the world beyond. It was just the two of us, our bodies chafing, our minds focused on nothing else but the rising gradient of desire steaming out of every pore.

We climaxed simultaneously, Karen screeching at the top of her voice and me letting out a guttural roar.

Fuck Callum and Chrissie!

The two of us collapsed against each other. I clung on tight, my arms around Karen. Her nails dug deep into my back but her hold on me gradually eased as our breathing calmed again. We rested together. I slid off her and lay by her side.

'Luke,' Karen muttered in a whine that warned me she was going to moan about *something*. I mentally went on the defensive, though I took care that my body didn't flinch and reveal it to her.

'I really enjoy you coming over, but I don't know if I can *afford* to keep having you here like this.'

I turned my head towards Karen's face, but remained shtoom. I let a slight smile play across my face to re-assure her. I knew that if I concentrated on listening instead of butting in, I'd gain some time to work out my answer and hear what she *really* wanted of me.

I held Karen's hand and played with her fingers to give her the impression that I was completely on her side. While, in actual fact, I was doing nothing but being a good hooker and playing her for all she was worth. As if I would've turned up at her door if it weren't for the cash!

The trouble was that that was exactly what it turned out she was asking of me.

'Luke,' she repeated my name as if she was pleading with me, which I suppose she was. 'I see you often enough.'

She was right there. This must have been the third week in a row when she'd called me out three times. The best part of five grand's-worth of my time. That was a record for any of my regulars.

'Yes,' I agreed with a determined warmth in my eyes.

'Well,' she mewed, and her whole tone went into little girl mode, 'can't you reduce the rate, pleeese?'

I looked down at Karen's naked breasts but remained silent. She clearly didn't understand that the very fact she *was* one of my regulars gave me all the more reason *not* to charge her a loyalty rate. Added to the reality was that it was damn exhausting work being at her beck and call so often, especially since I had to play the fucking boyfriend role.

Literally.

'I mean,' she continued, falling into the trap I'd set her of talking herself out and putting *all* her cards on the table, 'if I could guarantee you coming round this much *every* week, how about you reducing the fee to two hundred pounds a night?'

I swallowed a guffaw, which left me with a coughing fit. I jerked myself up to a sitting position and cleared my throat. Karen patted and stroked my back in an attempt to soothe me. Not realizing that it was her suggestion that had got me started.

'Come off it, Karen,' I joked to her with a twinkle in my eye to let her down gently, though I was deadly serious.

The maths was that she was currently paying me £500 for a standard overnight. And she was already asking me to do more than she was paying for really by expecting me to act as her real lover in front of Callum and her friends. Expecting me to cut my rate by more than half was some fucking cheek. Not to mention that it just wouldn't be worth my while.

'I like seeing you, Luke,' she whined, 'but I don't know how much longer I can afford to. What'll I tell Callum, and the girls? That you dropped me just like that?'

That wasn't my problem – that was the situation she'd got herself mixed up in. It had nothing to do with me. I was just her puppet on a string, dancing to her tune.

And that was the measure of it. For all the money I was getting paid, Karen needed me a damn sight more than I needed her. I could always find myself some more clients to fill the gap that her dropping me would leave in my income.

But she wouldn't be able to find another me – or anyone like me – too easily. Being a male escort remained very much a gay guy's arena. There'd be a definite gap in her life if she stopped seeing me, and certainly no *real* boyfriend to fill the gap. And how would Karen explain *that* to Callum?

Agnieszka

Summer solstice

'This is what I want of you, Luke. I want you to lie back so I can fuck you,' explained Agnieszka in a low, breathy voice.

I'd only just got through the door of Agnieszka's house-share out in Guildford. We were heading up the stairs to her room and she was already telling me what she wanted to do to me.

'Let me get my coat off first!' I joke-gasped.

'We need to get things going as quickly as possible!' she ordered. 'My flatmates could be back at any time.'

This was sure going to be a session and a half. Her on top and the two of us doing our thing while hoping the neighbours wouldn't find out. Not the most natural of setups, but since Agnieszka had called me out in spite of such hurdles, then who was I to complain?

From her faltering phone calls, I'd expected Agnieszka to be a nervy girl, out of her depth in a foreign country. But the young woman who had led me into her bedroom wasn't anything of the sort. She had striking dark looks, and her East European accent was sexy, like a Bond villainess. She looked a couple of years older than me and there was a fire in her.

Agnieszka directed me to sit down on her king-size bed. She stood over me. We were still fully clothed.

'This is how it goes, Luke.'

I noticed that she hadn't even offered me a drink.

'I broke up with my boyfriend,' Agnieszka continued. 'Which is why I called you out. This is how I get over a broken heart!'

Both her hands were pressing down on my thighs and she was looking me straight in the eyes.

'I want you to lie down, and I'm going to get on top, and then I want you to really fuck me hard, OK?'

Fuck, she's telling me my job!

I was impressed that Agnieszka had the confidence to spell things out for me. It sure made my work easier, even though it felt as though she was turning the tables on me. And the way she spoke, giving instructions, wasn't what I was used to at all.

I began unbuttoning my shirt, and in this instance she followed suit and undressed along with me. She had a firm, toned body that looked like it took no prisoners. I fell back flat on to the bed and got a grip of myself in readiness for the sex.

But it was as if all the forethought – coupled with Agnieszka's barking manner and certainty at what she wanted me to do for her – had intimidated my cock to the point of it remaining at ease. My hand action increased along with my flailing sense of nervousness.

Agnieszka knelt at my feet and watched with a

curdled air of contempt. Which didn't help one bit. The only sound in the room was a ticking clock counting down the time alone with her, and my desperate wanking. And the mental shouting echoing round my head, aimed squarely at my limp prick.

For fuck's sake, get your act together.

Agnieszka had the look in her eyes of someone mentally crossing their arms in peeved impatience. It felt like *hours*, but it must have been only a few minutes before Agnieszka spoke. 'Are you going to be able to do this?'

'Of course!' I threw straight back in a tone that was an octave too high. 'I just need a bit of warming up,' I stated with fake calm, as if taking an age to have an erection was routine to me and nothing for anyone to be concerned about. It might have only been a few minutes longer than usual, but below the surface I was bricking myself.

And then Agnieszka completely changed tack, as if she'd realized that the *way* she was talking, as much as the words she was using, were doing nothing to improve the situation. Her hand stroked my leg gently and there was a new element of compassion when she next spoke, her voice more gentle now. She was quieter, too.

'What's going to help make it work for you?'

Our eyes met then. *She's doing* my *job.* Agnieszka was using the sort of concerned expression and tone that I employed when putting a girl at her ease, trying not to scare her away. It bugged and ashamed me that a client was trying to reassure *me*.

Yet beneath my level of humiliation was one of steel – I felt fucking damned if this girl was going to get the

109

better of me. I owed it to her and myself to rise to the occasion and stay there if it killed me.

My wrist action quickened. It was strange if I thought too much about it – and I was doing my utmost not to. A woman like Agnieszka taking control in her 'evil vixen' accent would have got most guys going, but for me it was as though she was trying too hard.

Maybe she didn't realize the intimidating effect she might have on men, even ones like me who made sex their business. A domineering woman could make as many guys wilt as those she'd arouse.

I gave my cock a talking to: *'It's not you, it's HER. You know this game, no sweat. Ignore her and get on with the show!'*

Maybe it *was* Agnieszka's fault. Maybe she just didn't get how a guy achieved erection. I mean, I wasn't about to harden just because some chick decided it was time that I did.

Maybe she just assumed that men fell immediately for her; that even the very suggestion of sex with her was enough to get a bloke fired up.

Sorry, babe, but that ain't working for me.

My own focus on my dick at last did the trick. It was uniformed and standing to attention. I gave Agnieszka a glint of a smile: 'Hey girl, you come right on over.' She pawed her way towards me like a panther, and I speared her from beneath.

Agnieszka forced me back down on to the bed with a strong push at my shoulders. I lay there and let her do whatever she wanted to me. The heels of her hands were digging into my six-pack, and her fingers were clipped tight around my waist. The rest of her sat on top of me, rocking hard with vigour, as if she was aching with all her might to scratch an out-of-reach itch deep within her. While I felt like I was reaching for the last bit of jam at the bottom of the jar.

For a split second, her focus on her own pleasure flickered and our eyes met. It was an unspoken signal for both of us to simultaneously up our game and head hell for leather towards a mutual orgasm.

I gripped her wrists as if I was dragging her further onto me. She increased her hard rhythmic ride of my cock. Her jutting tits and my head rose and fell together with the quickening momentum.

And then Agnieszka's head was thrown back and a thin yelp crept up the length of her throat and I found myself mesmerized by the pulsating vein in her stretched neck. And then as the thrill started to surge through me too, I let my head drop back onto the pillow, blindly thrashing it this way and that, as if at the very same time that I was succumbing to the physical joy, something in me was willing it to calm down.

Agnieszka knew exactly where she had me. She collapsed, flinging herself on to my chest, my tired dick still inside her. Like the two of us had melded with the passion.

Our pounding heartbeats calmed with our own quietening.

'Thank you,' I muttered in her ear before I realized what I was saying. *What the fuck? She should be thanking me. Get a grip, goddamnit!*

'No need to thank me,' she crooned. 'It was all your doing,' she winked as she climbed off me.

I felt set up. Manipulated into giving her exactly what she wanted. OK, that was my job, for God's sake. Wouldn't I love all my clients to be so forward? It'd make my job a whole lot easier, for one thing. But the way Agnieszka'd got me there rankled with me. She only had to ask! But she hadn't, had she? She'd taken control from the moment I got through the door.

I looked over at her bedside clock. There was ten minutes left until the end of the session. God, she'd even timed the sex up to the wire. On the one hand that was fucking impressive of her. But the flipside was that I felt the ball had been all in her court. And for an escort, that wasn't a good or comfortable place to be at all.

Too fucking vulnerable by half.

Because though I'd just had some frazzling sex that topped boiling point, no doubt about it, it sure fucking well came with conditions.

I dressed and waited for Agnieszka to come back with my money. I shook my head a couple of times to clear my thoughts. This session had been damn confusing from start to finish. And I knew I didn't like that feeling.

I suppose I shouldn't have been so cut up about things. Agnieszka came back into the room and counted out the fee into my open palm. I'd still given her her money's worth, hadn't I?, and I was getting paid in cash for the privilege. What the hell was wrong with me?

This is my job, whichever way a session goes.

Yet the truth was, I was still smarting – or at least my dick was – at being hustled into submission. Agnieszka hadn't seemed to realize that it didn't have to be that way. But she'd been too caught up in her own 'dom' fantasy to work that out.

Tom & Claire

Tom was explaining to me what he *didn't* want at the forthcoming session with him and his wife.

'The thing is, Luke, we've done this before,' he boasted over the phone, 'and, to be frank, the escort was *hopeless*.'

There was nothing for me to be afraid of there, then.

'I have plenty of experience working with couples,' I reassured him, 'and no record of any of them being disappointed with my service.'

I thought of Lars and Eva and the pleasure I'd brought the two of them on her birthday. I knew exactly where my talents lay.

'Indeed, a good number have booked me more than once.' *So put that in your pipe and smoke it.*

There was a momentary silence on the other end of the phone.

'I'm sure that they have, Luke,' Tom said, 'but our last escort was *terrible*. It was like he lost his nerve. He couldn't even *perform* properly. He ruined everything.'

114

That got me. I cringed for the faceless gigolo not able to keep it up. *Poor sap.* But Tom had touched a nerve with me, too. Only days ago, my dick had been all but beaten into submission by Agnieszka's dominant manner – but at least it had eventually got its act together.

It had just been a minor blip, then. Past experience told me it was when I was way out of my depth that there was a chance things would go limp for me. And hadn't I been overwhelmed back then? Two gorgeous lesbians and me, still a newbie in the game. God, but I'd sure made up for it since.

So, why should I worry what Tom was telling me, or reminding me of? He would just be one other man who wanted me to service his wife for their mutual enjoyment. What could be simpler than that?

'As I said, Tom, none of the couples who've hired me have ever complained about me,' I repeated. 'You have nothing to worry about.'

'I'm glad to hear it, Luke,' Tom replied brusquely. 'We wouldn't want you to turn up and be like him. We haven't come all the way up to London, and hired a babysitter, for things not to happen.'

'I understand,' I replied, *not* fully understanding.

I was confused by his implication. The way Tom had gone on and on about the previous guy. He wasn't me, after all. I had a sneaking suspicion that all this talk was part of Tom's pre-session build-up. To show he was the one with the power as well as the money. That, while I was the one about to shag his wife, he remained in control. I was only doing it because *he* gave the permission.

I knew that without saying anything, but Tom obviously felt he had to make it clear. For his own peace of mind.

Tom and I were waiting for Claire, having a drink in the sitting room of his hotel suite. Tom was telling me how they'd spent the day 'doing Piccadilly', as he put it: the Royal Academy, Green Park, Burlington Arcade. I kept an ear on what he was saying, though at the same time I found myself wondering what Claire might look like. I hoped to God that I'd find her attractive. That was the bottom line, really.

Mind you, as an escort, that was my job. Finding something – anything – in my client that got me going. Not that I'd ever had a problem on that score. The girls that hired me weren't normally mingers, thankfully, and there was surely no reason for Claire to be any different. Deborah, with the ghastly skin condition, momentarily flitted in front of my mind's eye, but she'd sure turned out to be the exception rather than the rule. The chances of Claire being anything like that were remote. *Please God!*

Tom turned his head towards the bedroom as the door opened. 'Ah, here she is now.'

He set his wine glass down to better savour Claire's entrance.

I followed his gaze.

I'd had nothing to worry about. *Fucking nothing.*

Claire was completely naked and, what's more, carried herself with no shame. Not that there was any chance of *that*. She had nothing to be ashamed about.

116

In fact, she was drop-dead sizzling. I mentally licked my lips.

She headed straight towards my chair, then, halting at its corner, leered at her husband, jutting her pelvis out towards him so he had a full-on view of her. And then she turned, bent towards me so her tits were inches from my chest, and kissed me hard on the lips.

Claire stood up straight. 'That's for starters,' she purred, and stepped backwards into her husband's arms.

These two had obviously decided between themselves exactly what they wanted. As an escort, you had to be careful when it came to couples work. You couldn't be sure that being hired for the wife was the husband's fantasy rather than anything she wanted to do.

It would surely be quite a difficult thing to broach with your partner, after all? 'I'd love to see you with another man, darling.' *Fuck.* I didn't mind helping a couple out, but I couldn't get my head round my own sex life ever getting to that point. Seeing the woman I loved with another guy? *No way!*

Claire was standing expectantly beside the arm of Tom's chair, her hand on his shoulder. The two of them were looking straight at me. Tom was removing his tie.

'You ready to join us, then, Luke?'

Tom said it with an air of impatience. That riled me. It reminded me of his phone call. There was a part of him that seemed to be doing his utmost to rattle me. To my annoyance, it was beginning to work.

I'll fucking show you.

I began removing my clothes in unison with Tom's own undressing. Not that I much cared about him.

I was only showing him that I was at the same level as him; that he had nothing to worry about when it came to me pleasuring Claire. God, I'd prove it to the both of them.

Hand-in-hand, they led me into the bedroom. Tom pulled a chair into a position with a clear view of the bed. Without any prompting from me, Claire pulled the covers right down and went and lay flat out on the sheets.

This was far from new territory to me. It couldn't have been any easier. *Shouldn't* have been. Except in that short journey from the room entrance to join Claire to lie down next to her, the image of the other escort – the poor guy who, according to Tom, couldn't get his act together – filled my mind. I had no idea who he was or what he looked like. But at this very minute I knew *exactly* how he felt.

Oh God, NO!

I stopped dead in my tracks. How to explain that my dick had suddenly decided that it wasn't up to the game? I didn't dare look down. I feared that my cock had shrivelled into nothingness.

Tom only needed to give me a glance to notice that things weren't up to scratch. He must have been wondering what it was about male escorts and his wife. I wasn't about to look him in the eye, but I felt as sorry for him and Claire as I did for myself.

'What's going on, Luke? You're not just the same as the last man we booked?'

That was the measure of it, wasn't it? Both of us were thinking it. And him saying it wasn't going to make me think any better about myself. Or encourage my cock to rise to the occasion anytime soon.

It felt as if my dick was out to shame me. That, however much I wanted things to go smoothly and give Claire a good time, it wasn't going to be having any of it.

Oh, come on, fella. We're supposed to be in this together. Don't bail out on me now. I talked us up, for God's sake!

It was stalemate all round. Tom was staring crossly at me like he couldn't believe another hooker was wasting his time and money. *Again.* Claire's head was propped up on a pillow and she was watching me intently. I attempted to throw her a smile, but it only amounted to a feeble one at that.

I couldn't believe that my cock was playing up again so soon after my session with Agnieszka. Because that suggested I was losing my grip. And the fear that rose out of *that* was that I might never be able to rely on it ever again. That I had worn out my cock by sheer overuse. It was literally giving up the ghost.

And where did that leave me? What the fuck was the point of a male escort without a point?

I chose to show willing even if my dick was proving temperamental. I figured if I joined Claire on the bed that, by then, my cock might have got back in the game.

It wasn't as if there was much alternative. It wasn't as if I could close my eyes and conjure up some guaranteed sex bait such as Sasha and Mae. They might not still be on my client books, but they still were an asset for helping get me fired up when I needed it.

Trouble was, they couldn't be of help right now. I had to keep my eyes fully open, to show Tom and Claire that I was focused on *them*.

My bare feet sank into the deep pile carpet. When I reached the foot of the bed I slunk onto it, like a leopard going in for the kill. Claire's fine legs, her curves, her eyes watching, waiting for me to give it to her. She was everything I needed to get me going. By the time I was straddled over her I had nothing to worry about. Dick was back at my beck and call.

Time to party, mate.

So we did.

Lars

Lars's invite to see West Ham play could hardly have come at a better time. I sure needed something to raise my spirits.

I'd become deeply unsettled by how my escort work had been going this past month. My session with Agnieszka, and then the dodgy start with Tom and Claire, had certainly shown me that my mojo wasn't running at full speed. Thankfully, I'd eventually got myself going on both occasions. But, even so, not being able to depend on my cock being in full working order when I needed it was one of the worst things that could happen to a gigolo.

Clearly what I needed was a break. Or at least that seemed to me what my dick was clearly telling me. I might have been happy with the rate at which I was picking up work. But the trouble was that my prick seemed to be demanding a breather.

And while it was doing that, it sure had control over me. I was the one who ended up humiliated and

121

embarrassed and making excuses about how long it was taking me to get hard. 'This has never happened to me before.'

Yeah, right.

Lars and me walked from the car park to the West Ham stadium. It sure was a far cry from my escort life. Being surrounded by guys all heading in the same direction for the football was like a breath of fresh air.

'Lars, it's really good of you to invite me along,' I told him as we passed through the ticket barrier.

He turned to me as he flashed his season ticket at the guy behind the counter. 'You don't have to thank me, Luke. It's my pleasure. So you can watch some *proper* football, eh?'

'When in London, eh?' I threw back.

We headed up the steps to our seats.

'Mind you,' I mused, 'With all due respect, I'd have preferred seeing Arsène Wenger's lot. Now, *that's* what I call *football.*'

The words were still coming out of my mouth when I realized that Lars wasn't seeing the joke. He took a deep breath, but didn't say anything. I'd clearly touched a nerve. There were some things that were no laughing matter – and that included which London team you supported. That was one of the things Mark had warned me about when I'd got here. Even for non-Brits, like Lars, if they'd lived in any part of London for any time – like Lars had done before he was married – and liked football, they would have made that decision. And stuck with it.

When Lars next spoke, there was a tinge of hard

warning in his words. He scanned the stadium, avoiding my eyes, but his words sure hit home. 'Don't let anyone hear you saying *that*. Either Hammers fans or the Fulham lot.' He nodded at the crowd facing us across the stadium. 'That could get you lynched.'

I grimaced. 'I'm sorry. I was only joking.'

Lars turned slowly to face me and raised an eyebrow. Dead serious. He'd clearly meant what he said.

'Look, I was out of order,' I admitted. 'Chalk it up to me being an out-of-towner,' I grinned, attempting to lighten things.

He nodded.'So was I, once. But apology accepted. Just don't let it happen again, eh?'

He was letting me off the hook.

Lars had been very generous to treat me to the match. It was ironic that we'd met through him and Eva hiring me, yet he was now providing me with the break I was in dire need of. I appreciated that he saw me as more than just their escort. The least I could do was cheer on his side, for God's sake.

I swept a look around the stadium. The stands were packed out. It was difficult not to get caught up in the atmosphere, even if I didn't care which side I supported. Of course I'd back West Ham this time. But such was the rush from the crowd as we waited for the teams to come out and for the game to begin, that it didn't matter to me at all. It was enough to enjoy the game for its own sake – and savour the easy company of Lars and his mates.

From where I was sitting it seemed to me that Lars knew half the crowd. Or at least the lot in our stand.

They were practically queuing up to exchange slaps on the back and 'Great to see you's. And Lars was happy to count me in. He introduced me to each and every one of his friends. 'Meet my Aussie mate, Luke.' I felt really welcomed. It was as though they'd made a space for me, and I'd been absorbed into the crowd. *That* was as much what a decent football match was about – as well as the stuff that went on on the pitch. At a football match, nobody asked questions of each other. They were just happy that you were there. It wasn't like when I met Karen or Melanie's friends and they wanted to know everything.

I thought back to last year, before the lads had gone home, and how we used to kick a ball around of an evening. That had been friendship enough. Since they'd gone, there'd been no more of that.

Things were so different now. I was sharing a flat with three *girls*, and I got my football kicks at one remove: on the box, or sitting in the stands, like today.

The players filed on to the pitch and the whole crowd went bananas. Lars slapped me on the back. '*Now* you're going to see some decent football,' he roared in my ear to make himself heard.

I only really had my escort work, I reflected. That was the one constant since I'd been in London.

So I'd better make a fucking go of it.

That thought pulled me up. I wasn't really taking in what was going on on the pitch, though I was watching it. It was a flurry of men and ball shifting fluidly from one end to the other.

The point was that I didn't have any choice but to be a successful escort and collect some money together.

I couldn't now do anything else – certainly nothing that would bring in anything like the same amount of money I was earning by selling my services.

I was so lost in my thoughts that I missed the West Ham goal. Everyone around me roared and the stadium seemed to shift with the clamour. Even so, I found myself caught up by it.

Lars's hand was on my shoulder. His face was flushed. 'Fucking brilliant, wasn't it?'

'You bet!' I agreed.

I looked around at the crowd of men with their eyes wide open and heads thrown back with the thrill of the ball going in. It flashed across my mind right then that watching your team score could be as exhilarating as good sex.

I also had the sense that all these guys were on my side too. That, if they knew what I did for a living, why, they'd be backing me all the way. Slapping me on the back with a loaded wink. 'Put one in for me, eh, son?'

You bet!

That thought made me smile. Lars clocked it. 'You glad you came? Even though it's *only* West Ham?' he teased.

'Actually, I am,' I laughed. 'They're not bad, are they?'

He rolled his eyes and shook his head, as if I was beyond all hope.

When Lars had invited me to the match, I'd seen it as a breather from the current confusion my escort work was giving me. But it had turned out that coming here had raised my spirits way beyond my expectations. Lars didn't realize it, but I knew I wasn't about to forget his generosity in a hurry.

Gray again

The soccer match put things into perspective for me. It helped me relax and worry less about how the escort work was going. Yet deep down I knew I still needed some help with my failing cock problem.

Gray was the only person I could think to call. He was surely the right person too. The only guy I knew who was in my line of work – if only as my PA – and understood how much jeopardy my problem put me in. After all, if I lost it altogether, he'd be affected too.

'Hi, Gray, have you had anyone calling in?'

It was an odd thing to ask, I knew. Generally he called *me* to let me know the latest update.

He knew me too well. 'Luke, you OK? You don't have to call *me*. We've been at this long enough for you to know that. What's up then, mate? This isn't like you.'

I left a few seconds before I spoke. They must have sounded all the longer at his end of the phone. 'Luke? You with me?'

I gave a false chuckle. 'Ha! Yeah, I'm still here, Gray. You're right. There *is* something up. It's just, it's just—'

Gray put on a posh accent: 'Spit it out, man. Spit it out.'

It was his way of trying to lighten things and help me ease into what I had to say, to seem as non-threatening as possible.

I coughed. 'The truth is, Gray, that this isn't something that any guy likes to brag about. It's just . . . it's just . . . this past month' – *in for a penny* – 'I've had real trouble keeping it up. To be honest, even getting myself started in the first place.'

I heard his intake of breath: 'Fucking hell, mate. That's tough, really tough. Especially for *you*.'

That was just what I needed to raise my spirits and my flopping cock. The weight of the expectations and hopes of all the guys in the world on my shoulders. What Gray seemed to be suggesting was that if I of all people couldn't even *get*, let alone *keep* my act together, then what hope was there for the rest of the planet's lads? I owed it to *them*, goddamnit!

'Thanks for that, Gray. Don't I damn well know it?' I agreed with a forced lightness in my voice. Sure, it was easy to make fun of the worst-case scenario for any guy, but at the end of the day, it was still *me* who couldn't perform properly. And not only that, but unlike the masses of men out there with the same problem, my entire employment depended on it.

What on God's earth was the point of an escort whose cock had gone on strike? If it was any sort of joke, then it was humour of the pitch-black variety. A hollow laugh stuck in my gullet.

'Gray,' I blurted out in a whine, 'I need some help.'

There was a rigid silence from the other end of the line.

C'mon Gray, don't bail out on me.

Giving sexual advice to a mate wasn't something I'd want to do if I could help it. I'd certainly put Gray on the spot. I almost felt sorry for the guy, that I'd put him in such a position. *Almost.*

Gray gave out a slow whistle, which sounded like a tyre with a puncture. I pictured a limp inner tube.

'You're not helping, yunno,' I laughed. '*Say* something, for fuck's sake. I need help here.'

I was very aware that I'd now changed my tune by making light of my predicament. The truth was that I'd heard uncertainty in Gray's tuneless response and I didn't blame him. I was as confused and unsure about what to do about my sexual problem as he was.

'You know what, Luke. I'm not sure I know what to say that'll help your Limp Dick.'

Ouch! Those capital letters sure hurt.

The image he'd now presented to me of my sad prick was even worse than the inner tube. It might have been the truth, but even so.

'Bastard!' I laughed.

'Sorry,' he sniggered, 'but I couldn't resist the temptation. It *is* funny, y'know.'

I knew where Gray was coming from. I'd have laughed about it too if it hadn't been happening to *me*. But the trouble was, it very much was.

Just my typical fucking luck.

And at that very same moment I found myself thinking of Mark and my other Aussie mates. They'd have made light of it too, just like Gray. It would've fucking *killed* them. In my mind's eye I saw them spread-eagled on the grass in the park, roaring their balls off over my 'little problem'.

Bastards, the lot of them!

It would have been the flipside of Simon always calling me 'Stud'. God, he'd have had a field day, never letting me forget that I was no longer up to the game. He'd no doubt have come up with something like 'Limp Dick' too.

Gray coughed down the phone, and when he next spoke, there was a serious tone to his voice. 'I tell you what, you want to meet up? We'll sort something out, you'll see.'

I damned well hoped so. Part of me sort of believed that if I took things easy for a few weeks, laid off the sex by having a break from hookering and the one-night stands, then my cock would get back to business.

Trouble was, I couldn't really afford to take time off and lose potential punters. And there was a darker, deeper part of me too that wasn't totally sure that cutting down on sex for a while would do the trick. Suppose my prick was on the brink of giving up the ghost altogether? That overuse had run it into the ground? The possibility of *that* scared the shit out of me.

It had been four days since our phone conversation, and Gray had asked me to meet him to 'sort out that

Limp Dick of yours.' He now had a huge grin on his face like he couldn't wait to tell me his news. But he refused to say anything until we'd gone to the chippie and settled down on a bench on the nearby green to eat. A handful of teenagers were kicking a ball around in front of us.

He looked fit to burst, but at the same time I could tell he was getting pleasure from letting me stew.

'Come on, Gray. I didn't come here to enjoy the view,' I joked as we unwrapped our chips.

For a second I savoured the waft of vinegar that hit me full on in the face, then dug in. Gray stuffed his mouth, as if he was giving himself time to work out quite what to tell me. When he'd swallowed his food, he spoke.

'Well, I had a think about what we can do.'

'And?' I butted in.

He sighed. 'The thing is, there's really nothing I can say that will make things easier for you.'

I almost choked on my chips. I was seething. 'Then what the fuck did you call me here for?' I spat out, and regretted it as soon as I did.

Gray sat back and watched me. He remained silent for a little while, as if he was digesting what I'd just said. 'It's really getting to you, isn't it?' he said quietly, sympathetically.

I didn't know what to say. There was nothing *for* me to say.

Gray removed the pack of chips from his lap and placed it on the bench beside him. He put his hand in his pocket and fished about. 'There's something I've got you,' he said. 'I've got to be careful how I give it, *them* to you.' He was half whispering.

He looked across at the teenagers, and nodded in their direction. 'They're not to see what we're doing, OK? Now, give me your hand,' he instructed.

I did as I was told. For one thing I was intrigued. I wondered what he was going to give me. I slipped my open hand behind my chip paper so that anyone facing us wouldn't be able to see what was going on.

I watched as from between his fingers he dropped a handful of small blue tablets into my cupped palm. I didn't have to ask what they were.

Viagra!

Gray knew I'd guessed. 'Miracle-workers, my friend,' he gloated. 'The answer to your prayers.'

I wasn't convinced. 'I'm not sure, Gray. I know you're trying to help me, and I appreciate that, but I don't do drugs. You know that.'

'Pfah!' he exhaled. 'They're not exactly Class A, are they?'

To be honest, I wasn't sure what Class they were. But that wasn't the point.

'Number One: Where the fuck did you get them?' I shot at him.

He shrugged his shoulders. 'Oh, come on. Where does anyone get *anything* these days? Off the Internet, of course.'

I gave a hollow laugh. 'And that's somehow supposed to reassure me? How do you know this stuff's genuine?'

He didn't have an answer to that.

'*And*,' I continued, 'Question Number Two. Which

131

is related to your answer to my first question. Are you even aware of the side-effects these things have, even if they *are* genuine?'

Gray frowned. 'God, Luke. You'd think you didn't want to jump-start your game. I'm just trying to help.'

It was as if Gray had taken my asking more about the drugs personally.

'Look, I understand what you're going through,' he stressed. 'It'd be bad enough any of us having a refusal at the fence. It must be ten times worse if you're getting paid to be there,' he winced.

I winced in return. He was spot-on.

Gray sighed and admitted, 'Yeah, you're right. You do have to watch out for something when you take them. If you're not careful, you can end up rock solid with a long-term hot rod. Out of the frying pan into the fire.'

Ouch. If there was anything as bad as not being able to get it up, it would be the embarrassment and pain of not being able to keep your good man down.

'Even one tablet is too much,' added Gray, though I was only half listening. The rest of my mind was on my uncooperative cock. Frankly, a solid dick would at least get my job done.

I shook my head to get my brain back in gear with what Gray had just told me.

'One tablet is too much?' I repeated to ensure I'd heard him right.

'Yup, afraid so. You've got to remember to only take half a tab, and leave it at that. Oh, and you need some time for it to work,' he instructed. 'Give it an hour before your session, OK?'

I looked down at the clutch of Viagra pills in my palm, put my hand in my pocket and released the tablets. Gray was right. As long as I was careful, these would be the answer to my prayers. I felt like Keanu Reeves in *The Matrix*. There wasn't any alternative.

'It was good of you, y'know, to get them for me,' I said as we scrunched up the chip paper and tossed it into the litter bin and made to go.

Gray shrugged his shoulders.

'Look, I'm doing this for both of us, aren't I?' he replied.

'I suspected as much.'

'Yeah, well, I get a kick out of this line of work, even if I'm not in the front line. I want it to be a success for you, though. You know that.'

I nodded. 'Yeah I do, thanks,' I said, and I meant it.

I was scooting home, the little blue pills all but burning a hole in my pocket, a tremendous feeling of relief and renewed confidence bubbling up within me. I was on a natural high.

I reached the estate and parked my bike at the edge of the car park as I always did, and walked up the path to the entrance to my block. And then out of the corner of my eye I spotted a figure I recognized. My heart sank.

It can't be.

I stopped dead in my tracks. I was facing her, even though she wasn't supposed to be here. She was in the wrong scene of my life. None of my clients knew where I lived. But somehow Karen had tracked me down.

133

What the fuck?

How had she found out my address? Checked my wallet when I was last over there while I was otherwise engaged? It was possible, I could see that. If a client wanted to discover where I lived it wouldn't be the hardest thing to do.

Part of me wanted to go inside and shut the door on Karen and forget she was there at all. But I knew I'd still know she was here outside. Waiting. I had no choice but to confront her.

I marched across the grass verge towards her. She was leaning against a lamppost trying to look as nonchalant as possible. But it wasn't working.

'What are you doing here, Karen?' I asked with a hint of a snarl.

'Luke! Fancy seeing you here. I'm waiting for a friend.'

'I must know her, then,' I beamed. 'What's her name?'

Karen looked down at her shoes.

The thing was that I did know my neighbours. Well, not in any deep way or anything. One or two of them I could put names to. But I did know what they looked like. I'd made a point of sticking my head out of the door to introduce myself when I first moved in around six months ago. It was just something I always did whenever I arrived at a new place. It put both parties at ease.

'Caroline. Her name's Caroline, and she knows I'm waiting for her here,' gabbled Karen. 'She's getting ready. She'll be out in a few minutes, and then we plan on going shopping together.'

I didn't believe one word of it. I was pretty sure that there was no one called Caroline in my block. And if there was a Caroline in any of the *other* blocks on the estate, there was no reason for Karen to be waiting here.

I stood staring at her for a couple of seconds. Karen might have been genuinely waiting for a friend and it was just pure coincidence that she happened to live on the same estate as me. Or Karen had indeed tracked me down. Either way, her story included the elusive Caroline.

That gave me an opt-out clause. The truth was that I couldn't be bothered with Karen at the moment. I was too excited about how my sex life was set on full thrust again now I had some Viagra. And minus the fear and shame that had dogged me, along with the limpness.

Whatever Karen was on about could be dealt with some other time. I wasn't going to let her ruin my day. I'd had enough worrying to be going on with in recent weeks.

I put on a warm smile for Karen's benefit. 'Well, I hope you don't have to wait too long for your friend. Goodbye, Karen,' I said, and left her standing there.

Marcus & Rachel

Mid-July

I felt right on the money when I rang the Stones' door-bell. I'd swallowed my first dose of Viagra over an hour ago, and I felt buoyed up and ready for business.

Back in the game.

Marcus had booked me for a session to entertain his wife. Just speaking to him on the phone I knew what to expect. He'd sounded like Tony Blair, which meant a nice house in the wealthy London suburbs, down some pleasant, tree-lined side street.

Right first time. The house in Islington was detached and double-fronted. There was a metal plate on the doorpost. Turned out they were both doctors.

Marcus opened the door. He looked in his late forties or early fifties with friendly eyes. 'Ah, Luke, do come in. I trust you had no problem finding us? You look hot. You ran from the station?'

'Oh no,' I said, not sure what he was getting at. 'I came on my bike, my scooter?' I pointed to it outside on the road. 'You don't mind me parking it out there?'

He shook his head and peered past me. He looked impressed.

'You've got yourself a Vespa? God, that takes me back. Very *Quadrophenia*. Not that that was my thing. Punk was more my line. Nineteen seventy-seven and all that.'

I shrugged my shoulders and grinned. 'Before my time, I'm afraid.'

He looked me up and down. 'Don't tell me. You hadn't even been born then?'

I gave him an apologetic look: 'Sorry.'

Marcus shook his head. 'I should send you home now, before you make me feel too old.'

I was in my element. I smiled to put him at his ease. 'Oh, I can assure you, my job is to take years off you. After all, isn't that why you called me?'

He led me down the hall. 'Fair point, Luke. Fair point. Now, if I can introduce you to Rachel.'

Rachel was in her mid- to late-thirties and a few years younger than Marcus. She had quiet, classic looks even without make-up; some added colour would have made her stunning. They made a handsome couple.

'Darling, this is Luke.'

I reached out my hand to shake hers. 'Pleased to meet you – it's Rachel, isn't it?'

She took my hand and shook it back but there was a puzzled look on her face. 'Would you like a glass of water, Luke? You look a bit hot.'

I felt fine, but accepted her offer graciously. 'That'd be nice, thank you. It must be the stress of getting here. London traffic and all that!' I volleyed back.

When she left the room to fetch the water, Marcus

stood nervously, as if unsure what to do next. Then he rallied.

'Please sit down, Luke. I must admit that we've never done . . .' – he coughed – '. . . this before.'

He directed me to the sofa and I settled into it. He sat down in the armchair opposite, and clenched his hands together on his lap.

He'd just given me my cue for how to go about things – as much in his wound-up body language as by his words. I needed to guide Marcus and Rachel to where they wanted to go, but not force things, in case I scared them off.

Rachel returned to the room with a tray on which she'd set out a glass jug of water topped with lemon slices and ice, and three tall glasses. She set it down on the dining table, poured out the drinks and handed me and Marcus each a glass.

'Thanks,' we said at the same time.

I took a sip. I hadn't really wanted a drink, but the water was cool and refreshing. I didn't know if it was his earlier suggestion, but though I'd felt fine when I arrived, I was aware I was getting warmer. Like I'd caught a bug or something.

If I started to feel worse I certainly wouldn't be up to any escort work in the next hour or so. Sex might end up the last thing on my mind.

But as long as I hadn't yet reached that stage, I was sure I could wing it. Do my job and get out of here, get home and rest.

Concerned glances passed between Marcus and Rachel.

'Are you all right, Luke? You *do* look a bit flushed,' he said.

'I dunno,' I sniffed, 'I think I might be coming down with something. Your British weather can still get to me, y'know.'

I wiped my hand across my forehead. It was clammy. I took another sip of the ice-cold water. At this moment I wanted to be anywhere but here. The thought of scooting back to West London feeling like this didn't fill me with glee either.

Marcus spoke with a fatherly tone. 'Luke, I'm worried about you. You're not looking at all well.'

I half smiled to try and reassure him. 'Oh, I'll be OK. It's just something I've picked up.'

The truth was that I was feeling grottier by the minute. I hadn't eaten anything out of the ordinary. The only difference had been the half-tablet of Viagra I'd taken.

Oh fuck.

It had been a waste of time taking that little blue pill, then. Because no matter how up for it my dick might be, there would be no action given how foul the rest of my body now felt.

Marcus must have known *exactly* what I'd gone and done. He was a GP, for God's sake. Coming to the conclusion that the escort he'd hired might be taking Viagra was hardly rocket science. If he'd worked that out, then my cover was blown. I wasn't the expert escort I was pretending to be, was I? They'd had every right to assume they'd be getting a fit and healthy young buck, and here I was, dependent on artificial means to keep my act together.

There was shame in my red face, too. And that made

up my mind for me, though I felt terrible saying it. 'I'm really sorry, but I'm not feeling at all well. I need to go home.'

I aimed my apology at both of them. There was no further point in trying to kid anybody that I was up for anything at the moment – let alone having sex with Rachel, and putting on a show for Marcus too.

'Of course, Luke. You shouldn't remain a moment longer.'

He said it so matter-of-factly. At least being a doctor, Marcus had my best interests at heart. Any other client might have expected me to carry on once I'd got through their front door. Not that that had ever happened, thankfully.

'Finish off your iced water to cool you down a bit more,' Rachel added kindly, 'and then Marcus will run you home.'

In spite of feeling under the weather, I was still aware of the logistics of that.

'My scooter . . .'

Marcus shook his head. 'Don't worry about your Vespa. We'll take good care of it until you're well enough to come and pick it up, OK?'

They had it all worked out. It was sweet of them. God, they couldn't have been more understanding.

But I knew it wasn't just my scooter that was bothering me. The point was that I didn't want any of my clients knowing anything more about me than the person that turned up at their place. And I couldn't risk any of the Girls seeing me getting out of Marcus's car back at our flat.

'Look,' I stressed, 'that's very kind of you. But I'm going home on my scooter, thank you.'

I spelt it out, made it as clear as possible that I'd made up my own mind to go home my own way. I didn't want to give them any reason to ask me to explain myself any further. As far as I was concerned, I'd chosen to ride myself home, and that was that.

I stood up to go. Rachel got the message and left the room to get me my jacket. Marcus looked up at me from his chair.

'Your line of work, Luke. There are risks. I know you're a fit young lad, but even so . . .'

His words tapered off.

Even through my Viagra fug, I heard what Marcus was saying. It felt important that I acknowledge that.

'I really appreciate you and Rachel looking after me this evening,' I told him.

He gave me a wan smile.

What I didn't tell Marcus, nor his doctor wife when she returned to the room, was what I really appreciated was that neither of them had mentioned anything about me taking something, least of all Viagra, even though all of us knew. That was decent of both of them.

Marcus and Rachel looked after me up to their front door. Marcus patted me on the back. 'We'll see you again when you're well, eh?'

The two of them stood and watched me put on my helmet and step onto the scooter. There was a look of motherly concern across Rachel's face. Our eyes met as I turned on the ignition.

'Goodbye, Luke,' she mouthed. 'Take care.'

It was that look on Rachel's face that made up my mind for me. I wasn't about to use Viagra again, that was for sure. I'd learnt my lesson this time. And I'd been especially lucky that she and Marcus had been just the right people to have around when I had the allergic reaction. I couldn't be sure that I'd be so fortunate if I took it again. Nor what effect the Viagra might have a second time. Everything could be a whole lot more dangerous. Nope, it just wasn't worth the hassle. My mojo might be stuttering, but I'd stick to letting things happen naturally, dosed with masses of hope.

Nina

Late July

The late morning sun was streaming through my window but I was still lying on my back in my bed. I shifted my head to shield my eyes and looked over at the blonde girl there beside me.

I shut my eyes. *God, what was her name?* It had been a hell of a party and I had the head to prove it. *Nina, that was it.* Nina. Nina. An old college friend of Kirstie's.

Nina was still fast asleep. I raised myself quietly up on one elbow and leaned my head at an angle to get a better look. Not that I needed to. I could see her now in my mind's eye, from last night. I'd first spotted her leaning against our kitchen doorpost, her head down, trying to listen to some other girl above the thumping bass. She was a petite blonde with a cute pixie cut and she'd been dressed in a glittery green shift dress and matching ballet pumps. She'd sparkled.

God, my head was throbbing. I lay back down again and my drop on to the mattress woke Nina. She shifted

143

sleepily as an arm reached out blindly and played over the duvet like she was getting her bearings.

I held my breath and waited to see what would happen next. Her eyes opened so she was looking up at the ceiling and then she turned towards me and caught my eye. We both grinned at each other.

'Morning, Nina,' I whispered, and swallowed back the pounding in my head.

We kissed lightly on the lips. That was all I was up for.

'Urghh,' I grunted.

'My sentiments exactly,' she chuckled, then winced. Her laugh was a pretty sound. Like sleighbells.

Nina snuggled up to me and I wrapped an arm loosely around her shoulders. I rested my chin on her head. It was difficult to keep my eyes open. The two of us went back to sleep.

I didn't know what time it was. Around midday, I suppose. There was movement and chatter in the next room, and then someone switched the vacuum cleaner on. My eyes were wide open now and the pounding in my head was getting more pronounced.

'That's just too cruel,' moaned Nina.

'Bastards,' I agreed.

I ripped the duvet cover from the bed and stood up before my mind had a chance to grab back control of my body and keep me trapped under the duvet. Nina was still lying there, completely naked before me, looking delicious. God, bed was tempting.

But I was also starving. And I had my flatmates to

think about too. I wasn't sure if any of them had seen me and Nina get it on last night, but they'd sure notice if I wasn't around to help with the clearing up. It'd be rubbing salt in the wounds if instead of coming out of my room they found out that I'd spent the day hard at it with one of their old friends.

Nina was sitting on the opposite edge of the bed in her bra and knickers, stepping into her green dress. I watched her while I pulled on my jeans. She stood up and reached for the zip at the back. I stretched over the bed and got there first. 'Let me do that.'

She looked over her shoulder at me. 'Thanks.'

I drew the zip all the way up over the curve of her cute little ass and straight on to the nape of her neck. She turned on her heels so she was looking directly at me and smoothed the front of the dress down. She still carried some of the sparkle of last night about her but it was mixed with this morning's dishevelment.

Very sexy.

'You'll stay for breakfast?'

'You bet!' she shot back.

I liked that. The voice of a hearty eater.

Nina joined me at my closed bedroom door. I looked down at her standing nervously beside me.

'Ready?' I half whispered.

She nodded but said nothing, biting her bottom lip. I took her hand in mine and softly squeezed it.

'No worries, OK?' I winked at her.

She nodded again but there was a little smile across

her face. She winked back. I opened the door and led her across the hall, into the kitchen.

Carrie and Kirstie were sitting at the table and Laura was standing by the kettle, ready to switch it off when it boiled.

'Everyone, can I introduce Nina?' I said.

There was a choruses of 'Hello Nina's, which wasn't altogether played straight. 'I did go to college with her, y'know,' crowed Kirstie.

'But I didn't,' said Carrie, reaching forward to shake Nina's hand. 'I probably said "hello" last night, but I'm afraid it's all a bit of a blur,' Carrie admitted in a mock-groan, holding her head as if in pain, in her familiar jokey manner.

'Hello,' said Nina bashfully.

Laura nodded a welcome.

I gave Nina a reassuring smile. She had nothing to fear. My flatmates weren't about to dig up what the two of us might have got up to last night, even if, as far as I could recall, we hadn't. Or hold it against her or me. After all, it wasn't as if we'd done anything they'd never got up to after a party. Though not with me.

Nina hovered beside me as I poured us a couple of orange juices.

'Sit down, love, and I'll rustle us up some scrambled eggs, OK?'

'Thanks,' she said. 'That'll be fine.'

Carrie watched Nina join her and the others at the table.

'*Breakfast.* Crikey,' she joshed in a faux-Aussie accent.

Carrie raised her mug of tea to Nina. 'God, you have no idea how lucky you are.'

Don't, Carrie.

I cast her a hard stare, then smiled at Nina. 'Oh, don't listen to her,' I joked, stirring the eggs in the pan.

'You mean you don't normally get your act together? Dashing out of the house without your morning fuel – been there, done that,' threw back Nina.

Thankfully she'd got completely the wrong end of the stick. Because what Nina didn't know – and what I wasn't about to tell her anytime soon or possibly ever – was that she'd just passed my 'Morning After' test.

It was one thing for me to have a girl spend the night. *No sweat.* It was quite another for me to like a girl enough to ask her to stick around the following morning. That meant she meant something to me. The real intimacy was in us eating together.

And didn't my flatmates know that. I spooned the egg onto the slices of toast and took the plates to the table.

I decided to throw the ball Carrie had lobbed me back into her court and I sat down next to Nina, my leg touching hers.

'So,' I looked around at each one of them, 'was Nina the only lucky one last night, or did any of you meet any nice guys?'

A flush of red washed over Laura's face even as she was holding her mug up to her mouth with both hands. Hiding behind it.

'Laura met Bob, didn't you?' offered Carrie, nudging

147

her flatmate in the ribs. Laura blushed again over the top of her mug of tea.

'Well, good on you, girl,' I cheered, and when she'd put down her mug, high-fived her.

With that sort of support, she immediately brightened.

I was genuinely happy for her. Laura was the quietest of the three of them and better at one-to-one conversations than mixing it in a crowd. Maybe having the party at our place had been the making of her. Whatever, something had worked for her last night.

'So, where's he now?' I queried, looking under the table. 'You hiding him in your wardrobe or something?' I joked.

Suddenly I realized I was skating a bit too close to the edge, as much regarding my own situation as hers. I swiftly shut up, and reached below the table for Nina's hand. She took it and stroked the back of mine with her thumb.

'He didn't stick around for breakfast,' stressed Carrie, and I winced. I'd have to say something to her once Nina went home.

I turned to Laura. 'Oh, I'm sorry.'

Laura was having none of it. 'Don't feel sorry for me, Luke.' She looked happy. 'That's fine by me. I was only after one thing, anyhow. It was me who didn't ask him to stay. I kicked him out,' she beamed.

It had clearly been a triumph of a night for her.

'Well, congratulations,' I laughed, and we high-fived again.

'Yes, let him make his own breakfast,' threw out Carrie.

God, she was getting near the knuckle. I could only hope that Nina hadn't sussed what my flatmate was getting at.

I so feared Carrie saying something that would damage whatever might be developing between Nina and me. I was very aware that I was entering new territory with this girl sitting beside me – couldn't Carrie see that I needed all the help I could get?

Give me a chance, Carrie.

I finished off my scrambled eggs and knocked back the remainder of my orange juice. Nina had already pushed hers aside.

'Right,' I grinned. 'Fancy a walk to the station?'

I pushed out my chair and stood up so that Nina had no choice but to leave the table with me.

'Fast mover,' shot Carrie.

I stuck out my tongue at her and guided Nina out of the room. With relief.

And, anyway, I needed some fresh air. Taking Nina to the tube station would help clear my head and let us have some time alone to talk. And I'd get a chance to ask her for her number.

We both put our coats on, called out our goodbyes and left the flat. As I closed the front door behind us, I could hear loud laughter coming from the kitchen.

Nina and I were just out of the door to the block, holding hands and cutting across the grass verge, when I spotted a woman leaning against the lamppost across the path from us, watching our every move. That was unnerving enough. When a moment later I realized that it was Karen *again*, that sickened me even more.

What the fuck?

I don't know what then possessed me, but I felt drawn to Karen. I suppose I wanted to give her a piece of my mind so she'd know not to hang around my place ever again.

And then I remembered it was Nina's hand I was holding and she was the reason I was even out here at the moment. I stopped in my tracks.

'What?' Nina mouthed, looking confused.

Fuck, why now Karen?

'I'm afraid I've some unfinished business to deal with.'

I cocked my head in the direction of my client, though I could never let on to Nina who she really was. There was so much explaining I wouldn't be able to do with Nina if we ever got together – but the way things were going this morning, I was beginning to wonder if that was ever going to happen.

Just let me sort this out and we can get back to where we left off.

Nina was frowning. I could understand why. It looked as if I had another girlfriend not even hiding in the wings. She was here for everyone to see.

'It'll only take a minute, Nina, I swear,' I stressed. 'I've just got to have a quick word with Karen. You carry on, and I'll catch you up.'

Nina was in a good mood and accommodating in that on-their-best-behaviour way people are at the start of a possible relationship, but she still gave me a split-second dark look as she walked away from me. She had every right to.

I stormed across the grass towards Karen. 'What are you doing here again, Karen?' I seethed at her.

She tried to look unconcerned but I wasn't convinced one bit.

'I've got a friend in your block, I told you. It's co-incidence. I can't help that she lives near you.'

Yeah, right.

I chose to call her bluff.

'I tell you what, I'll wait with you until she arrives. Caroline, wasn't it? Keep you company on such a fine afternoon, y'know.' I shrugged as nonchalantly as I could.

Karen was playing the same game as me. 'What about that girl you were with?' She nodded her head in the direction of the path that Nina had headed along.

By now Nina had turned the corner on to the main road and would be a few minutes' walk from the tube station. I didn't want to give Karen the pleasure of knowing but she had hit a nerve. If I didn't move now, I'd miss Nina. And I was already fearful that she'd got the wrong idea about me and Karen. If she assumed Karen was an ex – and what else would cross her mind? – Nina would surely be horrified by such lack of quality control. And wonder what that said about *her*.

'I can't stop, Karen. But listen to me,' I spoke sternly at her. 'I don't care if you've got friends who live here, OK? I don't even believe there actually is a Caroline. But, whatever, I don't want to catch you round here ever again. Got it?'

I didn't wait for Karen's reply, but started pelting towards the station, desperate to catch Nina before the next train came. I reached the station foyer just as a train pulled into the station.

If there had been no station staff there, I would have jumped the barriers just to say goodbye. But unfortunately there were, and I could do nothing but stand and listen to the tube train drawing out of the station, taking Nina away from me.

Fuck. Fucking Karen.

Even when there was silence again, I found it difficult to head back straight away to the flat. I was fuming. Karen had damn well ruined what might have come to something between Nina and me.

I traipsed back to my block and prayed en route that Karen wouldn't be still waiting for me. Thankfully, she'd got the message, for now anyway, and was nowhere to be seen.

When I reached the flat, I let myself in dead quietly and headed to my room. As far as I could guess, the three girls were still gassing in the kitchen. But I wasn't up for finding out what they were talking about. I didn't need any smartarse digs in the ribs about me pairing off with Nina. As far as I was concerned, I'd blown it. She was history.

Jill

'So, how long have we been going out, and where did we meet?'

I didn't even have to turn my head away from the cab window.

'Oh, that's easy,' I replied. 'Just under two years. And we met on the ski slopes. Almost bumped into each other, ha!'

I looked over at Jill and we both smiled at each other. Both in on the joke.

Jill nodded at me in the dingy light of the cab, egging me on to finish my story. *Our* story.

'I was out of my comfort zone. An Aussie on the slopes, and because our chalets were practically next door and it turned out we went to the same bars, it made sense for us to all go out as a group. You and me weren't the only ones to pair up, were we, love?'

I stressed the 'love' as I winked at Jill and squeezed her hand. The sheets of notes she'd given me almost slipped off my knee and onto the taxi floor. I let go of her to bend down and grab at them to stop them from falling, then straightened them out on my lap.

'So, how am I doing?'

'How do you think you're doing, *boyfriend*?'

I kept my mouth shut but nodded at her with a rueful smile.

Because that was the crux of it. Whether I could convince Jill's colleagues I was her other half. That was my mission – should I choose to accept it.

Goddamnit, the two of us were in our black-tie gear and en route to her work's summer ball. There was no getting away from it. I couldn't come across as anything *but* her boyfriend. Whether or not I'd memorized our back story and all the facts about her no longer came into it. I was to be her lover, and that was that.

'Oh, I'm up for it. No problem,' I assured her, though I was saying it as much to chivvy myself up as to re-assure her.

Shit. I hope she believes that I'm going to do a good job for her, and that I'm not about to put a foot wrong.

I took a sideways glance at Jill. The lights of Holborn flooded the back of the car with different hues as we sped through the streets, emphasizing Jill's cheekbones. And taking pounds off her.

Jill was a larger girl than I was used to pairing up with, but once I'd got to know her, I could see she had an awful lot in her favour. She was almost as tall as me, only broader, but she was bright and enthusiastic and ran her own successful events-management business at the age of twenty-seven.

Tonight was a thank you to all this year's clients.

From what she told me about the long hours of her work, the only way she could have a social life was to mix business with pleasure, partying with the people she worked with. She'd told me that she'd spent so much time building up the business that she'd never found the time to even have a boyfriend.

Which was where I came in. Jill had hired me to fill in that gap and keep up the impression that she had her life sorted. But just sitting beside her now underscored the very real truth that it wasn't, was it? I was the damning proof of that. Sometimes my job just involved papering over the cracks.

I looked at her, sitting in the corner of the back seat, and reached over to run my hand up her thigh. Through the satin of her full-length dress, I sensed the tantalizing strip of flesh beyond the top of her stockings.

That was the extent of what I was getting tonight – Jill had made that clear when she booked me. I was here for the sake of her colleagues at the party, and then the two of us were to go our separate ways. It made a change, to be honest. A break from the sex games for a night and the chance to exercise the social side of my skills.

The cab drew up in front of the Savoy. I turned to her: 'You ready?'

She smiled back. 'More to the point, are you ready, boyfriend?'

I liked that she was in a light-hearted mood about this setup. It relaxed me too.

'Don't worry, Jill. I'm right here beside you.'

I slipped out of the car, held the door open for her

155

and offered her my hand. She took it and stepped out on to the pavement, then adjusted her dress and directed her attention to me. Jill straightened my tie and brushed down my jacket. Like lovers do. She took my hand.

'Right,' she said, 'here goes.'

It was Jill's show, so I held back a step behind her so the focus of her colleagues was all on her as we entered the ballroom. Each of was handed a glass of champagne as we arrived.

I stood at Jill's shoulder and allowed myself to be introduced to her workmates. I played the nice, polite boyfriend who shook hands with them but at the time held myself back, even though that was not my natural style. Or at least not my style in my escort work. My instincts cried out for me to be proactive, to reach out and be sociable. To put anyone I came across at their ease.

Jill turned towards me, touched my arm lightly and gave me a sweet smile.

'You all right, Luke? I'm sorry that I can't give you my undivided attention,' she apologized, 'but you know how it is. No rest for the wicked.'

I shook my head. 'No worries. Don't mind me. You just do what you have to do. OK?'

'Thank you,' she whispered, as she was approached by a guy a couple of years older than she was.

She turned her head abruptly to focus fully on him while I took a deep breath and returned to playing the strong, silent type beside her. They shook hands, and he hovered with his hand in mid-air, as if he was not quite sure whether or not to acknowledge me. At least he had the decency to consider my presence.

156

Jill noticed. 'Matthew, may I introduce my partner, Luke?'

I noted she'd upgraded me to a pseudo-husband.

Fast worker.

And neither was Matthew aware of that. Which suggested that Jill was flirting with me, at the very least. This was more in my comfort zone.

Matthew's hand reached out to shake mine. 'It's a pleasure to meet you, Luke,' he said.

'Pleased to meet you too, Matthew,' I replied and gave a slight tilt of my head. 'Isn't this a beautiful venue?'

I aimed the question at both of them; even as the words were coming from my mouth I realized that I'd slipped into escort mode – finding *anything* to move the conversation along, though I gave myself a minus point for not asking an open-ended question. Matthew took the bait anyhow.

'It's pretty impressive, isn't it? It's a great place to have a party, Jill. Tell me, Luke, do they have anything like this where you come from?'

There was a twinkle in his eye. I wasn't going to let his words rattle me, though.

'Australia might be a young country, but we're not *that* young, I can assure you.' I grinned to let him know I was in on his joke.

'S'funny,' countered Jill, 'but I thought Australia was ancient.'

She scrunched up her nose at me as she spoke. I smirked right back.

'Well, yeah, if you're an Aborigine, it is. But you know what I mean.'

I didn't let on to either of them that old buildings weren't something – even when I'd been living in Sydney, before I came to the UK – that I really looked out for. I supposed there must have been some fine places back home that were just as elegant as this one, but I hadn't made a point of searching them out once I got to the city. That wasn't where my interests had lain. Nor lay now. But I knew that it was something that would impress Jill's friends so I'd mentioned it. It was surely why Jill had decided to host her party here, wasn't it? To make an impression.

I cast my eyes around the ballroom. However much or little I knew about interior design or architecture I could tell that this place was something.

I found myself looking up at the ceiling. And then I looked straight at Jill. I'd observed her tonight and she'd shone among her colleagues in such a heady environment. She'd chosen well with the venue. It said that she had classy taste and enjoyed sharing it with others.

'This is the first time I've ever been inside the Savoy,' I admitted. 'I've seen the outside before in films, but to be actually here is something else.'

'It is, isn't it?'

A huge smile lit up her face.

Jill dwarfed a lot of guys but she could still look striking, I now realized. The guys she met in the line of her work couldn't have been looking in the right place. Even Matthew.

But there was no point me noticing if no other guy did. The trouble was, my presence here was double-edged. As much as I was helping Jill with her public image of a together woman who had a successful career, good looks and a cute hunk – natch – of a partner, I was probably deterring any of these guys from approaching her tonight on the off chance they might wangle a date with her. Why would they, with me, the 'boyfriend' around?

This was my first time out with Jill and I could see that she'd created her own tangled web with me slap-bang in the middle of it. Not only was I her man for tonight, but Jill would now have to keep up the pretence of her fake relationship even when I wasn't around to back her or her story up. As far as I could see, she'd conjured up a whole heap of trouble for herself.

It was the early hours of the following morning and we were heading home in the back of a black cab. Heading to Jill's place. It had been a pleasurable evening at the Savoy and the champagne bubbles had raised my spirits and set me up for the rest of the night. Had raised hers too, as it turned out.

She'd originally only hired me for the party, but changed her mind past midnight when it began to taper off.

She can't get enough of me!

If I was tired now as we leant against each other in the back seat of the cab, it was mixed with the headiness I felt I now shared with Jill. Going back to Swiss Cottage to finish off our session – however it might play out – was all right by me. It would be a great finale to a good night out.

I had a flashback from earlier in my career, of Sasha

159

and I returning to her flat in a black cab and the fast sex that had followed. I was dog-tired back then too, if I recalled rightly, but that had only made the sex more of an out-of-body experience. Mind-blowing! I could only hope that if I played my cards right in the next half an hour or so that I'd have just as heated an experience with Jill at the helm. She wasn't exactly in the same league as Sasha, looks-wise. Few were. But there was no reason why the sex couldn't be as passionate.

Neither of us spoke during the journey. It wasn't an awkward silence we shared, but rather one of contentment and comfort. I was looking forward to seeing Jill's apartment.

The car drew up outside a block of flats. Jill pulled herself up from the depths of the back seat, rifled in her purse for the fare and paid it. I followed her up her garden path. She put her key in the door.

'You'll come in for coffee, won't you?'

I trusted Jill was using a euphemism. That was where my head was at this point. The very possibility had shifted the cloud of sleepiness from my mind. I was ready for action.

Jill took my hand and led me quietly over the threshold and down the hallway to her flat. 'Ssh,' she put her finger to my lips as she said it. 'We don't want to wake any of the other flats up.'

'No,' I agreed, shaking my head vigorously and trying not to burst out into giggles or raucous laughter at the overplayed mime we were drunkenly enacting in order to keep the peace.

Jill let us both into her flat and, once we were settled,

she went to the kitchen to put the kettle on. Looking around the place, my first impression was that it was neat and cosy, a refuge from the hectic pace of her work life. I was glad of that. It suggested that, in spite of her long hours and her lack of a genuine social life, Jill was at least aware of her need to recharge her batteries and have time out.

Jill came back into her living room, handed me a steaming mug of coffee and cuddled up beside me on the sofa. 'Thanks,' she whispered, 'for tonight.'

I turned to look directly at her. 'It was my pleasure, Jill. I had a great time myself, you know.' I meant it. It had been a relaxing change to take a step back and simply play someone's companion for the night.

She nudged me. 'You did?' She sounded genuinely surprised.

We drank our coffee, our spare hands entwined in each other.

'This is nice, Luke.'

'Um?'

'Just sitting here, comfy on the sofa. It's a really nice end to the evening,' she sighed, and rubbed her hand over my knee a couple of times.

Hang on.

Did she realize what she'd just said? Was it a slip of the tongue, or did she know exactly what she was telling me? That I wouldn't be getting any nookie tonight after all?

She knew what I was thinking.

'Luke, look, it's been a wonderful evening. My colleagues thought you were smashing. You did a great job.'

161

'My pleasure, hon.'

I didn't voice my fears that our very success at putting on such an act would have had a detrimental impact on any interested guys tonight. She didn't need to hear that, especially while she was basking in the success of the party she'd thrown.

'I do like you, Luke, and I know I asked you in. It's got nothing to do with you.' Her voice got quieter. 'You're pretty special, you know.'

I cocked my head at her. *Well, yeah! That's my job.* She continued, her tone straight and serious. It made me tune in to what she was really saying.

'It's just this thing I have,' she admitted. 'I'm not into sex on a first date.'

I was momentarily taken aback by Jill being so blatant about it. But at the back of my dog-tired, dog-eared brain there was a muffled yelp of warning.

Date?

That was just the word she used, right? *She's joking. Or maybe she doesn't know what other word to call tonight?* And maybe there was a little yearning on her part for it to be something more than it was – a financial transaction between her and an escort.

Jill couldn't admit to herself that our evening had been all about cold hard cash – at least for me. Which meant that, at the end of the day, for all her success, the kudos of arranging tonight's lavish ball, and the thanks she'd got from colleagues, she still remained on her own. No, I wasn't about to query her use of the word 'date'. That would have been too cruel. *Not my job at all.*

Suddenly I was thinking of Nina. God, we hadn't even been on a proper date as such. But the short time we'd had together sure felt a hell of a lot different than me sitting here with Jill. A hell of a lot *more* than this, to be honest.

But who was I kidding? I'd ruined any chance I might have had with Nina by not catching up with her at the tube station – or rather, *Karen* had fucked that up. But what did it matter whose fault it was? It would have been too difficult to explain anyway. And, what's more, I hadn't even managed to get Nina's phone number. I suppose I could have got it from Kirstie, but the balls-up I'd already made with Nina stopped me from doing so.

When it boiled down to it then, I was in no better position than Jill.

Jill must have been watching me, seeing I was miles away.

'Look,' she said, 'I'll give you a call tomorrow or the next day and maybe we could go for a coffee or something like that?'

It was as if she was reassuring me that the fact that she didn't want sex just now was nothing to do with me. I knew *that*. Yet it sounded too as if she was still clinging on to something of what we'd shared this evening at the Savoy.

Put like that, her not wanting sex made all the more sense. She didn't like to have sex the first night she met a guy. *No, it can't be that, surely?* I sure didn't want that to be so. I was beginning to wonder which of us was the one full of wishful thinking.

We finished off the coffee, and she reached out for her mobile and called a cab for me. She drew herself off the sofa and went to get my fee. She paid me double. I knew not to query it. She knew my rate, and if she wanted to pay me more, a tip, then that was her prerogative. But while I'd never say no to extra cash in hand, that little voice at the back of my head was trilling that she was paying for something I wasn't yet even aware of.

As I went to the front door, I turned for one last time. 'Yes,' I said, 'call me and we'll go for coffee. Y'know, catch up on news. I'd be happy to.'

I'd been in this job long enough. Going for a casual drink with a client was a means of keeping them on side in the hope that they'd hire me for another session. I knew the score and how to remain in control. What could possibly be the harm in meeting up as friends?

Marie & Craig

Second week in August

The sea breeze was pleasurably cool against my skin as I leaned against the yacht's white railings, a glass of expensive whisky in one hand. Across the marina, the lights of countless other luxury yachts sparkled in the dusk along with those twinkling the height and breadth of Monte Carlo beyond them. And a beautiful woman, Marie, was standing up close to me, giving me her full attention.

Does it get any better?

This had to be pretty high up the league of escort experiences to be had, I was well aware of that. It was certainly my first time on a boat – a yacht – like this, anyhow.

Though it wasn't my first time in Monaco. A few months after coming to London, getting on for a couple of years ago, I suppose, me, Mark and the guys had treated ourselves to a cheap-as-chips bright orange easyCruise that had taken us along the French and Italian coasts.

Then, we'd been dropped off for a day in Monte Carlo, which helped us walk off the onboard excesses. And they *had* been excessive! We'd made a point of traipsing the length of the racetrack just so that we could tell ourselves and the folks back home that we had.

I'd never imagined that a break with the lads would ever help me get my bearings for an experience such as I was having now. But it also meant that I wasn't disappointed when we didn't leave this huge yacht the whole time we were here. It was an incredible place, and I was sitting in the middle of it all.

'The view's beautiful, isn't it? And this boat of yours is something else,' I sighed, languid in the heat.

Marie smiled but said nothing, as her long, manicured fingers wrapped themselves around my wrist. I gave a quick look around to check no one could see us; they were all at the other end of the boat, so I bent my head to hers and kissed her hair.

She pulled away, sharpish. 'Not now!' she gasped in shock. 'That's afters,' she mellowed, indicating with her head the clutch of couples. Some time fairly soon they would all be gone.

'Sorry,' I apologized. 'I got carried away. Y'know, I can't wait.'

'Well, I'm afraid you must,' she stressed, the lilt of humour in her voice showing she had no hard feelings about my mistake, 'but don't worry, there's plenty worth waiting for.' Maria smiled, and brushed at her neck so the loose kaftan she wore over her bikini fluttered to reveal the deep curve of her breasts.

* * *

166

I'd met Marie only a couple of days ago in a tiny coffee shop down a side road behind Harrods. She'd explained what she was after – or rather, what Craig wanted. When I arrived early afternoon on the Saturday, a number of their friends would be present, so I was to play their 'godson' to explain the age difference and my presence on their yacht. *That* was one hell of a euphemism. And once the evening began, we'd have the boat for just the three of us.

Craig had let Marie choose the guy, and was presumably happy with my pictures so had sent her along to finalize my trip. She was everything I could have hoped for, too. She was stunning, her beauty haloed by blonde, lustrous hair, and a tanned, honed figure. I just *knew* I was going to have an amazing time in Monte Carlo. When Marie handed me the business-class ticket, it was as if I'd won the lottery.

Even as I arrived early afternoon, the party was already hotting up. But Marie came to meet me with a big, welcoming smile that immediately set me at my ease.

'Luke! It's so lovely to see you again. Honey,' she called to Craig, 'Luke's arrived.'

She looked over at the guys at the other end of the yacht. The one with his back to us, who had his hand on another man's shoulder as he spoke closely to him, half turned towards us. He hovered for a second. I sensed that although he had been expecting me, that didn't mean he'd got himself comfortable with the reality of me now being here. He gave a couple of slaps on the back of the guy beside him as he indicated that he had to be elsewhere.

There was a marked and relaxed camaraderie among those men that noticeably fell away from Craig with every step he made towards me. He had the same tanned and wealthy air about him as Marie.

Craig shook my hand half-heartedly. 'Ah, Luke, you're here,' he said. 'We'll get someone to take you to your cabin, and then Marie will sort you out a drink.'

I noted him give a hurried glance to his partner, and then, as if as an afterthought, he cleared his throat. 'And then I can introduce you to my friends,' though there was an air of reluctance that hung about those last words. As though he'd be doing it under duress and that he'd rather I kept a low profile until our time together later this evening.

Craig looked around, as if searching for someone, then spotted him. It wasn't that hard to do.

'Ah, Mario, please help Luke with his luggage. He'll be in cabin four.'

Mario was wearing a white naval jacket with epaulettes and gold buttons, and beneath, nothing but a pair of trunks. His skin was a light golden brown. He had clearly been hired as much for his looks as for his service skills. For a split second, my male pride felt threatened.

Why call me?

But a moment later, I'd rallied. For some reason known only to themselves, Craig and Marie had been prepared to call *me* from London rather than make use of a local lad. That decision was benefiting me, so why should I worry?

I followed Mario and my trolley-bag through a small white-painted metal door and down a corridor to my room, where I quickly changed my clothing, going for smart/casual like the other guys on board. I wasn't yet ready to go to Mario's lengths.

When I left my room, locking it behind me, I turned to head back in the direction of the way I'd come. And there was Marie, standing facing me at the corridor's end. I wondered how long she'd been waiting for me.

'Please join me,' she beckoned, and I ventured towards her. 'You'd like a drink after your trip, I'm sure.'

Marie sticking with me was wise. It meant that when we actually got to the sex, she'd know me a bit more than as some guy she'd met in a London café last week. But it also gave me the opportunity to size her up too.

I followed Marie back up on deck, past the party-goers whose intrigued gazes followed us as they let us through, and into the cool of a darkened lounge. There was a deep red, horseshoe-shaped leather sofa, and a mahogany bar at the far end.

I hadn't quite worked out what either Marie or Craig did for a living, but I assumed it was something high up in fashion. Everything was beautifully styled, and on every available surface was a designer label. If they didn't work for this particular brand, I sure hoped they were being paid for the amount of space they were giving the logo.

Marie beckoned me to a bar stool and I sat down. 'What would you like?' she asked, her hand gesturing towards the stock of alcohol.

I might have felt as if I was in a Bond movie, but I

steered clear of asking for a martini. It was better to go for something straight and simple, so I asked for a whisky to get me into the right mood. I would keep my head clear by alternating with tonics and mixers. The worst thing I could do was drink too much and ruin the whole show. Though my dick hadn't played up, ironically, since my awful Viagra episode with Marcus and Rachel a month ago, I remained mindful that it was always possible that I could struggle to get hard again. Drinking too much would surely only increase the risk of such a fiasco. But a whisky in the company of Maria afloat in such a beautiful harbour as this – that could only put me in the mood for a satisfying bout of sex later on. Surely.

'This is a pretty impressive boat. Yacht, I mean,' I announced to break the ice as we drank together.

'You'd like to tell that to Craig? He'd love to hear it. It's his pride and joy.'

She came round to the other side of the bar to join me, and took my glass from me and set it down.

Maria took my hand to lead me back towards the deck. Sharp sunlight poured through into the lounge, and as I blinked to adjust my eyes, she let my hand slip out of hers. I got the message, but didn't draw attention to it. We had to take care that we didn't arouse suspicion among the couple's friends.

I fished my Ray-Bans out of the top pocket of my shirt and put them on as I stepped into the light.

'Now,' Marie half whispered to me, 'let's go and find Craig so you can tell him directly how much you enjoy being here.'

Marie stepped into the melee and I followed behind. Eyes turned to watch her as the group parted to let us through. She nodded back – 'Hello, Geoff'; 'It's good to see you, Malc' – but seemed to make a point of not stopping to indulge in any chat with any of them. Her focus was on Craig, as if it was vital that I spoke fully to him first before anyone else. There were a number of glossy women hovering with their partners on the edge of the party, but Craig's inner circle appeared to be solely male. There was clearly a pecking order here, as if he needed it underscored that he was Number One.

Marie was now by Craig's side. He was joking with a couple of men and they hung on every word, laughing in all the right places. Marie touched her partner's arm.

'Darling,' she said, and he immediately stopped in the middle of a sentence, and turned to look down at her with a smile. It was obvious that everything stopped for her. 'Darling,' she repeated, 'Luke was telling me how impressed he was with your yacht.'

Craig visibly gladdened. Clearly, after Marie, the boat was his prize possession. He cocked his head to one side and took a measured look at me.

'*My Fair Lady* impresses you, does she?'

His voice was rich, but I detected that he wasn't totally impressed with *me*. He reminded me of a lion with huge paws, like the ones in Trafalgar Square, toying with me before he went in for the kill. My hackles rose in self-defence, but I wasn't about to let him see that I was irked.

'Who wouldn't be amazed by a yacht such as this, Craig? It's something else,' I enthused.

That was what he wanted to hear, wasn't it? That was surely why he bought *My Fair Lady* in the first place. To make his mates green with envy, or at least to show he had the money to flash.

'You've been moored here long?' I added.

'In the height of the summer,' he admitted. 'But we like to cruise along the coast when we can, don't we, darling?'

Surrounded by his acolytes, Craig was holding Marie's hand and they smiled with their eyes at each other. I could see that I'd have to tread carefully tonight.

Keeping onside by being curious about his yacht would let Craig know that I was interested in him and his. And therefore that I could be trusted with his other favoured 'possession', Marie, and that I'd do my damnedest to make sure they both had a good time tonight; in other words: that it had been damn worth picking me to do the job.

'It's a beautiful coastline, isn't it?' I observed.

I thought back to me, Mark and the gang having the time of our lives on our budget cruise. Getting a look at the land the ship was passing certainly hadn't been top of our agenda then. Partying *hard* was. Yet, I could see how on a classy boat – *yacht* – like this, with a lover and your mates, that hanging out in Monte Carlo or in a quiet cove would be a pretty smart thing.

'You know the coastline round here, do you, Luke?' Craig threw out with a smile that I noted curled at the edges.

Fuck, where the hell did that come from?

I was only making small talk, nothing probing or

underhand. Couldn't he see that? Nothing to get competitive about.

'Why do you keep asking so many questions?' he sneered in front of his friends, as if my very presence was a nuisance. He was mocking me, trying to make me feel small and show everyone who was boss.

That certainly shut me up. I looked across at Marie, but she was looking up at Craig. His arm was around her waist. I wasn't sure where to look, or what to do.

Marie then turned to me but seemed to avoid actually catching my eye.

'Luke, let me give you a proper tour of *My Fair Lady*.'

She slipped out of Craig's hold and took me by one elbow, steering me away from the others. I felt Craig's stare boring into my back.

'My *godson*, huh,' I heard him say to the men around him, and they laughed along with him.

I felt stung. Marie gave me a sidelong glance as if she was reading my thoughts.

'I'll get you another drink. Come with me.'

It was an invitation back into the darkened cool of the main cabin. Which was just what I needed to get myself on an even keel again.

Marie shook herself a cocktail and I chose a fruit smoothie.

I was sorely tempted to knock back a swift pint just to steady my nerves, but I knew that was the wrong way to go about things. If Craig needed impressing that I was professional about things, then getting half cut within an hour of getting here wouldn't have done me any favours. And I needed to be absolutely in good shape for tonight's action, whatever Marie required of me.

That was always the downside of the glamour that others presumed was the escort's life. I could never one hundred per cent relax and just soak up the fun and the atmosphere of wealth I found myself swimming in. I always had to stay on my guard and make sure I remained on good terms with whoever was employing me.

And so, even when I was in a place like Monte Carlo, following Marie up to the roof deck – the cliché of the rich high end we were all supposed to desire – part of me would much rather have been back in my room in my flat-share in London. You could only keep the escort act up for so long, I'd found. A couple of days was probably the limit. After that, the real me kicked in, and I wanted my own life back.

Marie laid out a towel and I followed suit. She slipped out of her kaftan and her strappy heels. The bright red of her toenails matched the scarlet of her bikini. She lay on her back with her glass of drink and a book. I stripped down to my trunks – *eat your heart out, Mario* – and stretched out beside her. Sipping from my glass, I bathed in the sun's glorious rays.

I don't know how long I'd been daydreaming, but my ears suddenly tuned in to the sound of beer cans being opened and men's raucous laughter and loud voices wafting up from the deck below.

I sat up to reset my bearings. I could see other couples on the roofs of other boats doing exactly the same as Marie and me. She lay flat out beside me, engrossed in her Jackie Collins book. Just the sort of doorstep block-buster you'd expect to see someone reading in such a scene. Which blew my mind a bit. Why would she be reading it when she was *living* it?

Yet, at the same time, Marie's book was gesturing like a pointed finger at a big white circle around me with a speech bubble declaring, 'What's wrong with this picture?' It was fucking *me*, that's what.

It was always the way on these international jaunts. There would be a moment such as this one, when the scales would fall from my eyes and I would be only too well aware where I was. And that wasn't on equal terms with my clients. I was here because I'd been paid to be. The hired help. The sense that I was only renting time in someone's world of wealth would almost overwhelm me. For a few seconds, anyhow. And then I would swallow the ill feeling and the thoughts and the home-sickness and get on with my work.

I lay back on the towel and looked up at the deep blue cloudless sky. I had to admit that Craig had rattled me. My confusion about what he wanted from me meant I was now finding it hard to relax into my escort role.

And then I looked across at Marie, sizzling in her scarlet bikini, as she turned to the next page and sipped from her straw, and knew that things weren't all bad. I thought for a split second of Craig and his friends entertaining themselves without us down below, and knew that I'd definitely got the better deal.

I was looking forward to making love to Marie tonight, as long as Craig didn't make things too difficult.

I feared that he might change his mind at the last minute and order me to keep my hands off his woman. Not that that had ever happened before. I could only hope that as the night wore on and the drink got under his skin he would ease up so he could enjoy what I brought to the party. The *real* party that would begin once Craig's mates had left the boat.

Gradually the afternoon drifted into early evening and the sunlight mellowed too, as did the chatter and laughter wafting up from the lower deck. Couples were already beginning to disperse down the gangplank and wend their way back to dry land via the network of boardwalks. I watched them go.

Marie set her book down and sat up, as if she knew instinctively that it was time for us to reappear down below.

'You'd like another drink, Luke?'

'Yes, please, that'd be nice,' I said, sensing that things were about to get started *very soon*; once everyone else had gone. Presumably not long now. It was time then to get into gear. Spirits deserved to be raised.

'I'll have a whisky, please.'

Marie strapped on her stilettos and I admired her fine coltish limbs as she did so. She stood up and gave me her hand and pulled me up too. I handed her her kaftan and she slipped it over her shoulders. I picked up my trousers but her hand went to my wrist to stop me putting them back on.

'Stay as you are, Luke. I like you like that,' she ordered, though with a glowing smile.

We were definitely on to the next stage of the evening.

I followed her back down the ladder.

'Wait there,' Marie instructed, pointing to the front of the yacht, as she headed for the bar.

There were still a few of Craig's friends down the other end, and I could see Craig entertaining them at their centre. It was very clear that we weren't to mix.

I took the hint and walked the few steps to the boat's edge. I leaned against the metal railing and focused through the dusk. I couldn't help but be impressed by the vista stretched out before me. This place was another world.

I must have drifted into some sort of daydream, mesmerized by the lights strung out across the harbour, because what seemed like only minutes later, Marie was at my shoulder, her hand on my arm, passing me my glass of whisky.

'There you go, godson,' she trilled.

We chinked glasses and looked over at the marina and the luxury yachts bunched together between us and the mountain. Monte Carlo was turning golden in the evening light.

I sipped my whisky and took a sidelong glance at Marie. She was a handsome woman in her forties who'd looked after herself. Her body had clearly been toned by years of yoga. Which meant that the sex would be agile too.

It flattered my ego to think we made a good-looking couple standing together, in spite of the age difference. I was the six-footer fit Aussie and she was only a couple of inches shorter. We'd relaxed in each other's company during our time in the sun up on the roof, too. At least some of Craig's friends must surely have spotted Marie and me standing side by side; it must have crossed their mind that there might be something else between the two of us.

Maybe from the other end of the boat someone was watching us now, thinking that very thought. And then very likely shaking it out of their head and replacing it with something far more neutral. Yup, 'godson' was such a useful catch-all phrase.

I turned so I was leaning against the metal bars and to get a clear view along the deck towards the dregs of the party at the stern end. There was still a handful of couples yet to leave the yacht. And then the three of us would be alone and the play could begin.

Marie had turned the same way, and was thinking along the same lines. 'Not long now,' she whispered. Just the thought of it and the soft sound of her words got right under my skin.

I watched Craig say his farewells to the last of his guests. He was certainly all 'Hail fellow well met' with them. But for me, it seemed like Good Cop and Bad Cop with this couple. Maybe that was the point: he was acting aggressively so that I wouldn't get too complacent about why I was here. As if!

Yet if Craig didn't change his tune, it was sure going to be difficult to work with him for the rest of the night. How would I be able to tell if I was giving him what he'd paid for? I'd have to trust to Marie, since I damn well knew my practised sex technique would please her, no kidding!

Now his guests had left, Craig looked down the length

of the yacht towards us. At the same moment, as if he'd choreographed things, Mario came on deck with a fold-away table that he opened and placed beside Marie and me. Mario returned to the bar, just as Craig joined us, and returned shortly with a huge plate of light nibbles that wouldn't weigh heavily on us.

'Thank you, Mario. If you can bring us a magnum of champagne and glasses, please.'

Within minutes, Mario was back beside us, pouring each of us a glass of champagne from the magnum.

'That'll be all, Mario. You can go now.'

Mario bowed to us all, turned sharply and went back inside. Leaving us to the warm evening air.

'Here's to the rest of the evening!' toasted Craig, and we each raised our glasses to the night and its twinkling lights and the warm Monaco air. Craig knocked back his champagne and hurled his glass into the water. Marie did the same. So I did too.

And then Craig offered me his hand and we shook. 'Right, Luke, this is what you're here for,' he stated matter of factly. 'This is what *we've*' – he shot a glance at Marie – 'been waiting for.'

He didn't smile too well, but I realized at that moment that if I ignored his offhand manner and simply listened to what he was saying, it was clear his mood had now lifted, and he was no longer be-littling me.

I was wrong about Craig, then. I think. It was as if he didn't feel he had to pretend any more. Or feel embarrassed that this young buck squiring his wife was there for entertainment purposes that his mates could only guess at. It was as if, when night fell, my presence was at last fully appreciated.

The fact that I was alone with this hot couple raised my spirits, melting away any homesick thoughts of my London flat. Thrilling sex with Marie was on the agenda and there wasn't anywhere else in the world where I would rather be.

The evening was played out in slow motion. We drank and talked, and Craig and I languidly passed Marie between the two of us. She'd sit on one of our laps and then after a short while would slip away to wrap herself around the other. The man left with just his drink would take a sip and watch what the other two got up to.

It wasn't until the early hours that things really got steamy, even as the temperature cooled down a little. We moved out on to the middle of the deck. I had my arm around Marie's waist and she held her partner's hand, the three of us drinking in the luxury and freedom of this night.

We could hear others on other boats partying too, though they were at the far extremes of the marina, the water carrying their laughter and music in waves towards us. Presumably we answered back with our own night sounds.

Craig pulled away from Marie and leant against the edge of the boat to watch me with his partner. I sensed he was giving the both of us, and me specifically, permission to put on a show for him.

I necked Marie and she leant back into my arms as I did. I lifted her up, her long, loose kaftan dripping, draping fluidly around her, and carried her to the steps that led back up to the roof of the boat. It had been a siesta patio earlier in the day, but it sure would be party to something hotter this evening.

Marie gripped the white metal banisters in front of me and I shifted right up to her from behind. It was damn tempting to take her doggy style right there, but I was too mindful of Craig looking in.

Not just yet.

I wound my arms round hers so I was holding on to the banisters in front of her hands. She gripped my wrists, and with my body now firm against hers I encouraged her upwards with a strong hint of what she had coming to her. I could feel her own desire in the way she forced her ass back against my own hardening.

The two of us all but stumbled onto the smooth floor. Marie's earlier request for me to dress down made a whole lot of sense *now*. She slipped off her kaftan and the moonlight caught the two of us in its beams, casting dark, dark shadows.

I pulled Marie down onto me and, as I did, noticed out of the corner of my eye that Craig had joined us on the roof. He leant against the stair handles, arms crossed, engrossed in our action. I nodded silently to him to indicate that I would remain mindful of his enjoyment as much as Marie's. And mine.

Marie was just as much involved as I, the profes-sional, was. My whole afternoon, and the entertaining of the party guests, and the drink, and Craig's brusque manner, and the sunbathing only a short while ago – all had been leading up to *this*. We were now completely naked together, our white skin stark against the night. I armoured myself and gave it to her with gusto. I kissed her whilst sinking deep into her, her body rising up to meet mine. We rolled over on the deck, and Marie was now on top, though it was hard to tell where I ended and she began.

Despite the heat of the moment, I still had time to notice that Craig had stepped on to the roof and was looking down at our writhing bodies. His hand was in his pocket and he was rubbing himself, and then it was as if he'd had enough of that virtual wanking. He undid his belt and pulled off his trousers so he too was naked.

He was happy enough just to keep watching. Which suited me fine. Marie was a lithe yet firm sex partner. She pulled herself away from me, and before I'd sat up she'd sheathed my cock and had it in her mouth.

Marie was used to being in control. I could tell simply by the way she used her mouth, her tongue snaking round my dick and knocking me flat out on the deck in delight, all control of my limbs gone. She brushed her hands hard up my torso and I was all but lost to the world. She drew her lips away from me and then climbed on to my still erect cock.

My fingers sank into the cushion of her breasts and I nestled my head against them as her body rose and fell. Then, Marie threw her head back and let out a guttural shriek. I entwined my arms around her torso and drew her tight to me, and we rocked together until my own cries matched hers.

As our mutual climax subsided, we relaxed into each other's arms. Maria slowly disentangled herself and I lay back on the deck, well spent. It was then that I was reminded again of all the hassle my dick had given me only a month ago. It had certainly proved that it was back in the game tonight!

Marie trod over to Craig, and the two of them traded tongues. Soon, his hands were on her ass and he was drawing her close towards his own erect dick.

I was still flat out recovering when Craig pulled himself away from his partner and beyond my vision.

'What the fuck?' he seethed through his teeth. 'It's the police!'

That brought me to my senses. I sat up, and Marie grabbed up her kaftan from the floor and deftly wrapped it around her body so she was at least halfway decent. I scrambled to my feet and searched in the half-light for my trunks.

I was pulling them on, balancing on one leg, when the police boat drew up alongside ours. A powerful torch was shone across at us; its beam struck my legs and moved up to my chest and then my face. I had to look away to avoid being blinded by the bright light.

God, it could have been so much worse! Loudspeakers, sirens and flashlights or anything. The guys were talking loudly in French so I couldn't under-stand what they were saying, though I got the gist: that there were limits to the high life. Threesomes in full view of anyone out taking the air overstepped the mark as far as the local law was concerned.

Craig jabbered away to the police officers. I could tell from his body language that he was used to getting his way: he could be very charming, when it suited him.

The conversation between the men was light-hearted and the officers' eyes were sparkling in the darkness. Craig had worked his magic.

The police pointed to the lower decks and ushered us back down the steps to the deck. We complied with nods and laughs, and 'no problemo, officer' whether they understood or not.

They must have been used to this sort of thing. The marina reeked of wealth and was packed full of these large yachts, with people on them who had so much money they could choose to do whatever they damn well wanted.

The three of us had drunk so much that it was all a bit of a game. We turned to the police and nodded and waved back at them, and when they were satisfied that we were ducking inside and quietening down, they swanned off, presumably to have a nose around other boats to see what they could find. If you had to be a member of the water police anywhere in the world, it definitely wasn't the worst place to patrol, I could see that.

The police presence acted like a dampener to the rest of the night. Or at least it was a wake-up call for me to return to my own bed. It was now three o'clock in the morning, for fuck's sake, and I was bushwhacked. It had been a long day since leaving home early in the morning and then being out all day in the sun, not to mention the athletic sex-fest I'd just enjoyed with Marie.

I looked over at Marie and Craig who seemed to have forgotten I was even here. They were holding each other, eyes closed, dancing softly to a tune that must have been in their heads because there was no music to be heard.

I decided to mentally take credit for both delighting Marie enough for Craig to enjoy watching us have sex, but also for revving her up sufficiently for her to carry her uninhibited mood over to him. And to then silently slink away and leave them to it. If nothing else, I knew by now when to make my excuses.

The following afternoon, as I packed my holdall, I sighed. It was definitely time to go home. Craig and Marie entered my cabin, and I brightened into escort mode immediately.

Craig shook my hand with a firm, solid grip. 'Thanks for last night, Luke.'

Craig was sure whistling a different tune today. He looked at me, his arm round his lover, and gave me a big grin. It was as if he felt guilty at what had passed between us and his treatment of me yesterday in front of his cronies.

He'd barely spoken to me at all yesterday and he clearly wasn't going to start now, but at least he had something more positive to offer me. We'd had under five minutes of conversation during my time on his yacht – a quite remarkable feat in itself. But what made it strange to me was that Craig's previous hostility was such a contrast to the chattiness and warmth of his wife.

Marie herself certainly seemed well loved-up, which only added to Craig's delight. She was now wound loosely around him as if I'd disconnected her joints with my feverish sex moves. I certainly could take credit for unhitching something.

I was glad that I'd been able to help these two. And my time here *had* contributed something to their relationship; that was presumably why they'd asked me here in the first place. And now they were standing in the door of my cabin, blocking out the sunlight and facing me with warm, perfect-teethed smiles. Craig clearly now appreciated what I'd given Marie last night – and giving her a good time was, by extension, my gift to him too. I couldn't help wondering if I might get another invitation to Monte Carlo some time.

I knew I'd done an excellent job by the very fact that both of them now barely had eyes for anyone but each other. That was the success story I could notch up on my bedpost.

I was holding out for the football results on the Sunday night news, but my mind was on Monaco and what a weekend I'd just had.

God, that had been something to explain away to the Girls. I told them I'd been catching up with an Aussie mate in France who was travelling round Europe. That explained the suntan.

'Well, it certainly seems to have done you the world of good, Luke,' noted Kirstie, who was scrunched up at the other end of the sofa.

Hadn't it just?

'Yeah, it was a nice break. Y'know, get away from London for a day or so.'

The ends of Kirstie's mouth turned down in mock sadness. 'Hope you weren't wanting a break from us, eh?'

Laura, who was sitting in the armchair, turned to get a clear look at me, but said nothing. I felt cornered. I put my hands up in the air.

'Hey! Of course not!' I laughed. 'But I'm an Aussie. It's good to look around, see as much as I can while I'm here, y'know.'

'We know, we know,' smiled back Kirstie. 'But be careful that in all that travelling, you don't miss the fun you could be having right under your nose.'

I hadn't a clue what she was getting at.

'Oh, I've certainly been enjoying London, I can assure you. You don't have to worry about me on that score.'

A look passed between Laura and Kirstie. *What the . . .?* I looked at one of them, and then the other. I confronted them: 'What?'

There was a huge grin across Kirstie's face. 'Er, the party. Remember? We just thought there was something going on between you and Nina?'

Laura nodded in agreement.

'But if you're always swanning off to the Continent every weekend,' continued Kirstie, 'then how's it supposed to bed down?'

Blimey!

The fact that the Girls had mentally fixed me up with their mate, presumably while I'd been on Craig and Marie's yacht, making love to Marie, took me aback.

But it was sweet too that they were concerned about my love life – however out of touch they might have been.

187

'I appreciate your interest,' I laughed. 'But you need to know that nothing's on between Nina and me. I blew it.'

The two of them looked by their expressions as if they were angling for a better explanation. Not if I could help it.

'The point is, I didn't even get my act together to get her number,' I sighed, wanting to leave it at that. Just the thought of how *that* happened brought up images of Karen. *If only Karen hadn't been involved, would Nina and I have had a chance?*

Another look passed between Kirstie and Laura, but I could see them wanting to laugh.

'Oh, if that's all that's needed,' crowed Kirstie, 'you can have it right now.'

She fished her mobile out of her jeans pocket and handed it to me.

Talk about being put on the spot. I took it from her wordlessly.

Laura brought her right hand to her chin, her thumb to her ear, her little finger to her mouth: 'Phone her,' she whispered.

So I did. Watched all the while by Kirstie and Laura. At least Carrie wasn't here too. That would've been *too Witches of Eastwick*.

'Nina!' I called down the phone. 'It's Luke.'

Both Laura and Kirstie were smiling and nodding at me, happy for me that I'd made the move.

'Luke!'

In just that one word I could tell she was genuinely pleased to hear from me.

'Look, I'm so sorry I haven't been in touch. I missed you at the station . . .' I told her.

Laura stood up and Kirstie followed her out of the room so I could speak to Nina alone.

'I wasn't sure whether to wait to say goodbye and get the next train or not.'

God, she was taking part of the blame. Neither of us mentioned Karen.

I zapped the telly sound down. It was just me in the lounge room now and, feeling more confident, I jumped in with both feet. 'Nina, I'd like to see you again . . .'

'Me too, Luke.'

I mentally breathed a sigh of relief. I hadn't completely screwed things up with her, after all. I'd been given another chance. It wasn't as if I hadn't given Nina a thought since I'd last seen her. But it was as if the confusion with Karen, and me getting to the station too late to get Nina's number, had told me that juggling my escort work and a love life would be far too complicated. God, it had been bad enough that morning, and nothing had even got started! Kirstie and Laura pushing me to phone Nina had done me a kindness. It told me that maybe I should give the dating game a go after all.

We arranged to meet for lunch later in the week.

The call ended, I transferred Nina's number into my own phone.

Sorted.

Carla & Denise

I was nothing more than a cock. I could just as well have been a dildo for all that I was contributing – or was *allowed* to contribute – to Carla's pleasure.

She was straddling my erect dick and I was lying back, my arms at my side, my nails digging deep into the pink candlewick bedspread, staring tight-lipped at the ceiling. Wondering what the fuck I was doing here.

When I shifted my head slightly, I had a clear view of Carla's girlfriend, Denise, sitting in the corner. Her mouth looked as if she was sucking a lemon, her eyes were mean, and her arms were crossed, as though she just wanted it all to be over and done with so she could get back to having Carla all to herself . . .

Denise had made it very clear from the first time she emailed me that I was to do nothing to enhance what was going to be Carla's first time of having sex with a guy in at least five years. When she said that my job was 'to be there for her', she meant it in the most basic way possible.

Denise and I had discussed things in more detail on the phone a few days before the session. Or rather, she'd told me, and I'd kept my mouth shut and listened. While it had been Carla's desire to sleep with a guy, from the moment Denise had called me she'd made it very clear that our meeting was going to be on *her* terms rather than her bisexual lover's.

Denise had stressed that there was to be No Touching. I was to lie on the bed like a lump of wood, naked with an erection. A fence post with a nail sticking out. There was to be no fondling of breasts, or even kissing. Absolutely *nothing*.

Which would sure make things damn difficult. It had been hard to get my head around what she really meant and I'd spent the days between the phone call and our meeting trying to work out how I was supposed to achieve *that*. With my hands tied behind my back? If Denise had her way, I'm sure she'd be content that my dick was tied off too. I winced at the thought.

'You know what you're here for, don't you? What the deal is?' Denise interrogated me before I'd even got across the threshold of the Manor Guest House room. I nodded, struck by her stern demeanour.

Once I was squarely in the room, I had a chance to get a good look at the two of them side by side. These two fitted right into the butch/femme stereotype of a lesbian couple.

As I looked at Denise, dressed in denim jeans and a

denim shirt with cowboy boots, an image of Sasha and Chloe, and the hookers Emma and Louise, flickered across my mind. There seemed to be a fluidity about their sexualities. Like they enjoyed whatever they could get. A world away. Nothing like these two at all.

A miniskirted Carla hovered nervously in the corner of the bedroom, her neat figure haloed by the worn wallpaper she was leaning against. I identified – beneath her shorn hair, pierced lip and eyebrow – the slight, pretty girl who had no doubt drawn guys to her before she'd paired up with Denise five years ago and put all that behind her. Until I appeared.

I tried not to think of the possibility that she might have a matching collection of piercings down below that could snag.

Please God, no.

At the moment it entered my head, I swallowed that leg-crossing thought away. I could see that it wouldn't be my place to broach that concern with either of them anyhow.

The mood of this session felt all wrong. I decided to see if I could at least lighten our time together a little bit, though Denise's starchy requirements made it a difficult achievement.

'So, now I'm here, how do you want me?' I aimed at Denise, though I trusted that Carla might get the double entendre. I didn't expect Denise to have enough of a sense of humour to do so.

But, as soon as I said it, I regretted even speaking. Denise just gave me a look, her bottom lip stuck out. Clearly, I wasn't here to speak. Carla remained silent.

I wanted to be anywhere but here. But so, I suspected, did Denise.

'You can remove your clothes and lie on your back on the bed,' she ordered.

Perish the thought that she might instruct a fit young guy to undress. I swallowed a guffaw.

Denise seemed damned sure she was going to make today's session as unpleasant and unfulfilling an experience for Carla as it would very likely be for me. Even down to the choice of a seedy hotel on West Kensington's main drag. Of all the hotel rooms I'd visited in the course of my escort work, this had to be the skuzziest I'd ever been in. It didn't help that outside was brilliant sunshine, highlighting the shabby furniture.

This session would be memorable for all the wrong reasons, I was sure of that. I'd found it hard to believe that hotels such as this could still exist in a modern city like London. Weren't there laws against grotty wallpaper and unclean sheets, for God's sake? This was one of those dreadful experiences in ghastly environments that I knew I would one day look back on and laugh about. But for today, it was more of a life-sapping, soul-destroying endurance test.

I pulled off my shirt and trousers in as matter-of-fact asexual manner as I could muster, with my back to the two of them. Whilst I undressed, I couldn't help thinking of other threesomes I'd been a part of in anonymous hotel rooms, and the atmosphere of expectation and fun that had preceded them. Even with Martin and Fiona at the airport, when we'd been so rudely interrupted by their other halves. There'd been strawberries and champagne and a girl shared between two guys up to the knock at the door.

Each time, the guy had enjoyed watching me getting it on with the missus, and she'd benefited from my services. I could see it written on her face. Usually that had been the deal from the start. That was why I was there.

But if I thought about my presence here, as the third member – hah – of this trio, then it all seemed too warped by far. But then again, I wasn't here to think. Frankly, apart from the member in question, Denise would rather that I, Luke Bradbury, wasn't here at all.

I lay back on the bed.

'Give yourself an erection,' Denise bossed.

To be honest, Denise frightened me a bit. I had nightmare thoughts of her taking a machete to my dick. Or maybe she just looked like she would and I was doing her a disservice. It was hard to understand just what was going on.

I noted that Carla remained tight-lipped, in the background, silent all the while. I could see her standing straight, her eyes fixed on Denise so that there was no doubt that Carla wasn't – and *wouldn't* be – getting any pleasure out of today's session whatsoever.

The only words spoken were by Denise, and they were sharp with it. Between her orders, nothing was said. If it hadn't been for the sound of my hand-job – me making myself heard – Denise could have been the only person in the room. I stifled a laugh. Denise pulled up the lone chair and sat down. I heard it scuff the carpet. When I'd come in, I'd noticed it as the type we had at school back in Aus. Hard and square-joined. Like her.

'Carla, it's your turn,' she instructed her girlfriend through gritted teeth.

Carla didn't say a word but began to unpeel her clothes.

I couldn't mention to either of them that that was helping me, but the fact is, it was. Not watching her, of course. Just the thought and the sound of that petite boyish girl removing her miniskirt, top and her bra, boots, thong and black stockings. In the absence of any physical stimulation coming from Carla, I felt she owed me at least *this*. I was clutching at straws to keep myself going. To do the work I was being paid for.

I felt for Carla. She seemed half terrified by her lover, or at least incredibly submissive to her desires. Maybe that was how she wanted or needed her relationship to be. The trouble was, it seemed to me, that she still had a certain amount of her heterosexual tendencies troubling her. Which, presumably, technically made her bisexual.

I could see how the fear that her lover might one day leave her for a guy might scare the shit out of Denise. Maybe, then, it was the more feminine Carla who really pulled the strings in this couple, though neither of them seemed especially aware of the dynamic.

My dick at last stood to attention. I sheathed it.

'It's ready now,' I admitted, refraining from using 'I' and drawing any attention to the fact that there was a hot-blooded heterosexual male in the room. Though, to be honest, I wasn't exactly feeling on top of my game at the moment.

I could tell that Denise was completely naive about the working of a guy's dick. I was willing mine to remain firm for the entire time that Carla wanted. That was my worry, and the more I focused on the possibility that I would at some point flag, the more fearful I was that I might effectively will it into inaction. I tried not to think of my Viagra fiasco and the experiences that had led to it.

Carla clambered on to me. I sensed that she'd had a stern talking-to about what she could and couldn't do. There was to be no caressing, no tenderness. If she was holding on to me, it was only so she could keep her balance. Nothing else.

The irony was that not only would Carla not enjoy the experience, but by definition Denise wasn't likely to get off on watching her lover at it either. She had damn sure missed a trick. She was too incensed and wound up to get hot from seeing a naked Carla poked in front of her, even though it was by a guy. If Denise, upright in her chair and staring at us, was getting hot under the collar of her buttoned-to-the-neck blue denim shirt, it was because she was *fuming*.

Yup, this was the most grim, joyless and *sexless* sex I'd ever had. In fact, it demeaned what sex meant – yeah, even paid-for sex with an escort – to even call it that. I tried to blank out the whole godawful experience as Carla went through the motions.

I turned my head to look at the wallpaper. It had clearly seen better days. I wondered when the room had last been decorated. There was a worn horizontal tidemark where the bed had been shoved up against the wall. I tried not to think of the other grim couplings that were likely to have gone on in such dreadful surroundings. The whole place smelt of despair. I expected a cockroach to scuttle across the worn carpet any minute soon. That would be the last straw.

Just thinking about such hellishness threatened to send me into a fit of hollow laughing. But even the mere hint of a smile, however humourless, would be out of place in this setup. I returned to looking at the ceiling and tried not to think too much about what Carla was doing at my other end, though it was difficult not to. She gripped the sides of my waist, and rose up and down on my stiff, humiliated cock.

After about ten minutes of Carla bouncing up and down on top of me, holding on for dear life and me not moving a muscle, she stopped in her tracks, as if she couldn't quite see the point – *me neither, love*. She readied herself and drew herself off me. She'd been trying with all her might to orgasm, but hadn't. Given the circumstances, I couldn't see how she could have ever got in the mood. My dick relaxed too in relief that it had done its job for the moment.

Denise remained seated and didn't say a word. But on her face remained a hard glare that suggested she'd wanted the whole thing over and done with ASAP. And even though Carla was now off me, Denise wouldn't be completely satisfied until I was long gone out of there.

'Are you going to have a quick shower now, Carla?' Denise wasn't asking, I could hear that.

Barely looking her girlfriend in the eye, Carla picked

up her pile of clothes and scurried wordlessly to the bathroom. I meanwhile covered my cock loosely with my boxers, then slipped off the side of the bed away from Denise so I could get dressed myself without her needing to see too much of me.

I was intrigued how things would pan out for these two once it was all over and we'd gone our separate ways. Did Denise honestly believe that this depressing coupling in a seedy B&B would quell her girlfriend's sexual leanings?

The sound of a shower at full blast came through the thin wall, almost like a shrill comment on what had just happened here. I couldn't help wondering what Carla might be thinking to herself now she was in the bathroom and away from Denise's presence.

Surely, the very attempt by Denise to make this session such an asexual, ugly affair would instil in Carla the desire to do it better some day, presumably in the way she'd done before she'd met Denise. And next time, she might decide that things would be a hell of a lot better without Denise knowing or looking on. Denise, it struck me, had actually probably opened up a whole can of phallic worms. I couldn't help wondering if I might be the person Carla might call some day when her urges got too strong for her.

That was the tragic thing about what Denise was trying to do. The whole session could have been so much more pleasurable for everyone in the room, regardless of how successful or otherwise the sex was. There surely could have been room for us to just be nice and friendly towards each other.

I buckled up my belt, and I was doing up my shoelaces when Carla returned to the bedroom. She didn't say a word.

It was a shame she'd kept so quiet throughout our session, not even speaking to her partner. I knew that I could have helped relax Carla so she could have shown appreciation to her lover for hiring me. And I was quite capable too of reassuring Denise that I wasn't about to sweep her girl away from her.

In fact, if I'd had my way, I'd have given Carla the time of her life. Which was presumably what Denise feared all along. She was too wound up to realize that I'd have pleased Carla as much for her sake as to give Denise a good show too. And I would have enjoyed myself, too, just seeing these two girls lighten up a bit.

Now I was dressed again there didn't seem that there was a lot for me to say. Anyhow, I wasn't totally sure when – or even if – Denise might allow me to speak again. I imagined her shushing me like the evil guy in *Austin Powers* who won't ever allow his son to get a word in. Denise wasn't interested in what I had to say one iota.

I turned round to face the two of them, my mouth closed. Carla had her hand in the back of Denise's jeans pocket. Denise reached out her hand towards me with the wad of twenties, and I took them silently from her.

'Thanks,' Carla all but whispered, and I nodded at her, giving her the lightest of smiles so as not to threaten or disturb Denise.

'Can you go now,' suggested Denise bluntly.

There was still around twenty minutes I owed the two of them. But I wasn't about to argue, or, come to that, give them any of their money back. As far as I was concerned, full hour or not, I'd sure earned every penny.

And I damn well knew when I wasn't wanted. So I left.

Jill & friends

August Bank Holiday

Jill had invited me over to her flat in Swiss Cottage for dinner with some of her friends. We'd met over a coffee a few times since our 'date' at her company ball simply to touch base, and that had been fine, but this was more what Jill wanted my services for. To play her boyfriend.

I rang the bell, and she came to the door looking hassled. She was wearing a black cocktail dress, and had a knife in one hand.

Whoa.

She saw the look of unease flit across my face, looked at what she was carrying and roared with laughter.

'Sorry about that,' she grinned, 'I'm in the middle of chopping carrots. You'll help me?'

I hadn't even got my coat off and Jill was drafting me in to the 'helpful guy' role. *That* was new to me but, then again, hiring me as an escort meant that, as long as a girl was paying, she could ask me to do more or less whatever she wanted. I hadn't ever imagined being a chef's assistant, but that was all part of the deal.

201

She had me setting the table when the doorbell rang. 'That'll be them,' she hissed as she hurried from the kitchen to the hallway.

Jill opened the door and, from where I was standing by the dining table, I could hear the greetings of old friends, and laughter too. I swallowed hard, psyching myself up to play Jill's lover and be as friendly as possible to her friends.

A man a couple of years older than me walked into the dining room. He had a glass of wine in his hand. He stopped in his tracks when he saw me.

'Hello, I'm Luke,' I greeted him and shook his hand. 'I don't know if Jill's mentioned me?'

He looked me up and down. I wondered what he was making of me.

'I'm Christopher,' he told me. 'My better half's Miriam. She's in the kitchen with Jill. We live opposite. Jill told us she wanted to show you off.'

He looked slightly bashful about that. As he should. He'd just let on that *I* was tonight's entertainment. At the same time, I couldn't help wondering what he thought of me hooking up with Jill. It wasn't as if she wasn't attractive in her own way. She just wasn't my type; I generally didn't fall for the larger lady, so if he was anything like me he could well be wondering why I'd gone for her.

I suddenly realized that I was back in Karen territory, finding myself in a situation where I'd been hired to play the 'boyf' while being paired up with someone I'd have been unlikely to look twice at in any other situation. Being an escort wasn't always what it was cracked up to be.

A short brunette came into the room and hovered by Christopher's shoulder looking nervous. I decided to put her out of her misery.

'You must be Miriam,' I smiled. 'I'm Luke. Christopher was just telling me you were his better half. And may I say that he's absolutely right!'

Miriam laughed and squeezed her partner's arm fondly. 'He very often is.'

So, what I'd told her was corny, I damn well knew that. But it had cracked the ice a little, and that's what mattered. That was one of the most basic of skills in the escort armoury: putting people at their ease.

The doorbell rang again.

'I'll get that,' said Miriam. 'That'll be Siri and Ralph.'

She left the room, leaving her partner to deal with me. He smiled nervously at me, and fiddled with his half-empty glass while I finished off laying the table. I could tell that while Christopher was OK with the introductory niceties, he was unsure how to move the chat along any further. That was my job.

'So, how do you all know each other?' I asked.

Christopher relaxed his shoulders with relief that I'd thrown him an easy ball.

'Oh, Jill was really good to us when we first moved in across the way. And when there was a residents' meeting in the local pub, we met the other two. We were the only ones in our twenties,' he recounted.

I wasn't sure if I wanted to find out more about the meeting they'd all decided to go to, but it gave me a prompt for my next question nevertheless.

'You enjoy living round here?' I asked.

'Oh God, yes. It's just right where we are. It's on the tube but also is just the right distance from Central London. That is, not too close so that it's busy beyond belief, and not so stuck out in the suburbs that you can never join in real London life.'

Miriam re-entered the room with the new couple and we shook hands. Jill was still preparing the food. It was only right that I made it my job to relax the guests with my chat and friendly manner. I wondered if Jill realized the double advantage she'd given herself in hiring me.

I sensed that both Siri and her husband Ralph were sizing me up.

'So tell us, Luke, how you and Jill first met?' asked Christopher.

Ralph pulled out a chair from the table and sat down, all ears to hear my side of the story.

'Oh, hasn't Jill told you?' I parried.

'We just wanted to hear it from the horse's mouth, so to speak,' shot Ralph out of the corner of his mouth.

What was he saying? That he didn't quite believe Jill's story? Or now, having met me, could see that Jill and I didn't quite match?

'We were both holidaying in the Alps.'

Siri's eyebrows creased. 'That's a strange place to find an Australian, isn't it?'

'Is it?' piped up Jill, who had just entered with a steaming dish of lasagne.

Everyone turned in her direction. It was a relief that the questioning had stopped. She set the dish down in the middle of the table.

'Now, everyone, if you could sit down, please, and I'll just go and get the salad.'

I grabbed the opportunity. 'Jill, don't worry. I'll do that.'

I left the room. As I did I heard Miriam declare: 'You've got him well trained, Jill.' Jill laughed in response.

The bowl was sitting on the draining board where Jill had shaken off the excess water. I cupped it in both hands and stood for a couple of seconds, musing at the scenario I'd got myself up to my neck in.

This was Jill's fantasy. She had a nice home, good friends, a successful career – and had hired me to fill the final hole in the jigsaw of her life. And that sure made me feel an awkward shape.

I took a deep breath, lifted up the salad bowl and turned towards the dining room. 'Right, everyone, here's the *pièce de résistance*,' I declared as I entered the room.

'Give that to me,' beamed Jill, taking it from me, her eyes shining with happiness. She set the salad down beside the lasagne.

'Tuck in, everyone, and, Luke,' she instructed, her hand patting the seat of the empty chair beside hers, 'come and join me.'

It was the least I could do.

The red wine flowed. Christopher filled mine a second time. 'So, you're a good skier, then, are you? For an Aussie?'

I wondered where this might be going. It wouldn't take too many steps to go from this opener for someone to spark up and suggest that Jill and I join at least two of them on holiday in the New Year. I recognized the

205

possibility of relatively moneyed, childless couples sitting round a dinner table and where the conversation could end up.

I decided to play things as straight as possible to avoid getting into trouble further down the line. It was no good saying I was an expert skier when all piste meant to me was getting blathered of a Saturday night with my mates. I shook my head with an obviously fake sadness.

Jill read me well. Before I could say anything, she blurted out: 'To be truthful, he's *crap*, aren't you, Luke!'

There was loud laughter round the table.

Where the fuck did that come from?

I had to join in, I had no choice, but there were also sirens blaring in my head at Jill's blatant dig at me. I hadn't realized she was paying to belittle me.

'The truth is,' I countered, 'I'm not much more than a beginner. But I'm a fast learner, and I'm fit too, so I'm not afraid to up my speed and move up to the tougher slopes in time. Probably faster than most, I expect.'

That might or might not have been a return dig at Jill's own apparent fitness levels, and an underhand hint to the guys round the table that I knew just what they might be wondering – i.e., why someone like me might have paired up with *her*. Of course, only Jill and I knew the truth – that I wouldn't have been here in the first place if there hadn't been money involved.

Jill had sensed it too, I could tell. Beneath the table she was gripping on to my left hand like her life depended on it, as each of us with our other hand forked the pasta into our mouths.

We were drinking coffee, and had pushed our plates away from us. Christopher had lit up a cigar. I declined the offer.

'Sorry about having a dig at your skiing earlier,' he apologized.

'No problem,' I sighed, in a good mood after the food. 'It's the easiest thing to tease the Aussie in the snow. It's not exactly the usual idea people have of us,' I laughed. I held the moment for a couple of beats. I was very aware that I was walking a fine line. I didn't want to flag up my potential skiing skills, but on the other hand I was still smarting from Jill putting me down in front of everyone. I needed to lighten the mood. 'But, then again, there are plenty of images of you Poms we can find to laugh about,' I joshed. 'The cricket. The rugby.'

Siri's mouth was open in mock horror: 'Miaow!' she crowed.

Everyone laughed.

The party was over. I helped collect the coats and handed them out at the door. The guys shook my hand. I kissed the girls on the cheek. I might have known this crowd as long as Jill had done.

'See you around, Luke. It's been a pleasure to meet you,' said Christopher. 'You and Jill'll have to join us for dinner some time.'

'We'd like that, wouldn't we?' grinned Jill. She was enjoying the thought very much. At least I knew I'd done my job well enough to convince them as Jill had wanted me to. The job she'd employed me for. And the truth was that I'd enjoyed the evening better than I'd expected. They *were* a nice bunch of people who had helped me feel at ease, given I was the newbie among them.

The front door closed. I let my hand slip from Jill's.

'Well, I'm not going to be going skiing any time soon, I can assure you. I've had enough talk of it to last me a lifetime,' I laughed.

She cocked her head to one side. 'Oh, I bet you'd love it, if you took the trouble to have a go. We could get you started on the lower slopes. It wouldn't take you long to graduate from those, I'm sure.'

She nudged me with her elbow. I took it in jest, but I couldn't be altogether sure that she wasn't damn serious. That was the thing about Jill. There were a couple of times during the evening and some of the things she'd said to her friends that had gotten under my skin. It was as if she was *willing* me to be her real boyfriend, as though – if she only believed it hard enough – it would be true.

Not on your life, girl.

But that didn't mean that I didn't have to fulfil my escort obligations. The dinner party was only the beginning of tonight's session. Jill had decided to top it off with an overnight. Not that it would be too hot a night. The good food and the alcohol had put paid to *that*.

There were other ways of making a night of it. Hadn't my escort work taught me that? I could go quiet and gentle and build up the pleasure so I had them squealing at the tops of their voices by the time the night was out.

And I didn't have to exert too much energy to help them reach such heights.

God, I'm good at this game.

I took Jill by the hand and guided her back into her lounge room. She tried to pull away, to get back to the washing and the tidying up. I drew her back to me.

'Leave it, Jill. For tonight,' I suggested.

'But it won't tidy itself. And it'll be even worse tomorrow morning when I come down to it.'

No wonder she had trouble keeping men if she played them like this. She clearly had no idea that her domestic concerns would put a guy right off his stroke. *Literally.*

I gave her a firm gaze. 'Forget about it, Jill,' I growled and pulled her to me.

She heard my sex drive through that all right. I rifled my hands through the waves of her hair and took a deep breath of her perfume. Her hands were around my back and her lips were on my neck. She drew back her head so we were looking at each other now. Our mouths met.

When we drew apart, I shook my head at her: 'The house can clean itself. Come on,' I grinned, dragging her out of the room, and heading for her bedroom, wherever up above us it might be, 'we've got better things to do with our time!'

I was unbuttoning my shirt with one hand as I was leading her up the stairs. 'I have no idea where I'm going!' I laughed.

'Not much further,' she hurried, her head clearly already full of what I was about to do to her.

I pulled her to me as we reached the landing. The niggling worry that I might be laying myself wide open to facing 'girlfriend' trouble from Jill could shut the fuck up for tonight. Her hands were on my chest and she was nibbling at my neck. My hands were on her ample ass, fondling her through the sheer silk of her dress.

Big girls normally weren't my cup of tea, but then again, I was always up for trying new things. Getting lost between her huge breasts wasn't the worst thing that could happen to a guy.

'Behind you, Luke,' she gasped, forcing me backwards through the door to her room.

I almost tripped on the bed behind me. An image of being flattened by Jill flicker-booked through my head, but I quickly shut it out.

Don't.

I grabbed at her at the very moment that I flung myself on to the bed and the two of us tumbled on to the duvet. If Jill's body was anything like as fluffy and enveloping as her bed, then I had nothing to worry about at all.

And if there was something to admire about Jill, it was her confidence. That counted for a lot. She might have had trouble finding a real boyfriend, but the way she ran a successful business, and the way she was at ease with her friends said a lot of positive things about her.

But the way she pulled off her dress brazenly in front of me said it all. A confident girl made sex much more fun for the both of us. So, she might have been larger than the women I was used to, but I could see I was going to have a lot of pleasure via this new experience.

The two of us were lying naked together, looking up at the ceiling. I wasn't quite sure where to begin. Jill still seemed a whole new frontier compared to what I was used to. I turned on to my side and observed the expanse of her belly and her thighs. It did mean, I told myself, that there was more of her to enjoy. But I was also aware that I was trying to convince myself to go for it. I wasn't altogether sure why. I mean, there must have been loads of relatively small women who had to deal with bigger guys, whether in the cock department, or just them being larger-built men all round. God, hadn't I experienced that myself? Petite girls who were uneasy about my six-foot frame and all that suggested. Size to a certain extent *did* matter, no matter what anyone said.

But at the moment that I was deciding to go for it – *In for a penny, in for a pound of flesh* – Jill had made up her own mind. She wrapped her arms around me and pulled me to her breasts. In terms of all the tits I'd ever encountered, hers were the Himalayas. And, what's more, they were cushiony and *real* too. I had had nothing to worry about. I was in my element.

A low chuckle rose up from my gut. A giggle of relief bubbling up inside of me, so that it reached my throat to burst into a full-blown guffaw. I laughed heartily as I tightened my arms around Jill's girth, rocking in the humour of it all.

She joined in, though she wasn't sure what the joke was. 'What's so funny, Luke?' she giggled herself.

I turned to her in mock affront. 'Well, what are you laughing at, then?'

'I'm laughing cos you're laughing, silly,' she grinned, pummelling my chest softly with her knuckles.

'It's you and me, girl!' I shrieked at the top of my voice, and play-fought back.

'Shh!' she squealed. 'You'll wake the neighbours.'

'Ha, ha, and so we should. Spread the joy, I say!'

I collapsed on top of her, rolling with her like a boat on the high seas.

Entering Jill was a pleasure. She was curves and rounded edges and softness, and I felt swallowed up by the sex we were having. For the first time, I could understand fit guys who went for big girls. Jill might have been a potential problem with her desire to see me as her real boyfriend, but I was getting paid for it in cash and bodily delight.

Nina was waiting for me beside the little timbered cottage in the middle of Soho Square Gardens where we'd arranged to meet for our picnic lunch.

As soon as she spotted me coming up the path towards her, a smile lit up her face, and something sparked inside of me too. We hugged and kissed in greeting. I mentally thanked Kirstie for helping the two of us get together. She'd done both of us a favour.

I took a step back to look at her. 'Am I glad to see you!'

'It seems ages since we last saw each other,' she mused.

We found a bench to sit on and unwrapped our sandwiches. This was the right time as far as I was concerned to broach the issue of what had happened last time we were together.

'I botched things up, I'm afraid,' I admitted sheepishly. 'I got to the station just as your tube was pulling out. And I hadn't even managed to ask you for your number!'

Nina took a sip from her Coke can. 'Don't I know it?! I thought you hadn't wanted it, that you were just being polite, taking me to the station. And you didn't even manage that! That girl – was she a plant?'

There was a twinkle in Nina's eye but it seemed she didn't want to dig too deeply in case she got the answer she didn't want to hear.

If only.

'Karen?' I shook my head. 'Uh, uh. It was work-related. She shouldn't have been there.'

I was telling Nina the truth. Only not the whole truth.

There were a few moments of silence between us as we ate our sarnies. I feared that I might have said the wrong thing.

'But you got it anyway, didn't you?'

'Got what?' I queried, confused.

Nina set her sandwich down on her lap, and looked directly at me. 'Why, my phone number, of course.'

That was a relief. 'Oh yes, that was Kirstie. And I didn't even have to ask her for it, y'know. She *gave* it to me.'

That got Nina flummoxed. 'She did? Why would she . . .?'

'It looks like she – and Laura who was egging her on – want you and me to be an item!'

Nina sleighbell-chuckled to herself, then stopped

213

abruptly. She glanced across at me, a quizzical look in her eyes.

'And what about you, Luke? Do *you* want us to be an *item*?'

That was a question and a half. She was proposing a whole new ball game as far as I was concerned. Though I wasn't about to let on about *that*. Having a proper girlfriend as such wasn't something I'd ever been into. I liked my freedom too much. The freedom to shag whomever I wanted without answering to anybody. I'm not sure I could do 'boyfriend'. And then there was the 'getting paid for sex' issue too. That was the bigger problem. I hadn't even told my flatmates about my escort work for fear of what they'd think. I just couldn't see how being a hooker and having a girlfriend could be compatible. I'd end up living a double life, and probably I'd end up spreading myself too thin as well. Because the fact that women were paying me for sex didn't mean that it was always as simple as all that. I'd become friends with some of my regular clients such as Eva and Lars, and Melanie, which would be difficult to explain to another half: that I enjoyed sessions with my clients as well as sex with her.

God, if Nina ever found out, would she even want me?

But then I looked at our sandwiches on our laps, us sitting here in the sunshine, and other couples doing the same. This was all so different from the intense dinner setup experience I'd had with Jill and her friends. It was a world away too from the luxury of Craig and Marie's yacht berthed in Monte Carlo's harbour.

To be honest, I *liked* how relaxed I felt around Nina. It was as if a weight had fallen off my shoulders. I might have had to keep shtoom about how I made my living with Nina, but I didn't feel I had to put on any act with her otherwise. With my clients I was Escort Luke. I didn't need to be that person with Nina.

I took her hand and squeezed it. 'An *item*?' I gave her a knowing smile. 'I tell you what. I will if you will.'

Kim

Early September

When sex with a client wasn't on the agenda, I was still surprised by what was expected of me of an evening. Kim wanted me to accompany her to a nightclub all the way out in Essex just to make another guy *real* jealous. I was prepared for another test of my acting skills.

'Kim. After Kim Wilde?' she explained as she and I sat, legs brushing each other at the table on the side of the 'Sizzlers' dance floor. She saw my nonplussed look. 'My parents were fans. "Kids in America"?'

I shook my head: 'Afraid not.'

She playfully rolled her eyes: 'She wasn't big in Australia?'

'Well, if she was, she was off my radar. Or more likely my mum and dad's,' I grinned.

That was the light-hearted small talk over with, then. I shifted closer to Kim and slipped my arm around her shoulders and deep-kissed her.

This was all part of Kim's plan of action. That the guy she wanted to turn green with envy would see us

216

together and regret that he'd left her, since she was clearly having so much fun with her new man.

People could all get so fucked up about their relationships. It was clear to me that Kim herself was the envious one. Envious that her bloke had got away scot-free and left her feeling hurt.

Kim's lips tickled my neck, and we held each other tight. We relaxed into each other, and then Kim looked out into the crowd and she froze.

'He's here,' she stage-whispered to me out of the corner of her mouth.

I gulped back my snigger at the drama she was psyching herself up for.

God, it's just the same old boy–girl trouble, love. Nothing special.

'Which one is he?' I whispered back.

Kim turned to me. 'Don't look now, but he's on the other side of the dance floor.'

Her mobile phone rang. She drew it out of her bag and looked at the screen. And blanched. 'It's him! Philip,' she bleated.

She silently read the text. 'He's seen the both of us. He wants to know who you are,' she half smiled.

She'd already got her money's worth out of me, then.

As she tapped out a reply, I glanced around the club. I wondered which of the guys in the half-light it might be.

'I've let him know you're my friend.' She looked up at me and smiled. 'He can interpret that in any way he wants.'

'And so can I,' I replied, and went in again for the kill.

We locked lips *hard*. Whoever he was, wherever he was out there, I sensed his eyes boring into us.

When we'd set each other free again, I raised my beer bottle to Kim. 'Would you like another drink?'

I knew it was supposed to be Kim's call rather than mine. She was paying, after all. But I also recognized that somewhere out there we had an audience, and it was my job to act like I was the one in charge of things for his benefit. And, let's be honest, to wind him up big time.

Kim jumped up with glee. 'Don't worry about that, Luke. I'll order a bottle of champagne. That'll really put Philip's nose out of joint!'

Before I had a chance to say anything, Kim had hurried off to the bar, leaving me feeling like a lemon saving her table for her. I might as well be her bloody coat if this was all she wanted me for.

I had another glance around the room to see if I might be able to work out who was the guy I was there to make jealous. One of the advantages of escort work was that you soon learnt to read body language. My previous experience tended to be in a more local, intimate setting, but I reckoned that I could transfer it to a larger setup like tonight's. If I looked out into the crowd, I should be able to pick him out by the way the culprit – or was it victim? – was standing and looking, even if he was trying not to be noticed.

I flicked my eyes over the dance floor. There were a few guys looking my way, and among them I spotted a face I recognized, from the TV. He was somewhere between up-and-coming and a household celebrity but

I couldn't recall his name. I didn't want to look as if I was staring so I turned away.

Kim was coming towards me with a bottle of bubbly in one hand and waving a couple of glasses at me with the other. She set them down on the table. I took the bottle from her, filled the glasses and handed one to her. I lifted my own, raised it to her and winked.

It might have been a strange job that Kim had hired me for, but that didn't mean that I couldn't enjoy the night. And, let's face it, spending it with a hot babe – even though her mind was well and truly on her ex – still made me look good to anyone looking on.

The champagne bottle was empty. Kim jumped up from the table. 'I'll get another!' she chattered tipsily. I'd noted that she was drinking two glasses for every one of mine. I was drinking slowly, as I usually did while at work, but Kim had nothing stopping her as far as I could see.

I watched her weave across the dance floor, where she was waylaid by a couple of young women she clearly knew. They even looked the same as her. Long blonde straight hair, four-inch heels, tiny strappy tops and miniskirts that left little to the imagination.

She hugged them lavishly in that over-the-top manner that drunks do. And it was as if she'd forgotten why she was there because, instead of heading off in the direction of the bar, Kim began dancing with them. Or rather, falling about, with them holding her up.

Shit. Shall I go and dance with her? Pick her up off the floor? Or what?

219

'Do you mind if I sit here?' I turned my head towards the male voice – and hoped that the surprise wasn't written across my face.

'Sure, please do,' I stuttered and tried to act cool.

It was the guy off the telly. I racked my brains. Phil Hyde, that was his name. He was in his early thirties, and one of those actors who you couldn't identify with any particular role, but was on the box in enough decent programmes to have become well known. I'd seen him in the paper advertising some flash watch too. Nice work if you could get it.

He nodded in the direction of Kim. 'She's quite a one, isn't she?' he grinned.

I looked directly at him. *Oh God, Philip. Phil. He's her ex.* I hoped my discomfort didn't show on my face.

'Yes, she is,' I laughed, perhaps too loudly. 'Sometimes I can't keep up with her.' I shrugged my shoulders. 'Mind you, I'm not much of a dancer. Sizzlers isn't exactly my natural habitat.'

'I thought I hadn't seen you here before. I'm Phil, by the way.'

Fearing he might thump me, I jumped in before he had a chance to bring up the subject of what I was doing with Kim. 'I'm Luke. I tend to go to the clubs West London way.'

Out of the corner of my eye I could see Kim throwing the wild, uncoordinated shapes of a girl who was totally pissed.

'What, with all the other Aussies?' Phil asked, drawing my full attention back to him. He wasn't

220

threateningly handsome but certainly good looking enough for the box. He was wearing a quality suit and carried it well.

'Used to be. But I'm sharing with three English girls now. That's a whole new ball game,' I smiled.

'I bet,' he grinned back. 'That's every Aussie guy's dream, isn't it?'

I didn't need to reply. The two of us laughed.

I was surprised how well we got on since he had every right to hate my guts. I couldn't help wondering if he was used to losing a girl to someone like me. A young Aussie guy apparently on walkabout whose face wasn't plastered everywhere. On an obvious level, we were in different leagues, but what struck me about him was that at no point in our chat did he use that against me. Plus he'd had the balls to come and sit with a guy he could only presume was shagging his ex. He was talking man to man. That said something decent about him. I almost felt bad that I was only at Sizzlers to get up his nose. In any other situation, I'd have been happy to buy him a drink.

The table shook as Kim lurched towards me. 'Luke,' she slurred, 'can you come with me pleassh?'

I grimaced at Phil: 'Sorry. Excuse me.'

I must have appeared Kim's little man, at her beck and call – but it was the price I paid for being paid for: the raised eyebrows and barely hidden contempt from other guys. Though they wouldn't be thinking that if they knew what I was getting out of it.

I rose from the table and followed Kim to a quiet, barely lit corner where we could just about hear each other, even if I could hardly see her eyes or read her thoughts.

'What the fuck?' she seethed.

I was in for a right bollocking, then. I played dumb.

'What are you, stupid or something? I brought you here to make him envious. Not so you could suck up to him.'

I put up both palms. 'I know, I know. How did I know he'd come and sit by me and start up a conversation? What was I supposed to do? Pretend I didn't know you? How could I?'

Kim wasn't listening. In the half-darkness I could all but make out the smoke pouring out of her nostrils. I could certainly smell the fuel on her breath. 'Fuck,' she sneered, 'I'm not going to pay you.'

What the . . . ?

'I've come out all this way for you, Kim,' I spat in a heavy whisper.

'Yeah, but on the condition that you come here and stir up Phil. Why should I pay you anything? You haven't done what I asked you to do! I can't believe how unprofessional you are!'

Ouch. That stung me, the bitch. It certainly wasn't her place to tell me my job.

My face drew closer to hers. 'Fuck, Kim, but I did. I came here, I was all over you, as you wanted. He even started texting you because he was wondering who I was. I've done what you asked me to. You owe me,' I snarled.

And I'd had to watch her get more and more pissed the more the night went on. The whole setup was a mess from start to finish, and I'd been taken for a ride.

222

At that moment I saw things all too clearly. Kim was mad with me, and probably mad with herself to see Phil being so cool about things that he'd actually made a point of speaking to me. She had every right to feel short-changed with how things had gone tonight.

But I still needed to be paid, and I was damned if I was going all the way back to London without my money. Yet on the other hand I could see that if Kim chose not to pay up, there was nothing I could physically do to make her.

But I still held the trump card. I pointed to beyond the dancers to Phil, sitting at the table on the other side of the room and nursing his bottle of posh beer.

'I could tell him what I'm here for.'

'You wouldn't!' steamed Kim.

I looked directly at her and trusted that she could see the whites of my eyes. 'No, I wouldn't,' I stated, 'unless you don't pay me. And then I'd have no reason not to tell him, would I?'

She pursed her lips tight. I knew I'd got her over a barrel. 'I need a drink,' she snorted and stormed off to the Ladies; to euphemistically powder her nose, I assumed.

Phil was watching me as I approached the table. I rolled my eyes heavenwards as I picked up my drink and sat down. 'Pfff, she can be a real firecracker, can't she?'

'You bet!' he grinned, chinking his bottle against mine in brotherly support.

There was a few minutes of companionable silence between us as we drank our beers and observed Kim all but stumbling around the floor with her mates. When I thought about it, it was funny that she had two guys here tonight 'fighting' over her, as she was so off her tits that it was unlikely she'd be ready for any action tonight at all.

'So, Luke, how long have you been seeing Kim?' fished Phil.

'Oh, I dunno. A few weeks, I suppose,' I waffled.

He looked momentarily shocked, but rallied. 'How many weeks would that be, then?'

Phil was trying to speak in a nonchalant, calm manner but his words gave him away. No one would try and pin a relative stranger down about their dating history, surely. But I strung him along anyhow.

'Let me see, when did we hook up? It must have been two or three weeks ago, something like that. I'm sorry,' I smiled at him, 'I'm hopeless knowing what the date is.'

He peeled at the label on his beer bottle but said nothing.

'But who's counting, eh?' I shrugged. 'I'm not. I mean, she can be wild at times, but she's great fun.'

I'd lost Phil's attention. He was silently fuming at Kim who, completely oblivious to him, was gyrating in the middle of the crowd, her arms jerking wildly in the air and her head flung back.

Phil's head turned slowly in my direction. 'That's bullshit!' he sneered. 'Me and Kim only broke up a fort-night ago.'

It was my turn to look shocked. 'Fuck! That doesn't make sense,' I stuttered. 'I've been seeing her for . . . at least, at least that long.'

Phil shook his head a couple of times. 'Don't give me that crap, Luke . . .'

'I don't know what you're talking about!' I lied. Shit, I'd gone too far this time. He really was going to thump me. Surely.

He all but slammed his empty bottle down on the table. 'What are you saying, Luke? That you were seeing Kim behind my back?'

It was the bang on the table that brought me to my senses. What the fuck did I care? None of this was *my* problem.

'No, I'm not. I honestly don't know what you're talking about.' I lowered my voice for effect: 'But it's not me you need to be talking to, is it? This is between you and *Kim*.'

Phil's gaze was nonplussed. I lifted my bottle to my mouth and hoped that was the end of it. It wasn't. Phil was looking puzzled, as if he'd just realized something still didn't make sense.

'Why would you and Kim come to Sizzlers when she knows it'd be highly likely I'd be here too, eh? That'd be a real *bitch* of a thing to do, wouldn't it?'

I mentally took a sharp intake of breath. Phil had hit the nail squarely on the head but it was as if he hadn't realized what he'd just said. Or, more's the point, didn't want to.

If Kim was hurt enough to hire me to make Phil green with envy, not only was it well and truly working, but it revealed to me that Phil had strong enough feelings for her to be unable to imagine that she could be such a bitch. I wasn't sure if that was something to admire in him or pity him for.

He was looking at me now. 'So, tell me, Luke. What's

going on? Be a man and just be upfront about things,' he sighed, though it sounded to me like he was pleading.

God, am I earning my money tonight.

Which reminded me. I looked across the floor for Kim. Her dancing was more subdued and steady, like she'd worn out her furies. She gave me a lovely smile of recognition, and pushed through the crowd to greet me as I stood up to meet her. Her hands were on my arms.

'Look, I'm sorry about earlier. I was out of order,' she apologized.

'You were kinda,' I smirked. 'Yunno, I've given you what you wanted from him,' I whispered.

I gave a nod towards Phil who was sitting looking dejected alongside his empty bottle.

'Yeah, I know. Thanks,' she said, handing me my money in an envelope. I shoved it into my breast pocket. 'I'll order you a cab?'

'Yes, please, that'd be great, but I just need a few minutes if you don't mind.'

I went to buy Phil a pint.

I set it down in front of him. There was a look of surprise on his face. He hadn't expected that.

'I've got to go now. It's been nice meeting you.' I genuinely meant it. And it'd be one to tell the Girls back at the flat. I could just imagine their faces when I told them that, '*I bumped into that Phil Hyde off the box last night.*' It was just a shame it wasn't in better circumstances.

Phil nodded back with a muted smile, which made me realize I had to say what I was here to say.

226

'Look, I've got nothing against you. I'm just here to make you jealous.'

It wasn't as if Kim was likely to call me out again. I'd done the job required of me. But I'd also made sure that I'd tied up my own ends here. I liked Phil, and I wanted to do right by him and let him know his ex's little game.

Phil's whole body stiffened, but I didn't hang around to hear any reply.

I turned and went to look for Kim and my cab.

Shami

The following weekend

Revenge and jealousy had got me halfway round the world with a grand in my pocket and another £1,000 when I got back to London. That's what was blowing my mind as I stood on this doorstep in the middle of Texas State University campus and plucking up the courage to ring the bell. That and the fact that this was like a transatlantic version of my session with Kim only last week. It was funny how similar requests from clients sometimes followed close to each other. Mind you, none of them ever turned out exactly the same. That was what I liked about this job. No two clients were ever the same.

I pressed the button – it gave a metallic buzz that sounded like an electric shock – and waited. It sure was easy money, but it came with a certain level of confusion. Shami had sent me on this across-the-globe errand to get her own back on her ex, Jamie, who had left her in the shit. What she was asking me to do didn't make a whole lot of sense if I thought about it too deeply, but then again, that wasn't my job. As an escort I just did more or less what I was asked and got paid for it.

I heard someone's steps in the hallway and the twist of the handle, and a pretty student pulled open the door. She was in her early twenties and had long light brown hair tied loosely in a ponytail. She wore a university sweatshirt and jeans, her bare feet in grey felt slip-ons like she'd thrown the whole thing together. Presumably this was the 'Frances' whom Shami had wanted me to meet.

I started talking before I lost my nerve and before the girl even had a chance to say 'hello'.

'Is Jamie in? We've been seeing each other and he's been acting really suspiciously,' I garbled. 'Only seeing me at school and never any other time.'

She stood there watching me, but didn't reply. This wasn't what Shami was paying me for.

I tried again. 'I'm Jamie's boyfriend.'

I heard myself saying the words and cringed inside. I wondered again what I was really doing here, carrying out someone else's dirty work.

The gay identity had been Shami's idea. She had this suspicion, even while she was dating Jamie, that he wasn't altogether straight, so she wanted me to exploit her hunch. It wasn't as if I felt I had to put on an act or anything. I wasn't much into role play with sex or otherwise. I figured Jamie's 'boyfriend' could be straight acting. That was much easier.

The girl pursed her lips like she was repressing any shock she might have been feeling. 'Well, that's a co-incidence, because Jamie's my boyfriend as well.'

So, she *was* Frances. Her English accent sounded strange among the American voices I'd so far encountered. I'd arrived yesterday, had a night in a cheap motel, and then made my way to the campus.

I admired Frances's matter-of-factness. She seemed damned if she was going to get upset – or at least let me see her doing so. She was playing it cool, forcing me to explain what the hell I was doing standing on her front step. And I somehow had to play the part of Jamie's lover without letting slip that my presence had anything to do with an ex-girlfriend of Jamie's back in London.

Shami had ruined her own life when she'd fallen for Jamie and he had then eventually left her. So now she was seeking her revenge. Because, before her relationship with Jamie, Shami had been due to marry a fellow Indian whom her family all liked. She was in her late twenties and Krishnan had been her first proper boyfriend whom she'd loved dearly. She'd told me when we were arranging this trip that she knew she would have been completely happy with that.

That is, until Jamie – who had his own girlfriend – turned up, and the grass on the other side proved too green for the both of them. They had each left their partners and had had a passionate affair that lasted all of three months, until Jamie left Shami for the new girl here in front of me. To make matters worse, Jamie and Frances had then upped sticks for the USA to study there.

Which meant, as far as I could see, that Shami had

nothing to return to. She had thrown away her true love for a fling. No wonder she felt mad.

'Sorry, your name is?'

'Mark,' I lied.

Frances frowned. 'Jamie's never mentioned a "Mark". And certainly nothing about any Aussie friends. You sure it's *my* Jamie?'

I noticed the 'my', but then again she had a right to be territorial and wary in the midst of all this warped shit.

'It's Jamie I'm looking for,' I stressed. 'I got his room number from a college friend, because Jamie was being so arsey about seeing me outside school. Do you know where he is?'

I could see in Frances's eyes that she wasn't convinced by my words. I wasn't either, to be honest. I couldn't deny that the money was good, but on the other hand I was fast wishing I could be somewhere else ASAP.

The trouble was, Shami wanted evidence that I'd hammered a wedge between Jamie and Frances, so I had to keep the girl talking until I got it all down the wire hidden under my jacket lapel. God, sometimes this job really played to a guy's latent Bond fantasy.

I tried a different tack. I stood there in silence for a couple of seconds and bit my lip to indicate that I might be upset, and looked left and right, my hands in my pockets. 'You mean Jamie's cheating on me and he's cheating on you too,' I said in as troubled voice as I could muster. 'You know anything about this, about me?'

Frances seemed determined not to get involved, whatever she might have been privately thinking.

She showed little emotion on her face – certainly nothing that might mean anything to Shami when she listened to it back in London.

She shrugged her shoulders: 'Sorry, I'm not really sure what I can say. Your beef seems to be with Jamie, not me.'

Frances pursed her lips, showing impressive restraint. I also couldn't help being impressed by *her*. She wasn't bad looking, and in a parallel universe I would be here to service her. But in the here and now I couldn't help wondering if maybe she was planning on giving her partner a battering over this when he got back later on. Just wait until he got home!

'Look,' she continued, 'Jamie's away at the moment. He's out of the state; he's attending some conference? He's not going to be back until next week, I'm afraid.'

I knew that. Shami had deliberately sent me to America within this narrow time frame because she wanted to ensure he wouldn't be around.

Frankly, when Shami told me of her plan, I was tempted to call Jamie and warn him – whether or not I even made it over to Texas – about what Shami, his rather bitter ex, was intent on doing to him. But that thought quickly passed. It was simpler for me to stay out of things – or at least out of anything beyond crossing the planet to stand outside his house and talk to his girlfriend like I was doing right now.

The girlfriend was half smiling in satisfaction. 'You've picked the wrong time to come round here searching for your lover,' she sneered. 'Hanging around here won't help.'

Frances seemed remarkably casual about Jamie's absence. Maybe she just wasn't bothered, or had so much faith in him that she wasn't about to get hot under the collar about where he was – or who he might be with. I couldn't help wondering too whether they had some kind of open relationship that meant she was fine with him having stuff on the side. Or she knew he swung both ways and was OK with that too. It meant he wasn't cheating with a woman, for one thing.

But this was all guesswork on my part. The two of us had reached stalemate. There wasn't much else I could say, and it was clear by the expression on Frances's face that she regarded me as an irritation to be got rid of, with as little hassle as possible. I wasn't worth the time of day.

I walked backwards down off the step. 'Well, if you can tell him that Mark called,' I said, shrugging as I turned and headed off down the gravel path.

I realized as I crossed the grass verge that took me off campus and on to the main road towards my digs that Shami was the weirdest one of the lot of us, even as I was feeling damn uncomfortable about what I'd got myself into.

I might have tried to justify it by telling myself that I was only doing my job, but I knew that I was kidding myself. Because this was one of the worst ways in the world to be spending a couple of days. I'd come here with the sole purpose of playing with somebody's life and ruining a relationship. And that made me feel thoroughly dirty. It was one thing to sell sex for cash, but breaking up a couple was not something I did.

I was frightened at how easy it had been to travel halfway across the world to do the wicked deed. I cringed too at my sneaking suspicion that Frances must have regarded my efforts as some feeble student prank. That, or mistaken identity. Whatever she'd been doing before I rang the doorbell, I bet she went back to without a thought about mentioning anything of me to Jamie, except maybe to roll her eyes at it. I suppose that was some consolation, that I surely wasn't a good enough actor to have made a really harsh impact. I hoped so.

The money Shami was paying me cushioned the flat feel of the trip. I'd make a healthy £2,000 simply by going there and coming back. But since Shami was paying my expenses – the door-to-door transport, my night in a hotel, everything – she would be forking out closer to £3,000 just to *try* to bring down a guy who'd done her wrong a while back because life hadn't turned out the way she'd hoped for herself.

On the flight home, I listened to what I'd actually managed to record. It turned out that what I'd got down on the tape didn't make a hell of a lot of sense. An Aussie guy and an English girl having a standoff in North America. I was even more convinced that I'd caused little harm.

I turned off the tape recorder, pulled the earplugs from my ears and leaned back in my chair. I looked out at the field of clouds below and thought about what I'd just left. And the thing I was especially aware of was that for all the money, effort and mental energy Shami had spent in trying to rock her ex's world, I was pretty sure that she had had zero effect on Jamie and Frances's relationship.

Apart from the money, Shami's little plan hadn't been much good for me either. It had been an in-and-out whistle-stop tour, so I hadn't had the chance even to do any sightseeing. And it wasn't as if I got to sleep with Jamie's girlfriend, which would at least have added a bit of colour to the trip. To be blunt, this endeavour amounted to a complete mess from start to finish. Thousands of pounds going into my account, international travel thrown in which, admittedly shouldn't be taken lightly, but for all that I didn't get to have any fun. Not quite the escort high life.

I thought of the treat that Shami could have bought herself with that sort of money! Little did she realize that I could have remained in London and given her such a good time that the thought of Jamie and her relationship troubles would have been blown clean out of her mind. It could have been great for both of us.

Not thinking clearly, Shami, were you?

I shook my head, and nestled further back into my seat, stretched my legs out as far as the limited space would allow and hunkered down in an attempt to get some sleep. This trip had been a waste of time all round as far as I could see.

'It's a shame we couldn't have seen each other over the weekend,' moaned Nina.

It was Wednesday evening, and we were drinking in Nina's local pub. It was clearly an old boozer tarted up to appeal to a younger crowd. Which seemed to amount to a few fairy lights entwined around the old brass fittings and loud chart hits on the jukebox.

I was still getting back into gear after my trip to the US. I'd been out on another session since, so this was the first time I'd been able to see Nina for a week. The fact that the music was on the cusp of being too loud for us to have a proper conversation wasn't the worst thing. It put off having to make up a detailed story to explain myself.

'Yeah, I know. But I had work to do that I couldn't turn down, y'know.'

She nodded, taking it in, and picked up her glass of wine and sipped from it.

Once more, I was telling Nina the truth. It was just that I wasn't telling her the *whole* truth. I was well aware that this was becoming a habit – and not just with Nina – but I wasn't sure what else I could do. For one thing, I didn't want to hurt Nina's feelings. For another, I just couldn't see how revealing I was an escort would help anyone. Least of all me.

Nina frowned. 'What work were you doing that stopped us meeting up for such a long while?'

She was angling too deep for my liking. 'Oh, you know . . .' I played for time.

I took a gulp of beer. 'Y'know,' I repeated myself, 'the sort of stuff Aussies do to keep the wolf from the door.'

I'd told Nina that I did a range of jobs to pay my bills while I looked for something more substantial. Bar work, shift work, that sort of thing. That explained my strange hours, and the difficulty I had in arranging any dates, even at short notice.

'Look, I really did hope we'd have a free weekend. It bugs me as much as you, but I got a call from a mate asking me to help him out. It was about doing him a favour, y'know,' I shrugged.

Nina didn't look totally convinced. 'I thought all your mates had returned to Australia.'

I smiled at her in an effort to lighten our talk. 'Ah, but Steve's not an *Aussie* mate. He's a friend of Mark's. They worked on a stall at Camden together when he first got here.'

That seemed to appease her. It was all so fucking easy, it almost frightened me. I could come up with practically *anything* to cover the trail of my hookering. And what perhaps scared me the most was that Nina seemed to be accepting of anything I threw her way.

She was *so* trusting. And it touched me especially that she assumed I was worthy of such trust. I felt as much of a shit as I'd done out in Texas pretending I was Jamie's lover.

That gave me no choice. I was going to have to fence off this coming Saturday whether I liked it or not, even if it meant losing out on a wad of cash, and take Nina out.

'This weekend, eh, girl?' I said. 'You're out with me, OK?'

Nina visibly brightened. If she trusted me *that* much, among all my escort work, I owed Nina at least one of my nights off. And, let's face it, it wasn't as if I *didn't* want to spend more time with her. *That* was the problem. I really liked Nina. I wanted to see her, for God's sake. It was just that the job got in the way.

In more ways than one, if I thought about it. If it came to the crunch – the choice between being a boyfriend or a hooker, I wasn't sure which way I'd jump. Ready cash and sex without commitment versus Nina by my side. I hated to admit it to myself, but it'd be a tough call.

Haley

One day in September

I was giving Haley the works. And she was returning the favour with interest. But as much as we'd got deep into our stride, it was difficult for me to forget that there was Dale homing in on us with his video camera as we fucked. That, as much as I was enjoying myself, the bottom line was that this was going to be up on the Net for anyone who wanted to watch Haley in her element.

'Cut!' shouted Dale, and Haley and I collapsed against each other.

I'd been surprised to hear from Haley. When she'd called, I'd presumed she was just inviting me round for some easy, no-strings sex plus a little bit of friendship from a fellow escort, as had happened occasionally with girls I met on the job. I'd have been fine with that.

But Haley was introducing me to a different league altogether, one that I hadn't bargained for. She wanted to add to her website and saw porn videos as the obvious next stage to entice subscribers and their money.

239

And when she was thinking about guys to help her out, I was top of her list.

On the one hand I was flattered that she thought I'd make the grade. But moving into porn wasn't something that had crossed my mind. Certainly not back when I'd decided to advertise my sexual services. Yet now I'd been invited to join in, I couldn't help but be intrigued.

I was open to new experiences, and certainly more relaxed about things than I'd been back at the start. It would be something to brag about to my mates too – that I'd done porn with hot Poms. What guy wouldn't be impressed?

What's more, I wasn't about to turn down the opportunity for a sex session with Haley if I could help it. The point about escort-to-escort shagging was that it could be as no-holds-barred as we wanted to make it.

'You're doing great, Luke,' encouraged Haley.

I hoped so.

'You think so? I'd never saw myself as being caught at it on film,' I replied. I'd heard about those celebs whose private sex videos ended up on the worldwide web. *Anyone* being filmed like that was surely leaving themselves wide open to an ex-lover showing everyone. And what's more, I couldn't see how knowing a camera was catching your every move wouldn't put you off your stride.

Haley took my hand and directed me to the corner of the set. 'Oh, I wouldn't worry about *that*. You're a natural. Isn't he, Dale?'

Dale set down his camera and looked me up and

down approvingly before fixing his gaze on my dick. Haley looked from him to me with a knowing smirk.

'Oh *that*,' I laughed. '*That* goes without saying!'

Haley giggled. 'Well, yes,' she said. 'Why do you think I chose you?'

'Because I'm the only escort worth calling,' I strutted, grinning.

The truth was that escorts and porn stars weren't supposed to mix. It was too risky a business. There was a definite line that divided the two groups, involving protection. Escorts made sure to use condoms. That was the bottom line as far as any but the dodgiest escorts were concerned. Whereas the point of porn *was* the money shot. Seeing the guy come. Condoms would literally just get in the way.

Haley was asking me not to cross the line but to *straddle* it, like she was. Both of us were playing a dangerous game, even though we got ourselves regularly tested for STDs. We'd just upped the ante.

Dale showed us the shots he'd already got.

'Oh, God, I don't know if I can look!' I shivered, transfixed by the rushes.

'You can give it but you can't take it, eh?' ribbed Haley.

It was sure weird seeing yourself shagging someone. What I *looked* like when I was giving a girl one had never crossed my mind before. And then I remembered that this was going out on the Net.

What have I got myself into?

Dale picked up his camera again. 'Right, you two. Time for your close-ups.'

I looked over at Haley: 'You ready, gorgeous?'

'Course I am. If you're still up for it,' she teased.

What did I have to worry about working with Haley? We enjoyed each other's company. Doing this shoot was not much different to what each of us was more or less happy to do when the cameras weren't rolling.

We got back on the bed together. Haley stretched out and spread her legs ready for me. This time, I didn't have to rely on my imagination to get myself fired up. She was a beaut. I ran a hand from the round of her shoulders and down over the welcoming curve of her tits, just to hot her up, though she didn't need much help there. And then I shafted her again.

Dale had his camera pointed at Haley's rising and falling breasts as I rode her. He'd have got a better look from where I was sitting. A guy's-eye view.

Haley had known *exactly* what she was doing calling me. We were made for each other – both trained athletes in our element. And we were bringing the wealth of our joint experience to the show. That was a recipe for sexual fireworks if ever there was one.

I kept an eye on Dale. I was happy to show off my skills to him and any of Haley's subscribers. But while that would give some protection from anyone I knew stumbling across my latest work on the web, it could never be a total guarantee that I wouldn't be found out. Certainly friends would have to make a point of tracking me down. Which would incriminate them as much as me. But at the end of the day, that would still mean my cover being blown. And given the speed that news spread across the Net, I would only be a couple of mouse clicks away from *everyone* in Aus finding out. And whatever the extra money I'd be earning wouldn't pay for the cost of *that*.

Haley and I were sitting in our bathrobes side by side on the bed, one of my legs crossing hers. Dale's assistant was running around altering lights as he directed. Haley stroked my arm.

'You've done excellently today. I'll know who to suggest when my mates ever want to organize a shoot.'

I wasn't so sure. 'You think so?'

'Oh, God, yeah!' she stressed, as if she couldn't understand how I'd think otherwise.

The trouble was, I was very much aware that I'd taken like a duck to water to doing porn. Even in spite of the real fear of being found out, there was still a small voice in my head wondering if I should take it any further than I'd already allowed myself to do. But if I listened too much to *that*, I might end up questioning why I'd even said 'Yes' to Haley in the first place.

'Suppose I did do some work for other girls' websites. Wouldn't there be a problem with me appearing in too many?' I wondered aloud.

In my mind's eye, I could see my own sex fantasy come to life. A whole load of different porn films and little old me getting the benefit of each girl! That would make the subscribers green with envy at my luck.

Haley looked over at Dale and they grinned at each

other like they had some shared conspiracy. 'But that's the point. Guys will relate to you. Put themselves in your shoes,' laughed Haley.

Dale picked up his camera again. 'Anyhow, that's the British porn industry all over. It's so small it's practically incestuous,' he explained. 'Which means if you're any good, you'll soon make a name for yourself. And *plenty* of money.'

I wasn't sure I wanted to be known for pornography. It certainly flattered a guy's ego, but in the cold light of day it wouldn't be the wisest move. I still had to think of my folks back home somehow finding out. And, like escort work, it wasn't something to put on your CV either.

'The thing is, Luke, you're just the sort of guy that the porn world is crying out for. You're fit and good looking and straight, and from what Haley tells me the girls enjoy working with you . . . And, what's more,' he added, practically licking his lips, 'you can keep it up! That's a *real* asset.'

When he said that, I got the distinct impression that there were other things he'd like to do with his long camera lens than shoot me.

'I'm not sure,' I said, flustered, trying to avoid the lustful look on Dale's face. Though it was swiftly followed by a flashback to early summer when keeping it up had been one of my biggest worries. I shuddered. Thank God *that* was in the past – and I hadn't had to resort to Viagra after that one disastrous experience.

Porn work was so very tempting, I had to admit. The hot sex. The girls on tap. The potential money to be made. But the trouble was, I knew that it wasn't just about those things, it was where it might take me that bothered me. Even getting involved in *this* shoot was further than I'd ever imagined going. I could see myself being sucked so deep into this business that I'd end up too addicted to the easy sex and the money to ever find my way out again.

Dale could sense my hesitation. 'Think it over, Luke. There's no pressure.'

And then he flicked on a wolfish grin: 'But you're here making Haley's vid. It's time for you to get back to shagging each other stupid.'

Put like that, how could I refuse?

The bitch's here again, for God's sake!

I felt sick at the thought. And the sight. The silhouette of Karen was caught in the headlight of my scooter as I turned into the side street just in front of my block of flats. I steeled myself, my hands gripping tighter round the handlebars, and parked my bike. I hotfooted it up to the flat and let myself in.

'Hi, Luke,' chirruped Carrie from the lounge.

I didn't answer, but kicked off my boots and tiptoed to my bedroom door. I eased it open very gently but, as I did, Carrie burst into the hall.

'Luke? That was you, wasn't it?' she repeated, but stopped in her tracks. 'What the *devil* are you up to?' she mock-challenged me in that faux-posh way she had.

I turned to Carrie and put my finger to my lips. She closed her mouth, but one eyebrow rose in curiosity.

I entered the room. My hand automatically reached

for the switch but I held back from turning it on just in time. *That* was the point. Not to be noticed.

I crept to the edge of the window but held back from directly facing the glass. The curtains hadn't yet been drawn. Carrie had joined me in the room and was now at my elbow.

'What are we looking at?' she whispered, and then frowned: 'And why am *I* whispering?'

We both giggled, though the fact was that Karen out there, *waiting,* was no laughing matter.

'Don't let yourself be seen, but if you stand here' – we changed places – 'can you see the corner of the main road?'

'Just,' she strained, standing on tiptoes for a better view. 'There's nothing, nobody there.'

I closed my eyes for a couple of seconds. *Oh God.* I felt nauseous at the thought of having caught Karen in my bike light's beams.

When I opened them again, Carrie was looking at me, clearly concerned. She reached out her hand to touch my arm.

'Are you OK? You look as if you've seen a ghost. What is it?'

I took a step to the window and looked out across the estate, as far and wide as I could see, but there was no sign of Karen. I was in full view of anyone looking in, though I hoped I'd be sheltered by the dark of the room. Karen might have gone, but on the other hand she might still be waiting for me somewhere down below.

I was going to have to tell Carrie *something*, though

246

I wasn't yet sure what. But that could wait. Because what demand my attention at this very moment was *Karen* – and her tendency to hang around my flat. She hadn't seen me, but that wasn't the point. Karen was here, wasn't she? And this was the third time in a couple of weeks. It hadn't been my imagination. Karen *had* been lying when she told me she was waiting for her friend, Caroline. Which could mean only one thing.

I had my very own stalker.

Christine

Mid-September

It was a chilly autumnal afternoon and the sky was heavy and grey, but I hadn't seen a storm like this in all my time in the UK. My scooter was buffeted by winds all the way over to Ealing. Branches had been torn down, and rubbish – and even the bins it'd been in – were strewn across pavements. Christine was waiting for me.

Christine and I had met once before, on a hot sunny afternoon over coffee on the South Bank, so she 'could check me out', she said. She was a petite, busty brunette in a summer dress and sunglasses.

We'd clicked from the moment we'd started talking. I'd known we'd get on – I prided myself on how friendly I could be with clients. But with Christine, it had been like we were old friends, we felt so comfortable with each other.

Which is funny if you think about it.

Because Christine was a church girl. Which was why she'd called me in the first place. She'd now reached

248

an age where she'd 'waited until marriage' too long, so had tracked me down to help her fill that hole in her experience.

Literally.

It was weird that we were on opposite ends of the sex game, and by rights were supposed to have nothing to do with each other. Yet somehow we had hit it off.

I'd been nervous myself getting ready to leave home to meet her today.

She's waited so long. I'd hate to ruin it for her!

I buzzed Christine when I reached the front door of her block. She let me in, and I ran up the stairs to her private door, and there were smiles and hugs when she opened it.

'You had no trouble getting here?' she asked as we stood in the hallway. 'Isn't it a horrible day?'

'You bet. But it was OK. Thankfully the roads were pretty clear.'

'You'd like a drink?' she asked as we went into the living room.

'Whatever you've got,' I replied.

She fixed us both a vodka and tonic and we sat down on the sofa in the living room, knee to knee, and sipped from our glasses. I looked around the room. It wasn't giving a great deal away. There was the sofa, the small light wood dining table, and a crammed bookcase, all Ikea by the look of things. And there was a framed film poster on the opposite wall. A film starring Kate Winslet called *Hideous Kinky*, which I hadn't seen.

'So how are things going?' I piled in as if we were old mates.

'I'm fine, Luke,' she smiled. 'But you know the wind getting up? And the banging of garden gates?' There was a sinister edge to her words. 'Like something's going to blow?'

What's she getting at?

'It's all my doing, you know,' she said with a twinkle in her eye, and gave me a playful nudge in the ribs with her elbow. 'I'm about to cause a rift in the space/time continuum!'

I laughed with her.

'*And* I'm taking you down with me!'

She said it like she was a Bond villain. But I couldn't believe how she was making light of things.

So she's hired an escort, but the 'losing it' is still a big deal, right?

I turned to face Christine. Her eyes were as dark brown as her hair and she had small features that kept her youthful, making it difficult to guess her age, but I presumed she was around her mid-thirties.

'Is there anything you're worried about, Christine?'

She looked at me for a second. 'Not really,' and then she paused. 'Except that I'm five foot two and a half. And you're six foot.'

Size. This was her way of saying it.

And this is her first time – meaning she fears it's going to hurt.

Christine's legs were crossed, revealing pale skin above a black stocking where the silk of her wrap dress slipped away from her leg. I reached out and ran my hand along a thigh.

'I'll be careful,' I reassured her in a quiet tone.

She didn't flinch at all but just let me do it, and carried on talking like it was the most natural thing in the world.

She's so relaxed. When are the nerves going to kick in?

'It's difficult meeting a guy,' she admitted. 'At what point am I supposed to let him know I haven't done it? I'm embarrassed by it, to be honest. It was bad enough when I hit the Big Four O, but it just feels worse the older I get.'

Hang on.

She went on talking, not seeming to realize the personal detail she had just let slip.

Her age. She was physically small, but it wasn't just that that made me think she was almost a decade younger than she actually was. Sure, she looked well below forty, but there was a youthfulness in her manner too. While I, on the other hand, had seen a hell of a lot more than most guys my age.

Maybe that's why we get on. We meet in the middle.

I picked up my glass and pointed with it towards the bedroom door. 'Shall we?' I suggested.

She nodded, and led the way across the flat.

'You undress, and I'll get myself ready in the bathroom,' I instructed.

When I got back, Christine had just removed her bra and was hovering by her wardrobe with her back to me, still in her French knickers, obviously bashful and unsure of what to do. She didn't seem to realize that from where I was standing in the bedroom doorway, I could see a whole lot more of her reflected in the full-length wardrobe mirror. But her very nervousness stirred something in me.

Has she ever been naked with a guy?

Christine had requested a massage and for me to 'go from there'.

No problem.

'If you could lie on your front on the bed for me.'

It was more or less what I had planned for her anyhow. From my experience with other virgins, I'd learnt that it was a good way of easing them towards the sex. In truth, it was the quickest way to relax *most* women. Christine didn't raise an eye to me the entire time she was undressing. Eventually she lay flat out in front of me.

I began at Christine's feet and eased me and her into it. I climbed on to the bed between her legs and my naked leg touched hers.

'You'll let me know if you're uncomfortable with anything, won't you?' I asked as my hands pummelled further up her thigh.

'Sure,' she said in a clear voice, as if she was going to go with the flow of whatever came her way. But I couldn't help wondering at what point she was going to go tense on me.

It's going to happen, right?

'Can you turn over, please, Christine?'

She was on her back, ready for me to take things in hand. Which I did. Christine was slim with big tits. She had a waist for me to hold in my hands and tits made to be suckled by a guy. I reached out and took her right breast in my hand, brought my mouth up to Christine's nipple and traced my tongue over it. 'You've got a great body,' I told her seconds later.

'Thanks,' she replied, but said nothing else.

What is she thinking? What's going on in her head?

Christine gave little away, although I didn't get any hint that she *wasn't* enjoying herself. It was as if she was content to *sense* things rather than give any running commentary. Which was fair enough. This was presumably new to her. Maybe she was shy or maybe she simply didn't feel the need to speak. I however got into my stride. I explored her body, and her fingers rifled through my hair as I did. Our lips met and her petite mouth opened for me. There was more than enough room for our tongues to make their acquaintance.

'A good kisser,' I told her as I paused for breath.

There was a warmth in her eyes but she still didn't say anything, though she gave me a satisfied smile.

Face it, you've left her absolutely speechless with your overwhelming sexiness!

I parted from her. She lay there patiently, watching me step off the bed and rifle through my jacket pocket for the protection. I sat beside her and prepared myself, then lay down beside her, reached out and took her in my arms. She followed my lead and her own arms wrapped round my back, stroking and feeling their way. I slipped my fingers between her legs, then gently inside. She shifted. I removed my fingers to guide my dick to her, and kept my eyes on her all the while. I sensed her wanting to make this easy and comfortable for the both of us. She gripped me tighter in expectation, and she raised her hips to meet mine. I was inside her.

One giant leap for mankind.

She winced between gritted teeth.

There's the tension.

'You all right?' I wanted to make sure. For her first time.

'It's sore.' She said it like she wasn't expecting it to be anything else.

There was no clap of thunder. The sky didn't fall on our heads. We simply lay there entwined in the muted darkness of the room, its cream curtains closed against the late afternoon's fading light.

Locked in my arms, Christine nuzzled my shoulder with a line of kisses, and I further explored her body, my hands cradling her breasts and pouring over her belly. Christine's hands spread over my back and round to my chest. As I had fondled her tits, her own fingers sought out my right nipple. Her hands swept down to my navel but moved no further.

Some other time.

I slipped away from her in order to gear myself up for re-entry. Christine lay on her back, relaxed, and looking across at me seated by her legs, watched as I pulled the condom out of its packet.

'Your family, was it quite strict when you were growing up?' I gabbled.

I wasn't even sure why I asked. It was like I felt I had to fill some space. As I rolled on the condom, she told me a whole lot about her family tree, but she laughed as she spoke.

'I'm telling you about how my dad came here, and you're about to give me one!'

I noted I'd got her talking again.

Christine sat up on her elbows and gripped my wrists that were pushing into the duvet each side of her. She held them down further and her whole body tautened as my dick slid into her. She rolled on her hips, pushing into me like she didn't want to just lie there, but I could feel her discomfort. It spilled out from between her clenched teeth.

I'd done my job. I pulled away. 'Well,' I said, 'you're not a virgin any more.'

We hugged each other again and I told her I had to go. As I clambered off the bed on to my feet, she remained relaxed on the bed.

'Thanks, Luke,' she said, smiling up at me.

I shook my head. 'Don't say thanks, Christine. Because that sounds like I only did it for the money. And I didn't.'

She lay loose limbed and naked before me, like she didn't want to move a muscle, didn't want our time together to end.

'How do you feel?' I asked, looking down at her as I pulled my jeans back on.

'Comfortable,' she purred back.

Comfortable?

It wasn't a word *I'd* have used to describe *my* first time. But I stood at the end of the bed and observed her lounging in pleasure across it. She might have called it 'comfortable', but she looked like the cat that had got the cream.

Christine was hugging me goodbye. She gave me a bashful smile: 'A good job done.'

'My pleasure,' I smiled. 'Trust I didn't put you off.'

She shook her head strongly. 'Uh uh.'

She bit her bottom lip as if she wanted to say something but was still plucking up the courage. I decided to help her along.

'What is it, Christine?'

She looked down at her stilettos for a split second, and then she looked me straight in the face with a renewed confidence.

'Now I've got over that *hurdle*' – she let the word settle in the air for a couple of seconds – 'I don't want things to end there,' she confessed.

That suited me fine. 'You'd like me to visit again, Christine?' I fished.

She nodded. 'Um, I was wondering, um,' she stuttered, then composed herself.

'What I'd like is if you could also bring a female escort.' Her voice grew quieter with every word. 'And another man.'

By the time she'd got the words out she was all but whispering, and I'd bent my head so my ear was millimetres from her mouth. It was like we were sharing a secret. But, fuck me! That was a hell of a request!

'Another guy and another girl,' I repeated, just to make sure I'd got the right end of the stick. 'You'd like me to organize that for you?'

'Yes, please,' she answered. 'I would like that, Luke.'

Fuck me, she meant it!

On the threshold of her front door, I turned and overacted a bow: 'Then consider it done. I'll be in

touch so we can arrange our next meeting, all right?'
I winked.

'Thank you for everything, Luke. I really mean it,'
she said.

My head was spinning as I walked down the path
towards my scooter. I certainly wasn't expecting
anything like *that* from Christine. One bite of her
cherry and I'd unleashed a sex fiend!

Bloody hell!

Still, who was I to complain? I'd enjoyed tonight. I'd
been happy to introduce her to sex and help her get
over that barrier and she clearly trusted me enough to
go to the next stage.

Some next stage!

Yeah, I was happy to oblige. And, regardless of what
she'd asked of me, she'd requested another session. I
hadn't put her off. On the contrary, I'd introduced her
to a whole new world of experiences. As I stepped on
to the footplate of my scoot, I drew out my BlackBerry
from my jacket pocket. Who needed Karen on my files
when I had really appreciative, sexy, uncomplicated
clients like Christine? I blocked Karen's calls. I didn't
need her in my life *at all*.

Jill again

Jill's arm lay across me. She was fast asleep. It was time for me to leave, but I'd have to somehow slip away from her without waking her if I could. I much preferred leaving my overnights still in bed, half asleep, and dreaming of the night before with me. Rather than out of bed and observing me in the cold light of day and thinking of what we'd got up to.

I tried to shift but the dead weight of Jill's limb held me fast. There was nothing for it but for me to shove it away.

'Jill, honey,' I cooed as I pushed her arm, if only to soften the physical jerks I was forcing on her. 'I'm leaving soon.'

She snapped awake. I couldn't help wondering if she'd sensed my awkwardness beside her before I'd even budged.

'Luke,' she pleaded, 'you're not going just yet?'

We were both sitting up in bed.

I shook my head in reply. 'I can't stay. I've got to go.'

258

I wasn't about to explain myself so I let one foot slip from beneath the duvet and search out the floor. As I leant to climb further out of bed, Jill snatched my arm and held on tight.

'But you'll come on Saturday, won't you? We've been invited round to Ralph and Siri's.'

Oh, come on.

I turned my head sharply to fix my fuming eyes on her. 'You know I can't do that, Jill. I've got other clients, remember.'

I pulled my arm out of her grip. Her hands flopped on to the bedclothes in defeat. She dipped her head but raised her eyes at me like Princess Diana.

'But they've asked us,' she whined in a little-girl voice that made my flesh creep.

'You'll just have to tell them I can't come then, won't you?' I sneered. What the fuck did she think I was going to say?

'But it'll seem strange if you're not there. We've been invited as a *couple*.'

That fucking well stuck in my craw. I turned away from her, and placed my other foot decisively down on the carpet.

'But we're not a *couple*, are we, Jill?' I spoke the words in as clear and straight a manner as possible, keeping my cool. The steam was pouring out of my nostrils, though as my back was to her she hadn't realized it from my face. I couldn't help thinking of Nina, and how my escort work was interrupting our chance to develop our relationship. It was ironic that Jill had decided that she and I were a couple when, although both Nina and myself regarded ourselves as an item, it seemed far more difficult for us to arrange to see each other. I hated to admit it – and I was pretty sure I didn't want it to be so, but it seemed that arranging time with me was easier if you were a client who was paying than if your name was Nina and you were my girlfriend. Though Nina didn't know that.

Jill tried her luck again. 'But if I turn up alone, they're sure to ask where you are and I can't tell them the truth, can I?' she mewled.

She had a point. She'd got herself trapped in a web of her own making. The more she'd tried to convince herself and everyone she knew that we were a bona fide couple, the deeper the hole she was digging. God, she was practically shovelling the mud down on top of herself *and* trampling it down too.

But I couldn't see what I was supposed to do about it. Jill had already made up her mind about *that*.

'How much is your client paying you for Saturday night?'

She didn't even wait for me to reply, even if I had thought about doing so. Which I hadn't, since what I did with any of my other clients – and what they happened to be charged – was none of her damn business. And that was without considering Nina. Since we'd been dating, I'd become all too aware of how much I'd have to juggle escort work and seeing her if I wanted our relationship to go any distance. That was easier said than done.

'I tell you what,' Jill gabbled in all but the same breath, 'whatever she's forking out, I'll *double* it!' It was said almost as a cry of triumph, that she'd trumped whatever I could throw at her. That I was prey to her demands.

Not if I can help it.

I was standing and looking straight at her. She remained sitting up in bed.

'Don't do this to me, Jill. Don't do this to *yourself.* You don't know what you're asking.'

'I can pay over what you're charging *any* other girl.'

Not quite. That's where Nina would win hands down *every* time.

Jill was clean out of order, though she hadn't even realized. It was tragic really. As far as her experience with men had shown her, this was the only way she could compete with other women. If they weren't biting any other way, then it wasn't enough for her to occasionally hire an escort to play her boyfriend. She'd have him literally at any cost. And damn any other girl who chose to call me out.

'I don't work that way, Jill.' I turned to leave the room and get out of her house.

'Don't you get it?' she squealed, as if she was bringing out her last weapon. 'They're already having suspicions. The questions they ask about you. I can tell they don't believe me. And if they don't believe me, they don't believe you either, Luke,' she spat.

That halted me in my tracks. I enjoyed seeing her friends. I got on well with the guys. Which was quite a relief and a means of avoiding any romantic stuff Jill wanted to dump on me. We'd hit it off, which didn't mean I wanted to be their bosom buddy, but

I valued their company while I was with them. It made a nice change from all the girl talk I was surrounded by, especially since my mates had returned to Aus.

However, I'd had my own suspicions about them myself. That they might be wondering what the hell I was doing with Jill when I was clearly an athletic type – and she so obviously wasn't.

But even if they couldn't quite understand me and Jill being an item, there was a huge step between that realization and knowing what our 'relationship' was really about. Escort work was one of those jobs that people never assumed others were involved in until they knew someone who admitted they were.

Unfortunately Jill hadn't come to the same conclusion. 'Suppose they find out,' she hissed.

The real terror I saw in her eyes shocked me. I tried to calm her down. 'How on earth would they, for goodness' sake? Why would they even jump to that conclusion?' I turned the tables on her: 'You haven't told them, have you?'

Jill gave me a deep frown, clearly affronted by such a suggestion. 'Of course not. But you know what the Internet's like. Suppose they came across your website by accident?'

That shook me, but only because I couldn't work out any logic in what she was saying. 'Pass that by me again,' I frowned.

'The Internet. Your website. "Satisfaction",' she paraphrased. 'They could find out your job.'

I put my position straight to her. 'I have to admit,

Jill, that I can't see any reason why that might happen. The Internet's a big place, y'know. Unless they're searching for "London Male Escort", there's no reason why my name would ever come up.'

Was she threatening me? That if I didn't see her more frequently, she'd direct her friends to my website?

So I covered myself too, and offered consideration of her position: 'But I understand that it's a real concern and worry of yours. And that is important to me, y'know.'

She slipped out of her bed so she was now standing and looking right at me from across the room. There was a softness in her eyes, as if she was glad that I was at least attempting to listen to her concerns.

And then she went very quiet. Her voice became almost a whisper, though I could hear every word. But what she was telling me chilled me to the bone.

'If they found out about you and me . . . How we met, I don't know if I could bear it,' she murmured.

Jill's words hung in the air. I wasn't sure what I was supposed to say. It turned out that I didn't need to speak. She filled the gap.

'I'd have to stop seeing you, wouldn't I, Luke? And that would tear me apart.'

Jill wasn't looking at me any more, but she'd said enough anyhow. Her words were like nails down a blackboard. She'd been so busy putting on an act of a relationship that she'd fucking well grown to believe it. She actually *thought* that I was her boyfriend – and was giving me the emotional blackmail, to boot.

In your dreams, girl.

Trouble was, it was her dreams that had got the both of us in this position in the first place.

I just wanted out of that room. 'I'm afraid I've got to go, Jill.'

I wasn't about to get into any discussion or argument about what the hell she was thinking. Hadn't Karen been one stalker enough? I only hoped I hadn't laid myself open to collecting another with Jill. I dressed and was out of there.

It had got to the point that my hackles rose whenever Jill's name flashed up on my BlackBerry. She'd call between our weekly sessions, sometimes in tears, trying to get me to see her more often. Yet I couldn't simply ignore her since she was one of my regulars and I hugely appreciated the money she brought in.

Jill was calling now. I rolled my eyes before I replied but I put on my most charming voice by smiling as I spoke, even though she couldn't see me. It was a trick that gave a lift of welcome to my voice.

'Hello, Jill! How are you doing?'

I'd barely got the words out before she cut me off with her own: 'I've told Miriam,' she blurted out.

I pulled the phone away from my ear. Was Jill saying what I thought she was saying? I took a deep breath and placed it back at my ear. 'What are you telling me, Jill? You told Miriam what?'

'You don't need to worry, Luke,' she replied.

Which sure started the alarm bells ringing through my head. Jill was telling me that she'd told her mates something about me, but that I wasn't to *worry*.

Fuck off!

'I told Miriam that you'd told me you *used* to be an escort.'

You fucking WHAT?

I was fuming. 'And why the *hell* did you do that, eh?'

There was a moment's silence on the other end. I wondered if I'd been too hard on Jill and was about to back-pedal but Jill got in first.

'What was I supposed to do?' she sneered. As if she was blaming me for her own misgivings about our set-up. When she was the one whose feelings had become obsessive.

'My friends were bound to find out *sometime*. I told Miriam *half* the story. And I told her not to tell anyone. You *used* to be an escort. Which means you're not *now*.'

There was relief in Jill's voice, as if she felt that she now had all bases covered. And that she'd let one of her friends know at least some of the truth.

I, on the other hand, was *gobsmacked*. Did she really think that the issue would end there? God, she was so naive.

I was getting ready to go out when a text came through on my BlackBerry. It was Gray, telling me about Sarah in Highgate who had just called and wanted to touch base with me. I checked my watch. I still had an hour before I was due out the door. I phoned her number.

A man answered.

'Oh, hello. May I speak to Sarah? This is Luke.'

There was silence at the other end. '*Luke*, you say? Um, I'll just get her,' he gabbled.

265

I heard the receiver being placed down as he went to get her. I heard him a room away call, '*SARAH! LUKE* wants to speak to you.'

The voice sounded odd from where I was standing, as if he was trying out the names. I shook my head. Something was weird about this situation but I just couldn't work it out.

'*SARAH!*' came to the phone. She muttered, 'Here goes,' and took a deep breath as she picked up the receiver. I guessed I'd caught her at an awkward moment in which it'd be difficult to speak to me because someone else was present.

'Luke?' she queried.

'Hello, Sarah. I'm from the "Satisfaction" website. You called me? It's OK to speak now, isn't it?' I checked.

I couldn't help thinking about that male voice. A flatmate or friend, presumably. Surely not a partner? It didn't sound as though they were a couple who wanted to book me.

She laughed nervously: 'Oh, of course.'

There was silence, as if she was working out what to say next. I filled it for her. 'Would you like me to come and visit, Sarah? I'd be happy to.'

I beamed as I said it, hoping she'd catch my sheer enthusiasm at her end.

'Um. I'd like you to. I think.'

I didn't like that 'think'.

'I mean,' she continued, 'what are your rates? I need to decide what I'm after and get back to you?'

This wasn't new. I understood that a girl might be

nervous about hiring me and so needed to get round to it step by step. Almost to give her permission to do what she really wanted to do with me.

'That's no problem, Sarah. I charge £120 for an hour, and £200 for two hours. Or maybe you'd like me to stay the night?' I hinted.

'No, no,' she blurted as if she didn't want to think about *that*. 'An hour or so should be fine.'

I tried to push things along. 'Is there anything else you'd like to know, Sarah?'

I used Sarah's name as much as possible to stress the personal aspect of my work. To show that I was both a friendly guy but that I'd also be there purely for *her* when the time came.

'Er, how much warning do I have to give if I wanted you to come over?'

I needed to give the impression that she wouldn't have to wait too long while not implying that she was my only client. That I didn't have anything else to do.

'I can't guarantee that I'll be available the same day but a day or so before you'd like me to come over should be no trouble. I like to respond as quickly as possible. Not keep my clients waiting, y'know,' I chuckled, trying to bring some lightness to the conversation.

'Thank you, *Luke*,' she stressed. 'That's been very helpful. I'll get back to you soon. Goodbye.'

'Thank *you* for calling, Sarah. I look forward to hearing from you.'

I wasn't kidding. As far as I was concerned, the more work the better.

I went back to ironing my shirt. Five minutes later, my 'Berry rang again.

Had Sarah already made her mind up? She'd sent a text:

> Luke, this isn't Sarah. It's Christopher and Miriam.
> That's right. JILL's friends. Remember?

Oh fuck.

So they knew. Which meant that if they hadn't yet relayed it to Jill, they soon would. And it couldn't be long before they worked out how she knew me. I didn't need to read on any further. I had a good idea what the rest of the message would say. The trouble was, I couldn't stop myself.

> You tried to kid us that you were a nice guy but you turn out to be ONE FUCKING ARSEHOLE. We KNOW you're cheating on Jill. You FUCKING SCUMBAG WHORE.

I read and reread the message, running my teeth over my top lip.

It certainly wasn't damn worth answering. I wasn't about to justify myself to *them* any time soon. It was Jill I was wondering about – not *worrying* exactly. She'd got herself caught up in this crap in the first place.

I deleted Christopher's message, slipped the mobile back into my back pocket and resumed ironing.

A minute later my BlackBerry jiggered for my attention.

For fuck's sake!

I drew it sharply out of its holster. Jill was calling.

'Luke,' she shrilled like she was out of breath. 'The others told me they'd called you. You didn't answer, did you?'

I was at the end of my tether.

'God, Jill. What do you think?' I snarled.

There was silence on the other end for a moment.

'Shit. Shit. What can we do?'

Jill sounded as if she was talking to herself rather than me, though I was sure tuned in. It was as though she wasn't sure what to do next. Her friends were *so* close to discovering one hell of a truth about her. It could bring her whole make-believe story crashing down around her. It would show her up for the desperate-for-love girl that she was. How *sad* would that be? I'd feel sorry for her if she wasn't digging herself a hole as much for me as for her.

'Well, Jill. They know that I'm an escort.'

That was the bottom line. It wouldn't take much of a step for them to realize that Jill had hired me, surely? But for now, it seemed they were merely at the stage of knowing I was still working as one.

Strangely enough, Jill's mates hadn't made the obvious connection. Maybe that was simply too much for any of them to contemplate. That a dear friend was actually paying for her so-called 'boyfriend'. But then, who would?

'Since they now know you're an escort, why don't you get back to them and tell them that I put you up to it? That you were joking,' Jill suggested.

I had to admire her for *that*. She was sure doing her damnedest to sort out the mess. And it wasn't a bad idea given that there wasn't an awful lot of scope for much else. And the fact that she was fucking desperate to save face.

Let's face it, Jill had to salvage this situation. The gang she went around with had just discovered her boyfriend was a hooker. Which meant that her game was up, whatever happened between us. I certainly wouldn't be wanting to go to any of her dinner parties ever again, in case we ran into her mates. And it was likely that Jill wouldn't want to face such a scenario anyway.

If Jill was about to 'lose' me, then she was also very close to losing her mates if she wasn't careful. There was no way they could find out about her hiring me – that would be the end of everything, surely?

'Yunno, Jill, that's not a bad idea at all,' I gushed. 'And I tell you what, why don't you then tell Christopher and co that *you* put me up to it, that you'd already told me what he was going to do? Does that make sense?'

It didn't make perfect sense, even to me, but the more I talked, the more certain I was that I just wanted out – whichever way that might be.

'Yes, I'll do that,' agreed Jill in an upbeat voice.

She had to, really. For one thing, she was still desperate to please me, to keep me 'hers'. *That sure ain't about to work.* But it wasn't as if she had any other options.

The next thing I heard was that Jill had done exactly that, and so made out that I'd been stringing them along when I told 'Sarah' my rates.

'They believed me!' Jill exclaimed excitedly over the phone.

I couldn't believe how gullible everyone was. But not only that, I'd realized that Jill's friends, in going along with what Jill was telling them, were having to accommodate the fact that they'd gone along with my stringing them along hook, line, and sinker. They were willing to take that on board. That was *dead* generous of them.

'You've got some good friends there, girl,' I stressed.

I was damn sure I would be ducking out of this messed-up girl's life very soon, but Christopher and co were the type of friends who stuck around.

'Yes, I know,' she replied. 'But they're a bit embarrassed that they didn't trust you, you know,' she mused.

Nice to hear.

It was funny. In all Jill's desperation to find herself a guy, she was looking too far afield to realize that she had a group of mates who clearly loved her dearly, who wouldn't think the worst of her. The worst being the unthinkable truth that Jill might feel herself so lonely and adrift without a man by her side that she'd resorted to hiring me. No, it was my very presence that was what was wrong with that picture. There was nothing for me to do but make my excuses and leave the lot of them. Jill included.

Fiona & Co

Final weekend of September

This should have been the life. I was lying on my back in the water and looking up at the mosaic ceiling. And wondering what the hell I was doing here. The muzak pumping around the hotel pool was a muffled tinniness in my submerged ears. I was trying to work out what Suzy and her mates wanted from me. Or wanted me for.

On the surface, I was well aware why I'd accompanied the four girls to Manchester. It was Fiona's hen party weekend, and I'd been invited along for the ride.

How could I possibly refuse?

Suzy, the official 'Party Organizer' had called me a week ago, and since then I'd found myself excited at the thought of how the trip might turn out. I couldn't help thinking about stripper Sasha's hen night with her friends that I had turned down back when I'd only been a short while in this game – and had since so sorely regretted. God, I could still kick myself. That would have been such a blast, I was sure of it.

It was as if Suzy was giving me a second chance to

experience that sort of fun. Booze, a clutch of party girls, and a male escort for the entire weekend. Frankly, it couldn't be anything else but a recipe for some raw sex action – with me in the centre of it all.

I turned over and swam and swam, churning up the water. At the other side of the pool I relaxed on my back again.

What was irking me was that, as far as I was concerned, the party was taking an age to get started. We'd arrived last night and gone to our different rooms; it turned out that later they'd all gone out and left me behind. *What the fuck was that about?*

Of course, if they didn't want me around for any reason that was all there was to it. They *were* paying after all. But even so – I mean, forgetting the hooker? And if there was going to be so little action, then it would have been much better if I'd stayed at home and had some decent 'me' time with Nina, never mind the money.

Jackie and Suzy had looked suitably sheepish when we met over breakfast this morning. And then flattered me into a corner, by telling me that I didn't need any spa treatment. Which was why I was swimming alone this afternoon.

At least the girls weren't regarding me as the gay best friend who would want to do everything they wanted to do. That'd be worse, wouldn't it?

Maybe tonight would be different. There were supposed to be some really good clubs in Manchester. I wasn't a great dancer by any means, but I liked the vibe. And the mass of hot women. Though presumably tonight I'd be on a short leash, but I was sure the four of them would more than make up for it. They were a couple of years younger than me, and in any other circumstances I'd have homed in on fit, fun blondes like them any day of the week.

I turned on to my front and crawled back to the pool's opposite edge, then drew myself out, collected my towel and dried myself off. The girls would have finished their spa treatments by now. It was my job to go and find them and see what I might do for them. If I made myself available for them, then surely they would repay the compliment all the more, later in the day. I could only hope.

'Luke, you're coming with us. Right?' shot Suzy, jangling her room key as she shut the door. The four of them were lined up outside her room and looking my way with huge beckoning smiles.

I nodded: 'You bet!'

The girls were heading to the shops in the city centre and I felt in the mood to join them for the ride. I had some money to spend myself and was keen to see what Manchester had to offer. I'd developed an eye for clothes since doing this job. Let's face it, I had to look the part, whether that meant visiting a wealthy couple's luxury yacht, or blending in at a top hotel. And you never knew, the girls might even treat me. Clients had been known to in the past.

We stepped out of the hotel and crossed Piccadilly Gardens, the sky looking overcast and threatening a downpour. There was already drizzle in the wind. I pulled my jacket tighter around me.

'Y'know, they say it's always raining in Manchester, Luke,' offered Fiona, helpfully.

She waited a beat, and then added a little too archly: 'This is one of its sunny days.'

Which confused me: 'So, why come here for your hen night?'

A look passed between Suzy and Caitlin.

'Because we're not here for the outdoors,' stated Caitlin slowly, as if it was the only way the penny would drop.

We ducked into a coffee shop to get out of the rain, making a beeline for the deep brown leather armchairs in the far corner as Jackie ordered the drinks.

Suzy pulled out a notepad from her bag and with pen poised turned to Fiona. Drunk as the others on the train up here, Suzy was now acting the image of organization. No wonder she'd been picked to sort out this weekend.

'Now, is there a particular shop you want to visit?'

'Shoes.'

The lot of them laughed.

'Er, we guessed that,' shrieked Caitlin. 'Any favourites?'

'I want to start at King Street and work my way upwards!'

The girls all roared.

'I know you're the bride and have cash to spare, but I'd like to begin a bit lower down the scale. Gear myself and my credit card up for the big spend,' admitted Caitlin.

She let her words hang in the air for a couple of

seconds. 'But I'm with you otherwise,' she giggled. 'Shoes. Definitely.'

Jackie had arrived at our table with the tray of coffees. She'd caught the end of the conversation: 'That's it?'

She handed out the drinks to each of us. 'Yup, that's it!' Caitlin, Suzy and Fiona chorused in unison.

Suzy chewed the end of her Biro, then held it out, as if to draw the meeting to a close.

'Right, then,' Suzy laughed, 'we'll work our way through the department stores and the Arndale Centre and stop when we drop.'

I felt excluded. This really *was* girl talk. I noted too that nobody had mentioned what I was there for. And then Suzy turned towards me and ran her hand along my thigh. That was more like it.

'Sorry you have to listen to all this shop talk, Luke. You don't mind, do you?'

'Of course not. You enjoy yourselves. I'm happy to tag along. There's plenty for guys too, isn't there?'

The girls looked at each other but said nothing for a few seconds.

'Yup,' spoke up Caitlin, 'there's plenty for a guy like you to do, Luke!'

Fiona stood up abruptly, her chair scraping across the floor as she did. She was clearly raring to go. 'Right, drink up, everyone. Let's go spend some cash!'

There was a whoop from the others, and they downed the dregs of their coffee and stood up too. I followed them out of the shop.

*   *   *

276

If I hadn't had much idea of what Manchester was like before coming here, apart from knowing it was some northern industrial town, I damn well knew it now. I felt as though I had walked every available metre of its shopping streets. I looked at the girls in front of me tottering on their heels through the Arndale Centre and wondered how the fuck they managed it.

But then, they weren't laden down with bags like I was from all the stores we'd trekked through in the last couple of hours. I took a swift glance around at the glass and the shop fronts and the chain stores. It seemed to go on for miles.

I trailed behind and tried not to look straight ahead, or at least not beyond the gaggle of girls that had brought me here. My shoulders ached, and my fingers were sore from clinging on to the bag handles. I was beginning to wonder when this hen weekend was going to start hotting up for me. Up to now, the girls had been the ones having all the fun.

They had certainly got plenty of kicks by spending their hard-earned. I just felt I'd *got* kicked. I was their shopping slave for the afternoon, carrying their wares. A real donkey. Ironically, the one part of me which I liked to think might bear any resemblance to such a creature seemed to hold no interest for any of them.

Just watching their four asses sashaying in unison in front of me along the walkway, the thought struck me that just maybe these girls weren't as up for things as much as they liked to kid themselves. For all the booze, larging it, and the fact that they'd hired a male escort for the weekend, they weren't in any way going to take real advantage of me being here.

I suppose they'd always be able to tell their mates back home that they'd put money on the table for a guy like me, while leaving it up to those mates' imaginations to fill in the gaps.

The whole setup was way too strange. No other word for it. I was that close to freezing in my tracks right there, whether they noticed or not, dumping the bags, turning my back and just walking away.

What's the fucking point?

But I knew I couldn't, could I? It was damn unprofessional for one thing – even though leaving right here, right now was so damn tempting. And I was still waiting for my money. Suzy could have paid me upfront, but must have known how I might feel about things once I realized how little was wanted of me. Which meant I had no choice but to stick around for the entire weekend, with no sex in sight – however much I felt I was being screwed.

Fiona hovered at the entrance to Dune.

'Yes, please,' she cooed to her mates, as they crowded into the shop and I followed on behind. I slumped down on the nearest white leather cube surrounded by the hordes of bags of clothes, and let the girls get on with their fun. If there was one thing I'd realized from this time, it was that I never wanted to see another shoe as long as I lived.

I watched them as they selected what they wanted to try on. I even shifted along on my cube so that Fiona could squeeze beside me to try on a pair of gold strappy sandals, but I was damned if I was giving up my hard-earned seat for anyone.

I couldn't quite work out who was the mug. Me, for all the hard work I was putting in with apparently no added fun. *Not yet anyhow.* Or the girls themselves for not getting their full money's worth, or their friends back home for believing it all?

'Luke, Luke, what d'you think?'

I blinked hard to bring myself back to the job in hand. Fiona was demanding my full attention. Her hand gripped my shoulder hard to steady herself, as with the other she made sure her foot sat properly in the new shoe. She set her foot down side by side with its pair. I looked down at them. Her nails were cutely polished in a pearly pink and her feet looked healthy and tanned. It crossed my mind that she didn't need shoes.

'What do you think, eh?' she said to the top of my bent head.

For a split second I felt included. I wanted to kiss those feet, actually, though I didn't say. I looked up at her and into her eyes. She had a big friendly smile across her face. She genuinely wanted to know what I, the sole guy, thought. I couldn't help wondering if she'd fancy one last fling with me before she tied herself down.

'Your feet look beautiful. The gold really sets off your tan.'

I thought of the girls on the beaches back home and the way the sand slipped between their toes. *Yeah, beautiful.*

* * *

279

Fiona was dancing in her new shoes. She was holding Suzy's hand and they were doing a jokey, loose-limbed jive-type thing to Girls Aloud. Jackie and Caitlin were bopping along beside them.

I took a slug of beer from its bottle and watched the four girls enjoying themselves from the sidelines. They'd at least invited me out clubbing and paid for my drinks, but it turned out that I was only bag monitor.

'You don't mind looking after our stuff, do you, Luke?' Suzy stated more than asked.

As it happened, Suzy was right. I was past caring. I just knew that there was to be no real playing for me anytime this weekend. I watched the clubbers and the lights meld into one in the semi-darkness of the dance floor. Whichever way I looked at this weekend, the setup was deeply peculiar.

If a groom and his mates hired a girl for a weekend, sex with her would have been top of the agenda. What else was a hooker for? Even in the twenty-first century, some women weren't as up for loose sex as they thought they were. I wasn't altogether sure whether they'd bottled it at the last minute. Or they'd really only hired me to carry their bags – though they could still claim bragging rights with their mates given they'd hired me.

I knocked back the dregs of my beer. Yup, for all this lot's supposed sexual freedom, it was obvious that now they'd got themselves an escort, they hadn't a clue what to do with me. Nor the balls to try and figure it out.

The return on the train to London was subdued, as if the girls had realized that this pre-wedding lark became forced after a while, and that you could only have so much fun before the bride's thoughts turned to her groom – possibly being stitched up elsewhere by his mates. I wondered if I'd have had a better time with them. And there might well have been some female escorts in the mix to add to the fun too.

I surveyed the chairs around me, filled with the girls' shopping bags I'd lugged round the city. They reminded me that I needed to work out how I was going to explain myself to Nina, and my flatmates – if I was going to explain anything.

The girls in my flat knew I was travelling to Manchester, but I'd been cagey about why, and they hadn't really asked. They still didn't know my line of work; I'd taken care not to let that slip. I still wasn't sure whether I could ever let them know that much about me. What with my flatmates, and now Nina, it seemed to be getting increasingly difficult to keep my double life going. I feared that one day I might buckle under the pressure of juggling both worlds. I'd tell them I'd been visiting a distant relative, that was it.

I nestled deeper into my seat and looked at the fields and the green hills out of the train window. It lightened my mood. This was one way of seeing the countryside, anyways. I glanced briefly at the girls. They had no idea what they'd just missed.

And me? Let's face it, I'd had so many hot dates in this line of work. An occasional duck, even being treated as nothing more than a slave, I could live with. It was damn pretty good odds as far as I could see. I'd tick it off as a lesson learnt.

281

I put my key in the front door, shoved it open, and entered the flat, dragging my trolley-bag behind me. It was great to be back.

The telly was on in the living room, and the soft murmur of voices crept through the slit in the door. I let loose my luggage, and went and put my head around the door.

'Honey, I'm home!' I crowed to whichever of the girls happened to be in.

The full quota had turned their heads in my direction, but none of them said anything. It was as if I'd barged in on some secret they were keeping from me. The stiffness of Carrie, Kirstie and Laura's body language gave the game away.

Carrie was the first to speak: 'Hello, Luke.'

Blimey.

It was like *Invasion of the Body Snatchers*, the way she said my name with no emotion.

'Hello, *Carrie*,' I replied in a robot voice, wondering if she'd even get the joke. I coughed, half out of awkwardness, half hoping to bring the three of them back to normality.

'It's good to be back in London. Manchester was an experience, I have to say!'

Laura spoke. Which I wasn't expecting: 'You went to Manchester?'

'Uh huh, visiting distant rellies, you know how it is,' I chattered.

'That must have been *nice*,' she replied.

The words were left hanging in the air.

I hadn't a clue what had got into them, but I wasn't

in the mood for sticking around. My weekend with Fiona and her friends had been enough of an exhausting mind-fuck. I didn't need any more of the same just now, thanks very much.

I took a step back towards the living room door.

'Anyway, I'm due for an early night. I'm bush-whacked,' I chuntered.

'Well,' piped up Kirstie, 'whatever you got up to in Manchester, I'm sure it was satisfactory.'

Satisfactory?

I wasn't about to let on to them what I really got up to up North this weekend. Even I was flummoxed over what had quite happened there. It was certainly 'an experience' but I'm not sure that 'satisfactory' was any way close to describing it.

'Yeah,' I countered, 'I can now tick off Manchester. Been there, done that.'

I took a glance round the three girls. I couldn't help feeling I wasn't wanted round here. It was one thing to know how to be fluent in the language of a woman's body, quite another to fully understand what went on in their heads. Whatever secret they might be covering up, must have been a big one.

'I'll say my "Goodnights" then.'

'Goodnight, Luke,' they chorused.

I shut the door on them, picked up my luggage and went to my bedroom.

Christine plus three

Early October

Christine had jumped in feet first. Or rather, she was letting Sherry do so. Everything was so different from my last session with Christine. Then it was just her and me, and the reason I was there was to deflower her. But things had moved up a gear since then.

Rich and I looked on, except Rich kept throwing a glance at me from his armchair across the room. Not quite believing what he was watching, what he was part of. Two naked girls making out in front of two naked guys, and what's more he was being paid to be there.

I was leaning forward in my own seat, both hands clasped around Christine's right paw. She wanted me to be there. Someone to hold on to while she experimented with the next sexual level.

Christine's other hand was gripping Sherry's shoulder tight as the girls' lips locked together. Their bodies were tight together, and one of Sherry's arms was sandwiched down low between the two of them, her fingers deep into Christine and Sherry riding her own wrist. I yearned to dive right in.

I released one of my hands from Christine's, and lay down beside her on the bed. She was still snogging Sherry but her eyes were following me. I kissed the knuckles of the hand I was still holding, then ran my other hand over Christine's hip and her thigh. Her leg buckled in response to my touch.

I slipped my hand in between the girls so my fingers massaged Christine's right breast and my raised thumb circled, brushing the soft, smooth flesh beneath Sherry's tits. I cradled Christine's neck in my palm and licked it. Her free hand was inching down my torso towards my cock. When she clenched her fingers around it, I almost punctured her throat with my teeth, like a vampire, such was the thrill-bolt she sent through me.

Christine and I were now tonguing while she manhandled me. My eyes were fixed on Rich, inviting him, instructing the novice to join in. Sherry was turned towards him too.

'You know you want to,' she cajoled.

My fingers were both flickering against Christine's clit and slipping as far as they could inside her. Sherry's leg had crossed over the leg of mine that was furthest from her, and her pussy was positioned over me.

'My turn, Christine,' she mouthed, and the ex-virgin took the hint and drew her hand away from my hard dick. Sherry pulled herself onto me.

Sherry gripped my waist in both hands and rode me hard. Christine's whole body shifted on the bed to face Rich, tempting him to join her. He was standing next to the bed, plucking up the courage to plunge right in.

I was lying back, just soaking up the pleasure, letting Sherry take complete control of me. My dick was enjoying every second of it.

I looked up at Rich. 'C'mon mate. She's all yours,' I indicated towards Christine.

I understood his nervousness. I thought back to that night in the club earlier in the year when Rich had caught me out on the town with my client Heather. He'd been shocked when I'd later let on to him what my work involved, but he was also damn intrigued – like most guys would've been. And since then, whenever I'd bumped into him, he'd always ask how the escort work was going.

When Christine had asked me to find her another guy for a session, Rich was the guy I thought of to fill that gap. I'd be calling his bluff, seeing if he was really as up for it as he assumed he would be, but I'd also be watching out for him. I knew what it was to be a novice too, after all. I recalled being in exactly the same position as he was now, back when I was watching Chloe and Sasha, not knowing quite what to do. There was a point in group sex where joining in made perfect sense. I trusted that Rich would seize that moment.

Christine took it upon herself to grab it for him. There was *so* much boldness in that girl that had been stifled during the years of saying 'No' to all-comers. She was clearly keen to make up for lost time. By hiring us three she'd proved herself more daring than many of my regular customers. There was nothing vanilla about *her*, that was for sure. I sort of wondered how she squared it all with her God.

'Rich, come here,' she purred.

That got his full attention. It was as if it woke him up from his own dream world.

A massive smile filled his face. He couldn't believe his *fucking* luck.

If there had been space enough on the bed, I swear he'd have dived right on top of her, but instead he took it a bit more graciously, slipping beside her as he clothed his already-hard cock.

Christine spread her legs for him and he shagged her. Afterwards they lay tangled together, Rich now on his back and Christine lying against him. He was looking at me, grinning from ear to ear. I'd never seen any of my friends having sex before, nor they me. I didn't want to think too much about what it would be like when Rich and I met again. Hopefully, this was an experience we'd be able to laugh about over a drink.

Meanwhile, I lay back against the pillow, my hands behind my neck and elbows sticking upwards with casual pride as Sherry went down on me. God, this was the life.

I turned to Rich. Christine was licking his nipple. I smirked at him.

'Welcome to my world, mate.'

We couldn't stop laughing.

We were saying our goodbyes.

I hugged Christine. 'So glad I could help you out. *Again.*'

She returned a smile that flooded her whole face. 'I really enjoyed myself, thanks.'

She turned to Rich who was standing a step behind me, bashfully.

'It was lovely to meet you,' she beamed. She kissed him forcefully on the lips.

Fast worker.

For a split second, Rich looked taken aback. In spite of his new experience and sharing in the pleasure of this evening, he was only dipping his toe in the escort water. I wasn't sure if he'd want to do it again, but it was an experience he could definitely tick off. One that plenty of other guys who thought themselves cool never got anywhere close to.

Sherry was hovering beside Christine.

'You going home too?' I asked her out of politeness more than any real need to know.

Christine slipped an acquisitive arm around Sherry's waist. 'Oh, she's staying with me for a little while longer. Aren't you?'

I looked from one to the other. Sherry held her head up high, a knowing smile across her face.

Good on you, girl!

It struck me as pretty impressive too how Christine had chewed off her cherry. From no sex at all to a foursome in two sessions was pretty hot work by anybody's standards. I could only wonder where she'd go from here.

Rich and I were standing next to my scooter. I'd just paid him his share for tonight, and we were chatting before we went our separate ways.

'So, you had a good time tonight, then?'

'You bet!' Rich enthused.

He still couldn't believe his luck. A foursome!

He looked at me out of the corners of his eyes. 'Y'know, Simon never told me what you got up to. I'd have seen you in a completely different light had I known!'

I looked down at my feet and kicked away a pebble. 'I had to be so careful, back then,' I admitted. 'So did my mates. They knew full well, but you never know how people are going to react once they find out.'

I thought of Christine inside her flat this very minute, having sex with Sherry.

'Y'know Christine? The last time I saw her she was a virgin. Now look at her!'

Rich shook his head from side to side: 'Really?'

'I *know*.' I laughed. 'Christine the Christian. I doubt she's going to let on to her church friends what she's been up to any time soon!'

Rich turned to look back at Christine's place. Imagining, as I'd just done, what she and Sherry were getting up to in that bedroom.

'Aren't there laws against that?' he joked.

I nodded: 'That's *exactly* my point. As I said, "Welcome to my world". Whichever end of it you are, you can't be too careful who you let on to.'

The meaning of my words wasn't lost on Rich. As much as he might have been bursting to tell his mates about tonight's *sex*perience, he'd have to take real care. It could blow some people's minds.

I decided to let on to him about Haley's porn video.

'I tell you what, a foursome isn't the half of it.'

Rich's eyes widened. He wanted to hear about this.

'Oh yeah,' I shrugged, as if what I was telling him was the most natural thing in the world. 'I helped out with a sex tape for Sherry's friend, Haley. It's up on the Net as we speak.'

Rich's jaw dropped: 'Fuck me. You didn't?!'

I raised my eyebrows in an 'Oh yes my friend' gesture.

Rich was looking at me but not saying anything. His silence puzzled me – I'd expected him to be impressed.

'What?'

'Bloody hell, Luke. You don't know when to stop, do you?'

He said it with no emotion. Like he was *telling* me.

'What do you mean?'

'Oh, come on,' he sneered. 'I mean, being an escort is one thing. I'm certainly not going to judge you over that. How could I, after the great time I've just had?' He nodded towards Christine's place: 'I mean, fair game, mate.'

That was dead generous of him. Not. Because I knew exactly what he was going to say next.

'But porn movies? That's a completely different ball game.'

'Literally,' I grinned, trying to lighten his mood.

He wasn't biting.

'Nope, it's not something to laugh about. It's *porn* for God's sake!'

And?

'And your point is?'

He shook his head. 'Oh come on. Do I really have to spell it out? Don't you see? You're getting in far too deep,' he pleaded.

290

I appreciated his concern.

'I can handle myself. Don't worry about me, Rich,' I lobbed back.

'Where's it going to end, though? Everyone knows the porn industry is full of scuzzy people. Why the hell would you want to have anything to do with the likes of *them*?' he spat.

My hands were gripped around the scooter's handle-bars and I focused on them as I shifted my knuckles up and down in front of me. I spoke as calmly as I could to get my point across whilst holding in my boiling anger.

'I know what you're saying. But it's not how it looks. Haley's a friend of Sherry's. That's how we met. When we were all doing a job.'

I thought of Aidan and bit my tongue to prevent myself spilling anything more about that *particular* session.

'And it stops there, does it? You're not going to do it any more.'

I coughed: 'She and the director liked what I did. They like my attitude. They said there'd be more work if I wanted it. And the money's not bad either. I didn't say "yes". I'm thinking about it.'

Rich placed his hand on my arm. 'Well then,' he said in a quiet and measured way, 'I rest my case.'

I heard what Rich was saying; I could see where he was coming from. It's how most people regarded the porn business. I'd been a fool to tell him, then, hadn't I?

I stepped on to my scooter and turned on the key.

'Look, thanks for your concern. But I do know what I'm doing, y'know.'

He took a step away from my scooter to let me turn so I was facing out of the drive. 'Yeah, well . . . Take care though, eh?'

There wasn't much else either of us could say.

'See you around,' I waved as I scooted off home, though I wasn't sure I would.

My BlackBerry rang while I was nearing my flat. I waited until I'd parked my bike, and then drew it out of my pocket to check who'd called. It had been Jill. I was about to return it to my pocket when it rang a second time. I checked who was calling. It was Jill. *Again.*

I put on my best smiley escort voice. 'Hello, Jill? How can I help you?'

I wasn't about to suggest we meet up any time soon. I'd had my fill of the mind-fuck that our regular sessions and her incessant whingey calls were turning into.

'Hello, Luke,' she said, and it wasn't in the friendly manner I expected from her. Something was up. I let her speak on.

'I just thought you should know. I went to my doctor, and I'm pregnant.'

What the fuck?

I took a deep breath to steady myself, and bit back. 'Why are you telling me this? After all, it couldn't possibly be mine.'

I wasn't kidding. I was damn sure I had *nothing* to do with it. She was having me on.

'No, Luke, it's definitely yours,' she replied, as though she was talking to a small child.

I bristled. Her fantasy that I was her boyfriend had gone way too far this time. There was nothing for me to do but to spell out the truth to her. Once and for all.

'Well it can't be, can it? Because for one thing, during the *few times* we had sex' – I rubbed it in – 'we always used condoms . . .'

'Condoms can fail,' she sulked back.

'You're right there,' I agreed, 'but that might count for something if in those times we had sex I'd actually had an orgasm. And I didn't.'

There was silence at the end of the line. That'd stunned her.

'That's just not true,' she whined, *so* wanting it to be so.

'I'm a bloody good faker, Jill,' I threw back, not caring one bit how that might sound to her. I'd had it up to here with her manipulation. 'And so are you, aren't you? There's no pregnancy. You're lying to me, Jill,' I sneered.

'I'm not, I'm not,' she wailed.

I couldn't be bothered. I flicked my 'Berry off. However much money Jill had paid me over the months, it *hadn't* been worth it.

I was glad of a quiet night in. My head was still spinning from the spat with Jill a couple of hours ago, but a can of beer and *Match of the Day* on the box helped calm me down. The girls were out for the evening so I splayed myself across the sofa and indulged myself. A boy's night in. It made a pleasant change from wheeling myself across London to some chick's flat for the sex and the money. It was a great, lucrative way to make a living, but sometimes I needed a break to recharge my batteries and get my feet back on the ground.

My mobile rang. I pulled it out of my jeans and flicked it open. Nina. Just her name was a relief. A sweet break from the hassle I'd got tonight both from Rich and then Jill.

'Hey, gorgeous!' I beamed.

There was an audible sneer from the other end. My shoulders tensed.

'Don't you "gorgeous" me, you fucking bastard,' snarled my girlfriend.

She knows.

The thought whistled through my head. I could see no other explanation for Nina's anger. I was about to reply.

'Did you honestly think I'd never find out, you lowlife shit?'

I could smell alcohol on her breath in the tone she was using. This was a completely new experience. I'd never heard Nina in such a temper before. I could hear shouting and traffic in the background, as if she'd just fallen out of the pub and wanted to have a pop at me. Sure, Nina was angry, but it was fuelled by drink. This wasn't the girl I knew at all. But then again, she'd thought she had some idea of who *I* was.

'Find out what, Nina?'

I wanted her to spell it out, to tell me everything she now knew about me.

'That you're a fucking *whore*,' she spat, with all the venom she could muster. 'Kirstie told me.'

294

Kirstie? How'd she know? When . . . ?

'You make out that you're my boyfriend, that I can trust you and care about you, and all the time you're fucking other women. *For money.*'

Yup, she'd got the measure of me. And I'd been right not to have told her. My hunch that she wouldn't be able to take it had just been proven right. I wasn't sure what to say, though.

'It was different with you,' I stressed.

'Fuck, you really know how to flatter a girl, don't you?' she mocked. 'Do you honestly think that's going to impress me? That you treat me better than one of your *punters*? You haven't a fucking clue, have you?'

There didn't seem to be anything else I could say that'd make Nina feel any different. I admitted defeat. 'I'm sorry,' I said.

'And you think that makes it fucking all right, do you? Stop kidding yourself.'

The phone went dead. Nina had ended the call. She might well have slammed down the phone or flung her mobile across the room. I felt numb all the same and sat staring at the footie on the telly, even though I wasn't registering any of the action on the screen. I accepted that from where Nina was standing I had definitely done wrong by her. I supposed she was right, but her reaction had still stunned me.

I was lounging back on the sofa half asleep, the telly burring away, until the sound of a key in the door shook me fully awake. I straightened myself on the sofa, finished the dregs of my beer and threw the can at the wastepaper basket.

Kirstie put her head round the door. My hackles shot up.

'Oh, I thought I'd find you here, I saw the light under the door.'

She pushed it fully ajar. Standing behind her was Nina, glaring at me, her arms by her sides, her fists clenching and unclenching as if she was doing all she could to control her raging fury.

I jumped up to greet her, confused. 'Nina!'

I threw a 'what's she doing here?' frown at Kirstie. My head was still ringing from Nina's outburst. I also couldn't work out how Kirstie had found out about me – but that would have to wait.

'Nina wanted to speak to you.'

She turned to the woman behind her with a pointed stare: 'You didn't want to leave seeing Luke another minute, did you?'

Nina shook her head slowly from side to side.

'I'll leave you two to it,' Kirstie pronounced bluntly. 'If you need anything, just call.' She left the room.

I pursed my lips and stepped forward. 'It's good of you to come round to talk things through.'

I reached out, without thinking, to touch Nina's shoulder. She forced my arm away with a shove.

'You just don't get it, do you? You really think the crap you're involved with is that easy for me to forgive and forget? Fuck off, Luke,' she spat, and took a swipe at me with her clawed fingers.

I went to grab her wrist but she thumped me with her other fist.

296

'Calm down,' I begged her. 'Listen, we can talk about this.'

'*Talk*, you fucker? *Listen*? Don't make me laugh,' she seethed.

Nina took another swing at me and her punch sank into my upper arm.

Bloody hell!

The girl sure knew how to use her fists. Yet I wasn't in the habit of hitting women and I wasn't about to start now. Whatever Nina threw at me, I would be man enough to take. I'd fared worse in fights with guys back home in Australia.

I made a lunge for Nina and gripped both her arms, pinning them against her sides. That only served to frustrate her more. She struggled and swung her head, knocking hard against my jaw with a blow that sent my own head spinning. She followed that with a bite down on my shoulder at the base of my neck.

'Fuck, Nina!' I screamed.

I drew my hands away from her in shock to instinctively cover the gash with my hand, and in her anger she lashed out again at my bent head, breaking the skin of my forehead with those sharp nails of hers.

'Fucking hell!'

I covered my face with my arms. Nina picked up whatever came to hand, throwing magazines and cushions at me. She frisbeed a photo in a frame. I ducked just in time and it hit the wall behind me with a clatter and fell to the floor. Fortunately only its metal frame was dented.

I bent down to pick it up to put it out of harm's way

and Nina came charging towards me, her fists hard-pummelling my chest. She was roaring and shrieking. Tears of fury and hurt were streaming down her face.

'Nina!' I screamed, my hands on her shoulders, forcing her away.

Kirstie, with Carrie coming up fast behind, burst through the door and tried to pull us apart.

'Just get out, Luke. Leave her alone.'

What the . . . ?

It was Nina who was laying in to *me*, but that didn't wash with Kirstie *at all*. All she could see was her good friend mad with pain over her shit boyfriend. *Me.*

'Get out, for God's sake! Get out!'

Cassie grabbed at my arm and attempted to drag me out of the room. But any fight I might have had in me had fled. I simply wasn't wanted round here. Kirstie wrapped her arms around Nina and Nina collapsed sobbing in her arms. Kirstie gave me a hard stare over Nina's cowed head. 'Fuck off,' she mouthed.

I went into the hall and Carrie followed to make sure I wasn't sticking around. Laura was standing in the kitchen doorway. She didn't say anything, but glared at me and shook her head. Carrie pulled the front door open and shoved me through, then slammed it behind me.

That was it, then. Thrown out. Nina had violently dumped me. My day job had been found out. My flatmates had turfed me out. *This* was the worst-case scenario.

It wasn't just the fact of it, though. I sure felt sore

inside. It was as if I'd just been shown what being an escort *really* meant for the first time. It might have brought me plenty of money and sex, but it came wrapped in the stress of trying to live a double life. And now the wraps had come off, there was a whole heap of disdain and humiliation dumped on me from the people I cared about the most.

I racked my brains for what to do next. If only Mark and Simon and the lads weren't on the other side of the world. They'd have been on my side. But Gray was the only good friend I could think of to go to, even though I'd never seen his place before. I hadn't a clue where else I could turn.

Gray's place

The following day

'Gray, are you in there? Open up, will you?' I shouted.

I was banging away hard at Gray's front door. The clatter of the knocker rang out in the quiet early morning darkness. But I didn't give a fuck about his neighbours. I just wanted Gray to let me in.

I took a step back and looked up at the upstairs window. The bedroom light flicked on.

Thank God!

I pushed open the letterbox again and called out his name, even as I could see his pyjama-ed legs rushing down the stairs in front of me.

'It's Luke, Gray.'

He flung open the door, but not before he'd given me a belly-full directed at the bit of me he could see through the slot in the door. 'Fuck! Have you any idea what time it is? This had better be good.'

But as soon as he fully caught sight of me in the lamplight, he stopped dead in his tracks. 'Bloody hell! The Mark of Cain. What the fuck happened to you?'

I reached for the gash in the middle of my forehead where Nina had torn me with her nails. There was blood on my fingertips.

'Nina.' That was explanation enough.

Gray gripped my arm and pulled me into his house, shutting the door behind me. 'She's a real goer, ain't she?' he all but laughed, and then stopped himself.

'I've been thrown out,' I moaned. 'The Girls, they're her friends. I've nowhere to stay . . .'

He got my meaning. 'Come in. No worries. You can sleep on the couch.'

He switched on the front room light and ushered me in. 'Sit down. I'll put the kettle on.'

He left me, and I collapsed on to the sofa. I heard him rushing up the stairs.

I hadn't seen Gray's place before. There were piles of books, and a computer on a large table surrounded by loads of paperwork. Gray darted back into the room, brandishing a green box.

'Have a look through this. That cut needs something on it.' He handed me the first-aid box.

'Nothing in there I'm afraid for broken hearts.'

'It ain't broke. Don't need fixing, mate,' I flicked back in self-defence.

I'd taken Nina's angry attack on me as a matter of course. I mean, it wasn't as if I hadn't deserved it, was it?

'I didn't mean *you*,' he stressed. 'Nina's. The damage she's done to you? That's how much it's hurting *her* etched on your body.'

He headed out to the kitchen to make our drinks. And left me thinking about what he'd just said.

He was right, of course. What Gray had just said cut me to the quick. God, I'd really *hurt* Nina, hadn't I? There was an aching emptiness in my gut. I'd really blown my chances with her.

I opened the box and had a dig around. I wasn't up to covering myself in plasters. It was more my pride that had been wounded. Mind you, Nina had left her fair share of bruises and even bite marks on my upper body. Not that I was going to tell Gray that. Nor was I going to let on how my heart was sinking. He didn't need to know the entire extent of the damage she'd done to me.

I pulled a tube of Savlon out of the box and closed the lid and set the box beside me on the sofa. I was squeezing a dab onto my fingertip when Gray returned to the room with a couple of steaming mugs of tea.

'Just what I need,' I sighed.

'You can't beat tea in a crisis. It's what runs this country!' he jested.

'I'm learning that,' I winced while I spread the antiseptic across my forehead.

He set the mug down on the coffee table in front of me.

'Oh, and Savlon. That's a cure-all.'

'I hope so,' I moaned.

Gray sat down in a chair opposite me, his elbows on his knees, holding his mug in both hands. His eyes were fixed on me. He pursed his lips.

'She found out what you do, then?'

I rubbed at my bruised arms. 'What do you think?'

He nodded in sympathy. 'I'm sorry, mate, I really am.'

'Thanks, I appreciate that.'

I picked up my mug of tea. Gray was right. God, it tasted good.

Neither of us said anything for a few minutes while we drank our tea. I was still stunned by how this evening had gone – from a hot foursome, to Nina scrapping the shit out of me, and everything in between. And now it was looking as if I might be on the brink of being thrown out of the flat for good.

It was as if life was speeding up too quickly. Rich had been right, then. Porn or not, I was getting in far too deep.

'I don't know if I can do this any more,' I whined.

'Nina doesn't want you to, you mean?'

'What do you think?' I corrected myself. 'No, it's not just what I've got, *had* going with Nina. The escort work, the stalkers – I've just being accused of getting a client pregnant – it's all getting a bit too much. This wasn't what I got into it for.'

Gray's eyes were like saucers. 'Pregnant! You didn't?'

I shook my head, though at this precise moment that was the least of my worries. I just hadn't believed Jill, whatever she'd been telling me. It wasn't simply male pride. Making her pregnant didn't add up. I'd been too damn careful on every level.

'I don't see how it's possible. Do you remember Jill? Stalker material. I didn't even *come* with her.'

Gray roared with laughter. I was glad someone could see the funny side.

'Fuck, Luke, you *are* up to your neck in it!!'

I looked at him laughing away. It was as if he'd

switched a light on. That reminded me. I had something to tell him too.

'Oh, before I forget,' I said, putting the Savlon back in the box and closing the lid, 'd'you remember how I told you I'd get you some escort work?'

He looked at me sideways: 'Yea-ah?'

'There's a couple I go to? Eva and Lars? I won't be able to make my session with them? Would you go for me?'

Gray's mouth dropped open. 'God, Luke, you'd do that for me? I thought you were kidding.'

So had I, up to a point. But things had changed. My heart wasn't in my escort work any more. I sighed deeply. 'I need a break, y'know?'

I touched my forehead and checked my fingertips again. The wound was sore but at least it wasn't bleeding any more.

'It's more than that. This Nina shit. It's made me think about closing down the "Satisfaction" site,' I admitted.

A wave of disappointment swept across Gray's face. 'Really?'

'I know how much you enjoy helping me out, but I don't think I can carry on this lark for much longer. It's doing my head in,' I admitted. It was a relief just to get the words out, to at last be able to say what I'd been increasingly been realizing.

Gray nodded, deep in thought. 'Sure, you're right. I *do* get a kick from doing the site, but let's face it, this is your game at the end of the day. Not mine.'

'Thanks, Gray, for being so understanding. I've appreciated your help. I couldn't have got so far without you, you know that?'

That was one weight off my mind anyhow – that Gray remained on my side even if he wouldn't be working with me any more. But knowing that didn't stop me from still wanting to explain myself.

'The thing is, I'm sort of hoping that if I wind down the escort business, Nina might have it in her to get back with me. After all, that's why she's called things off.'

Gray didn't look convinced. 'That cut on your forehead. She sure meant business. Are you *certain* she'd want to get back with you even if you weren't on the game any more?'

Gray had a point.

'I dunno,' I sighed, looking down at my nails. 'You could be right.' I put on a brave face: 'But I can only hope, eh?'

A night on Gray's sofa certainly did the trick. He woke me up with a mug of hot coffee. I peeled back the duvet and raised myself on to my elbow, and took the drink with a 'Thanks'.

'You slept all right?'

'Yeah, I did. It was just what I needed, to be honest.'

It was as if Gray had given me a cocooned space, away from the flat and therefore all my worries. The girls' disfavour, Nina's red-hot anger, the whole escorting business . . .

'I'm glad I could be of help.'

'Yeah, you have been. I don't know what I'd have done without you, y'know. Ended up on a park bench or something,' I smiled.

He shook his head: 'Uh, huh. Not while you're a mate

305

of mine, you won't. You do know that, even if we close down the site, the invitation remains open.'

'Yeah, I know.'

'Like the *next* time you have a quarrel with the girls,' he winked.

I shook my head a couple of times but there was a smirk on my face. 'And the offer remains open for you to go out to Eva and Lars. Don't worry, I'll let them know you're coming.'

'Thanks.'

'I just don't think I can do this any more. It's my way of winding things down. Passing the job on to a good mate, y'know.'

I finished off my coffee, and climbed off the sofa. 'Anyway, I've got to get back to the flat. Face the music.'

'Well, if they're not ready for you, you know where to come.'

'Thanks,' I nodded, 'I'll bear that in mind.'

And I meant it. If there was one good thing that came out of escorting, it was my friendship with Gray. He'd been there practically from the start. I wasn't going to forget that in a hurry.

I'd decided to get the return to the flat over with as soon as possible. Like getting back on a horse after a fall. Or driving a car when you'd just crashed it. I wasn't about to think too deeply what might be waiting for me. Heap-loads of girl-wrath. But at the same time, this was the only way to deal with the shit I'd caused. And maybe Nina would be calmer after a good night's sleep too. We needed to talk to each other and clear the air.

As I said, I could only hope.

My phone rang as I was putting my bike helmet on. I pulled it off again sharpish so I could hear Nina speaking.

She sounded in a good mood. 'Good morning, Luke.'

I could see us back on an even keel again. The thought made my heart feel warm. She didn't give me a chance to reply.

'I've managed to sleep last night off,' she said.

That sounded promising.

'Yeah,' she continued. 'I've been thinking.'

'So have I, Neen,' I butted in.

She said nothing for a moment, collecting herself. 'Well, no doubt you'll have come to exactly the same conclusion as me.' She stopped as if for effect. 'Yeah, I've decided that things are going nowhere. Things can't be the same again. They just can't.'

What?

'I'm letting you go, Luke.'

The phone went dead. She'd ended the call. *Again.*

Jane

I was at a loose end.

God, wasn't I?

I'd lost Nina. That was the bottom line. I'd tried the dating game and solidly blown it. Hadn't I suspected that the escort life and having a girlfriend were incompatible? If only because most people just didn't get it. Expecting someone, who thought of you as something special in their life, to be content with you selling sex was too much to ask.

Part of me couldn't help wondering if going out with Nina might even have been a way for me to prove how much a relationship *wouldn't* work. I shook that thought out of my head. Anyhow, what did the whys and wherefores matter?

I needed to go for a walk. I didn't tell anyone. I didn't expect the Girls to care what I was up to. My name was mud as far as they were concerned. It was bad enough me working as an escort. That was a big shock when they found out *that*.

To be honest it had made me laugh, thinking of them fooling around on the Net and, out of curiosity, checking out London Male Escorts. Laura had let on that they'd clicked on the 'Satisfaction' site and found me there! Suddenly, their whole idea of who they had sharing their flat had shifted completely. Just because of that one mouse click. She told me that when I'd come in that evening, they hadn't had a clue what to say to me.

I understood their shock, though, and their feeling that Nina needed to be warned about me. Some of her violence stemmed from her trying to deal with her hurt at the truth of how I made my living.

That was something I'd sure given a lot of thought to since she'd left me. Thank God Gray was on my side. I'd be even more in the shit if it weren't for him. I was back at the flat, though keeping a very low profile, but if it ever got too troubled between me and the Girls again, I knew I could always go and stay with him.

I was standing beside my scooter in the car park. I hadn't meant to go for a spin, but my legs had unconsciously brought me here. I'd blow the cobwebs and the worry out of my head. And try and decide what to do with myself now I was cutting down on the escort work. At least I'd built up a decent amount of money to fall back on. Not that I wanted to dig too deep into it. I still planned on taking a wad of it with me to Aus to cushion my new start there.

I turned right out of the estate and put my foot down as far as the speed limit allowed me. I had no idea where I was heading, but that was part of the scoot's attraction. *No worries.* I mean, how lost could anyone really get on London's roads?

I was trolling along the local high street when a hand shot up from a girl on the pavement. 'Luke!' she yelled.

I couldn't for the life of me remember what *her* name was, though she looked vaguely familiar. I racked my brain as I slowed my bike to a halt beside her.

She must have recognized my confusion. 'Luke? You probably don't remember me. I'm Jane. I used to go out with Simon?'

Now, I placed her. I clicked my fingers.

'New Year's Eve!'

That was over a year and a half ago. Simon hadn't been much better at relationships than I was, but at least he made it to the three-month mark. He cut and ran at the point where girls started getting serious, whereas I shivered at the mere thought.

'That seems ages ago,' she smiled. 'I thought you'd be back home by now?'

I shook my head: 'Uh, uh, I still had work to do. And my visa's still got some miles on it.'

Jane's hands were in her coat pockets and she was scuffing her feet on the pavement. She was a low-maintenance girl. Fresh looking, with loose, shoulder-length hair, and dressed in jeans and ankle boots as though it didn't take any time at all.

'Do you fancy going for a coffee?' she asked.

It wasn't as if I had anything else going on. It would be nice to while away an hour or so chatting about old times, when London life didn't seem half so confusing and complicated as it was now.

'I'd like that,' I agreed.

I parked my scoot and we headed to the nearest chain coffee shop. We bought our drinks and collapsed in the red leather armchairs by the shop window so we had a clear view of the world going by.

'You still hear from Simon, or any of your Aussie friends?'

'Mark, you remember Mark? He was my closest mate, The emails have been getting fewer and fewer. You know how it is. Mind you,' I shrugged ruefully, 'it's not as if I'm any better.'

I drank some of my coffee and looked out of the window. The streetlights had just come on and were still warming up.

'Simon ever get in touch with you?' I asked, though I sort of already knew the answer.

She chuckled. 'What do you think? We only dated for a couple of months, y'know.'

There was an easy-come, easy-go air about her.

'It was nice while it lasted, though, eh?'

She nodded, smiling to herself as she looked down at her coffee, then upped her head assertively at me. 'Yeah, it was.'

'S'funny,' I laughed, recalling Simon and the lads and the times we'd had, 'he was always calling me "Stud".'

'I remember that!' she guffawed. 'I was torn between fearing you didn't have anybody, that he was being ironic . . .'

I raised an eyebrow. *Excuse me, do I LOOK like I can't draw the girls?* But then I thought of Nina and the crap I'd brought to that situation, which meant that

311

Jane was part right. That I didn't really have anyone, couldn't keep anyone in the conventional sense. At the end of the day, for all the sex and the people I met as a gigolo, I could see it could end up a lonely life.

'. . . and wondering whether you *really* were a stud. That you'd sleep with any girl with a pulse!'

Only if they pay me enough, hon.

I cocked my head, and put on my best Scottish accent. 'The namesch Bond. Jamesch Bond.'

We both cracked up.

I'd got her laughing, which was always a shortcut to my next move.

'You fancy going *somewhere*?' I suggested, making the most of my escort skills, even though they were otherwise redundant.

A knowing smile flickered across Jane's face. She ran a finger across her lower lip from one end to the other. *Very* seductive.

'Would you like to come back to my place?' she whispered.

I nodded *very* slowly in reply.

We both stood up from the deep leather chairs. I took her hand in mine and we left the coffee shop.

Jane and I were lying side by side in her double bed. If I smoked, I'd have had a cigarette in my mouth at this point. I was staring at her ceiling while Jane snuggled close to me, hugging my right arm to her.

My entire body felt relaxed, released of all the tension that had built up in it since Nina and I had had our spat. Meeting Jane had definitely been good for me.

It was as if Fate had given me a bit of a break. For a change.

The two of us were lounging, not worrying about how the afternoon would pan out but happy to remain in bed when my 'Berry kicked up a stink.

Fuck, just what I need.

I was tempted to remain beside Jane, except the bell kept ringing. As if whoever was calling me was desperate to speak to me.

'Sorry, but I'm going to have to get that.'

Jane released my arm grudgingly. I was back in Escortland, being called at the most inappropriate moments.

I rifled in my jeans pocket and pulled out my BlackBerry. I was taken aback by the name spelt out. It read 'Jill'.

What the fuck does she want me for?

I'd made it clear, hadn't I, that I wasn't responsible for getting her pregnant? Couldn't she tell that I wanted nothing more to do with her? God, I'd been so blunt with her, anyone else surely would have crawled away out of shame. But not Jill.

I slipped out of Jane's bedroom, indicating to her with a wave of my mobile that I had to take the call. She was fine with that.

'Jill, what are you calling me for?'

I spoke deadpan, with no enthusiasm. I had a look around Jane's hall as I spoke.

'Guess what, Luke,' Jill babbled, 'I'm not pregnant after all. It was a false alarm!'

Surprise fucking surprise.

'You can't imagine what a relief that was,' she gabbled on.

'Of course it was a false alarm,' I sneered. 'I never expected it to be anything else.'

I still couldn't believe how mean-spirited that had been of Jill, to try and tie me up with the oldest trick in the book.

'That was a real bitch of a thing to dump on a guy, you know that, don't you, Jill?'

'I didn't mean to cause any trouble, Luke. I really did think I was pregnant by you,' she whined.

Jill wasn't worth arguing the toss with.

'Well, you weren't, and I had nothing to do with any of it. Get this into your skull, Jill, I don't want to hear from you again. I'll be blocking your calls from now on. Goodbye.'

I didn't wait for her to reply. I flicked off my 'Berry. That was it with her.

I re-entered Jane's room, once again feeling laden down with the stress Jill had just thrown at me. Jane was propped against a pillow with a welcoming smile on her face. God, it was *so* tempting to join her for another hour or so and shag away all the ill-feeling Jill had stirred up.

But Jill had also set me off thinking about Nina again. The ex-fake-girlfriend client had reminded me of my real-life ex. Whom I was still deeply missing when I allowed myself to think about it. Jane had just been a distraction. Though I wasn't about to tell her that.

I picked up my clothes and padded across to Jane's side of the bed. I kissed her on the forehead.

314

'I'm afraid I'm going to have to go. Something's cropped up. It's been a lovely afternoon, Jane.'

I dressed and let myself out. For all her wrong-headedness about being pregnant and all the rest of it, Jill, unbeknownst to her, had just done me a huge favour. She'd brought home again the confusion and hassle that surrounded being a hooker. And in that she'd reminded me of someone who had offered the complete opposite. Jill had set me off feeling sore, again, but I couldn't help thanking her too for showing me who was really important in my life – it was still Nina.

Whether she wanted me back or not.

Nina & Luke

Almost Hallowe'en

I was pushing open the door to my block just as Kirstie and Nina were coming out. I hadn't been expecting *that*.

Kirstie threw me a frown as she barged past. We had barely been on speaking terms since the Big Bust-Up, even though it had little to do with her, and, anyhow, I'd been keeping a *very* low profile. But Kirstie felt sort of protective towards Nina, I think because she'd invited Nina to our flat party in the first place. And if she hadn't done *that*, then Nina wouldn't ever have met Luke the Shit.

Nina, it turned out, wasn't singing from the same song-sheet. 'Hello!' she exclaimed, before she remembered herself and soured again.

'I didn't expect to see you here,' I told her. 'But, look, I'm sorry. I fouled up. I don't know what else I can say,' I spluttered, very aware that in a minute or two I'd have lost my chance.

Nina's hand was on the door handle, and she was

hovering as if she was torn between following Kirstie or stopping to talk to me.

Kirstie wasn't having any of it: 'C'mon, Neen, we need to go.'

Everyone knew she was saying that she didn't want Nina to have anything to do with me ever again.

Nina stretched away from the door. 'You just getting back from one of your "dates"?'

It was if she was finding something to say, just anything to keep talking.

'*Sessions*,' I laughed. 'And, no, I'm not. I'm not doing . . . *it* any more. It's too much trouble, it's not worth it, y'know.'

I felt bashful then. I only hoped Nina could see that I was genuine. That I *had* put my escort life behind me.

I looked over at Kirstie who was impatiently fuming. I jerked my head in her direction. 'You're wanted,' I said. 'Don't keep her hanging on.'

'No,' she agreed. 'You are too, y'know . . . Wanted, I mean,' she stuttered, then frowned to herself. 'We need to talk. I'd like to talk.'

She headed towards Kirstie but turned her head. 'Call me,' she mouthed, making that thumb and finger symbol.

I flitted up the stairs towards the flat with a grin across my face. Nina was giving me another chance.

Nina was sitting at a pavement table outside Costa Coffee in Dean Street, where we had arranged to meet for lunch. Nina worked nearby. The weather was mild for this time of year and there were plenty of people milling around Soho's streets.

I saw her before she saw me and I approached her from behind. 'Nina! Lovely to see you,' I greeted, placing a hand on her shoulder.

Nina turned her face upwards and I bent and kissed her full on the lips. Like old times. I pulled a chair out from under the table and sat down close to her. It felt right. To me, anyhow.

'You ordered anything?'

'Not yet,' she admitted. 'I was waiting for you to turn up.'

I checked my watch. I was on time. But I felt nervous just being here. I feared that I'd already put my foot in it by arriving later than her; that she might have been having a dig. But I was bang on time, and she hadn't been. Which suggested that maybe she was as nervous as me at this minute.

We ordered our lunch.

'There's a real buzz around here,' I pointed out for something to say.

'Yeah,' she agreed, chuckling to herself as if she knew exactly what I was doing. As if she could figure out my moves. 'I couldn't imagine working anywhere else now.'

I threw a glance across the road. There was a euphemistic sign for a 'Model' directing clients up a staircase between two shops. One of the stores was called 'Dirty White Boy'.

Oh fuck.

If Nina needed any reminding of who she was sitting

next to, those signs were bloody well spelling it out. They might as well have been pointing directly at me. Not that I was about to point that out to her. I could only hope she didn't make the connection.

Our ciabattas and cappuccinos arrived. I dug in heartily, as if eating fast would draw attention away from the obvious truth about Soho that was staring us in the face. That among the media haunts where Nina made her living, it was a place where sex and money danced hand in hand.

I felt I had to say something.

'Nina, I'm so glad that we've managed to meet up again. I'm so sorry for all the hurt I caused you. I want you to know that *that*'s' – I couldn't bring myself to use the word 'escort' in front of her – 'all in the past. That fight we had – it made me realize what I'd lost. You're too important to me.'

Nina let me say my piece while she remained silent. My 'Berry burred in my pocket. I wasn't about to check who was calling and spoil the moment. Whoever it was, they could wait.

Nina set down her lunch, and stretched her hand across the table to tenderly brush my wrist. 'Don't let's talk about that,' she said.

It sounded as if she was just as embarrassed by the physical damage she'd dished out to me as I was for the emotional hurt I'd caused her.

'I'd like us to give it another go,' she declared very quietly, as if she was hoping against hope that we could start afresh. Again.

'I'd like that,' I replied.

A few minutes later, having finished her ciabatta, Nina jumped up.

'I just need to visit the Ladies,' she explained.

'No problem.'

She was gone in a flash. I remembered my BlackBerry and the call someone had just made. I drew it out of my pocket, and gave it a covert glance beneath the table.

Lars!

Gray was a lovely guy but the two of us still prefer your visits, ha ha. Sometime soon, eh?

That made me smile. Of course I'd known they'd be able to tell the difference between an amateur and yours truly.

I am SO good!

Nina was back standing beside me. I hid the gizmo. She stroked my hair, and sat down.

'I'll have to be going in a couple of minutes. No rest for the wicked, eh?' She drained her cup of coffee in one gulp.

'But you take it easy. Don't feel you have to finish off lunch on account of me,' she smiled.

Nina stood up to go, so I did too to kiss her 'goodbye'. She gave me a hug.

'I'm so glad we had lunch together, Luke. See you soon, eh?'

'Definitely,' I laughed.

She slipped out of my arms and I watched her head round the corner into Old Compton Street, past Dirty

White Boy and towards Wardour Street where she worked.

When she was out of sight I sat down again, and pulled out my BlackBerry and reread Lars's message. He had been so good to me, it would be rude not to answer. But some other time.

Read on for an extract from
Luke Bradbury's debut book, UNDERCOVER

All in a day's work

For fuck's sake, how much longer? Ring the bell, you bastard!

There's me and this gorgeous girl at it on the floor. Carrie or Emily or something, I can't remember her name. It's a bit of a blur by number six. It's not as if she isn't good at what she does. She's been hired, after all, same as me. So she knows all the moves and is fit to boot. It's just I don't know how much longer I can keep it up. Literally.

I'm trying my hardest. And both of us are into our stride. Hammer and tongs, wearing the creaking floor away. It's like we're swimming together in our sweat, our damp bodies sawing against each other. We're barely coming up for air, and a strand of her long blonde hair is in my mouth, and everything else is drowned out except for our panting, heavy breathing and thumping heartbeats.

And all I yearn for is the tiny silver jingle of the bell, held between Brian's index finger and thumb. He's silent. Watching us.

When he finally shakes it, satisfied, both of us

collapse, dead spent. As we catch our breath, Brian comes out from behind the curtain and tosses us both bathrobes. I help the girl to her feet, my arm around her narrow shoulders.

'You okay?'

'Yeah,' she mouths through a half-smile, catching her breath. She's pretty. She must be about twenty-three. Same as me.

'Luke, you stay here a while,' Brian instructs, tightening the belt of his dressing gown. 'Emma, come with me.'

Emma. That was it.

Brian guides her out of the room. I look at her go, her bare legs glistening.

As they leave the room, Emma turns to me. 'Nice meeting you, Luke. See you again, maybe.'

'You too, Emma.'

Maybe.

I stand there, waiting. A short while later, the front door slams shut, and I head to the bathroom and wash Emma off my skin. The warm jet of water is like a curtain between her and the next one.

Is that it for tonight?

I step out of the shower and dry myself down and wrap myself in the bathrobe again. I like the feel of its softness against me. I'm still tying it up when I enter Brian's lounge again. He pulls his armchair out from behind the curtain and sits low down in it, his legs stretched out before him. He raises his beer bottle to me.

'Cheers!'

'Bloody hell, Brian, I thought you were never going to ring that damn thing!'

'I thought you enjoyed sex,' he teases.

I sit down in the other armchair across the room, and pick up the open bottle that's been sitting there since before Emma arrived.

'Up to a point. It's easy for you. You don't have to put the effort in.'

'Guys your age are supposed to be gagging for it!' he smirks.

I lift the beer bottle to my lips and knock some back before answering.

'Well, yeah,' I laugh, 'but even so. That doesn't mean I don't need to come up for air!'

My muscles silently scream in agreement.

With Brian, I gave as good as I got. We'd built up a rapport since I'd started working for him. Let's face it, we'd had to. Because although he hired both me and some girls, we weren't all there on an equal footing. Because Brian was a voyeur. Which, I suppose, made me his Tester.

Brian had once hired me as many as twelve girls in one night. He would call me early evening and we'd have a drink together, and then he'd phone for a girl for me. And the bell was his method of communication, of control. If he wanted the sex to stop, he'd ring the bell. It might be after twenty minutes, it might be after five. She'd go, I'd stay, have another break, and then Brian would phone the agency for someone else for me. And a quarter of an hour later there'd be another girl on the doorstep.

Brian never joined in. All he wanted to do was hide behind the curtain and watch. And whatever else he got up to back there. Everyone gets their kicks some way. Sometimes the sex went on for so long that, like with Emma, I was willing that damn bell to ring. You can have too much of a good thing . . .

Still, I couldn't quite believe I was getting paid to do this. My mates would be up of a morning to go to work in offices, schools and cafés, whereas I could lie in bed all day or do whatever I wanted to. Until the evening. When I might have sex with five different girls Brian had selected for me. And earn in that night what my mates would in a week. It was almost too good to be true.

Brian was looking at me. His beer bottle was empty. Mine was still half full and held in mid-air on the way to my mouth. I could tell what he was going to say. He was pushing back the armchair with his bare feet even though he was still sitting in it, even as he was opening his mouth to speak. He held his mobile in the other hand. He'd put the agency number on speed dial so it took no time at all.

'Right, Luke,' he said with a wolfish leer. 'Get ready for number seven.'

Beginnings

Early August

'We've been shafted, the bastards!'

Mark spat the words out across the kitchen table. He'd just shown me his bank statement, and the evidence was there in bright red. I looked down into my mug of tea and nodded. I knew what he meant. But the truth was, we well and truly hadn't been. *That* was the problem.

'Meet loads of girls. You'll be sent out on six dates a week, and make £90 an hour . . .'

That was what the freesheet ad for the internet escort agency had promised us – and no doubt hundreds of other guys like Mark and me. Guys with too much male pride and not quite enough money to live on, who just assumed there would be women falling at our feet, and who were mugs enough to fork out £180 to register.

But in the three weeks since the two of us had coughed up our money, not one girl had called for Mark's services. Nor mine.

I took a sip of my tea and looked across at Mark.

It wasn't even as if either of us was that bad-looking. Not that I'd ever admit I was *good*-looking. You got a clip for that in my family, for puffing yourself up. I'd been told that I looked a bit like the *Spiderman* actor, Tobey Maguire. Which was good enough for me. I was six foot tall with dark blond hair that bleached easily in the sun back home in Australia, while Mark's hair was brown and he was slightly shorter than me. We worked out. Both of us had a reasonable Saturday-night success rate.

Mark shook his head. 'This is London, for God's sake. Where are all the girls?' He took a digestive from the packet upended on the table and bit into it. He had a right to ask. It wasn't as if we hadn't seen enough of them falling over each other on any of our weekends out on the piss.

'Not choosing to call out for a guy, presumably. That's what blokes do.'

I could see the callbox windows in my mind's eye, completely covered from floor to ceiling with brightly coloured 'whorecards'. Blocking out the muted sunlight. That'd been my introduction to England nine weeks ago, dialling my mum to let her know I'd got here in one piece.

'We can get a number for a girl from any phone box. But they can't . . .' I was working out the problem with our plan as I was saying it.

'But that's what the internet's for!' Mark spluttered, spraying crumbs. He swept them off the table with his forearm.

I ran a finger along the edge of the pine tabletop

330

until it hit a dent in the wood. I drew my nail again and again through the groove and looked Mark in the eye.

'Yeah, but they're not looking because they're not even aware that there's a service for them. They take their chances on a Saturday night.'

Mark nodded: 'Or go without.'

'Exactly. And even if they knew there were guys they could pay for via their PCs, that doesn't mean they'd do anything about it.'

I picked up my mug and took another gulp of tea, and thought of the callbox again and all the sex phone-line ads in the freesheets that I'd seen when I was trying to find somewhere to live. That'd been a grim time, sleeping on friends of friends' grimy floors while all the while I could sense they didn't really want me there. Sharing a room with Mark in this house for the past month had been a damn sight better than *that*, even with the beer cans clustered on the floor round the bin from when we hadn't thrown straight. He'd been looking for someone to make up the rent and I'd seen his ad on Gumtree. It'd helped that the two of us had hit it off as soon as we'd met over a drink. Same small-town Aussie background, I suppose.

'I mean, have *you* ever phoned for a hooker?' I raised my eyebrows at him as I said it.

He shook his head. 'Course not. As if I need to . . .' he crowed.

I put my mug down. 'Well then.'

And that's when it hit me. *What had we been thinking?* There was not even a market for sex with straight guys.

Or not one that involved money changing hands. On the girl's part anyhow.

'They've well and truly buggered us, haven't they?' I sighed.

A grin crept up Mark's face. 'Thankfully not. And that's something to be damn grateful for.'

We both laughed, but it couldn't disguise the fact that each of us was seriously out of pocket. We'd taken a gamble on making easy money and lost.

'Well, at least we can't be the only ones who've fallen for this scam,' said Mark. 'Think about it. There must be hordes of guys across London,' he continued, flinging his arm out as if to embrace the whole city and not just our poxy kitchen in a crappy area of West London, 'just like us, weeping into their tea at what might have been!'

I sighed. Surely it was the ultimate part-time job. Screwing girls for cash. We could have waved goodbye to the crummy minimum-wage waiting and bar jobs and selling stuffed pittas while hung over from a stall at Camden Market for friends of friends who always paid shit money. God, London certainly hadn't turned out to be all it was cracked up to be.

I looked down at my half-full mug and felt the cogs whirring even as he was saying it.

'Well then, that's how we make our money back, isn't it?' I suggested.

'What?'

'Look, there's clearly enough money out there to make it worthwhile setting up an agency that gets guys to pay to sign on.'

Mark's face momentarily fell. 'What, and rip people off just the way we were? Come on.'

Miserably, I nodded. 'I agree it's not exactly ethical.' I thought for a moment. 'But then it's not exactly *not*. What if we *were* to set up an agency, y'know, advertise our services to women, and ask guys to sign on? The blokes cough up, and of course we'll give them work if there's enough going, but we'll always have first call. What *is* wrong with that? We can't lose.'

Mark cocked his head to one side and shook it. But he was also smiling. 'God, Luke. A couple of months in this country and you've turned into a London spiv!'

I smirked back. He raised his mug to mine and we chinked.

My mind was already in overdrive. We'd advertise in the London freesheets. We could do it cheaply, surely. Advertise for clients, and put something on the internet to draw in the men as well. And photos. Me, Mark and the lads, to give the girls something to choose from.

'Face it, Mark. We're broke. We might as well make a go of it. We've got nothing more to lose.'

I suppose I expected it to happen overnight. But of course it didn't. And when it didn't, it meant it didn't seem real. It was just mates mucking about. Even after I'd spent fifty quid I couldn't really afford on a box ad in a London magazine; even after we'd put a whole lot of our pictures up on the net. Seven of us had spent an afternoon taking photos of each other, all of us with a big grin on our faces in front of the drawn curtains in our lounge room so it looked like we'd hired a studio or something. So we were able to still kid ourselves that we were only having a laugh.

But we weren't, were we?

Or, as it turned out, I wasn't.

The phone rang. Mark and I were lounging on the sofa with our cans of Stella and having our last-night debrief. We looked at each other for a beat, and since he didn't get up, I did and sauntered across the room.

'Hi?'

'Male Escorts Esquire? I saw your advert.'

Shit!

I pulled up a chair and sat down, half out of shock. The name we'd come up with wasn't the greatest, but it had clearly done its job. I struggled to get my head into gear. She was the first to call – though I wasn't about to let her know that, of course.

'Hello, how might we help you?'

What have we got ourselves into?

'Uh, I've never done this before,' she mumbled. 'I was wondering if you might be able to send me someone tomorrow evening?'

What was I thinking? *I can't do this. This isn't for me.* That was why I'd volunteered my phone number in the first place, so I could act the receptionist and palm off anyone who rang onto one of the others.

It was one thing to fantasize about girls phoning you for sex, it was quite another to be faced with the sheer reality of going with whoever happened to ask. Suppose she sounded better than she turned out to look? What did you do then?

This one wasn't too young – I could tell by the tone of her voice – and she was clearly nervous.

Join the club.

I sat up straight on the dining chair and went into professional mode.

'Is there anyone on the website you liked the look of? Sorry, your name is –?'

Mark's ears pricked up. He stared across the room at me with excited saucer eyes and a smirk. I shook my head as a sign to him to ease up, and tried to focus on what was being said to me.

'Jenny,' she replied. 'I don't have a computer.'

Ah, definitely an older woman. Okaay.

'Nice to talk to you, Jenny, I'm Luke. That's not a problem. What would you like him to look like? We have a range of young men on our books.'

Mark stifled a guffaw and I shot a glare at him.

'I'm not – I'm not sure,' she stuttered.

So, she was indecisive. That wasn't a problem either. All I had to do was make sure she was satisfied with the service. She didn't sound as if she could cope with someone too bullish, like Simon, our resident rugby player. She needed a gentleman who wouldn't frighten her off.

'You sound nice.' She laughed nervously. 'Are you available?'

Fuck!

'Thank you, Jenny, but, sorry, I'm not.' I tried to sound calm and friendly though I felt out of my depth. 'I tell you what, though, I'll make sure you have a pleasant surprise.'

335

I took down her details and we said goodbye to each other.

As I put down the receiver, Mark started clapping.

'Congratulations. You've just nailed our very first client!'

'Yeah, and now we've got to decide which of us'll have her. Will you go?'

I sat down beside him, and picked up my can from the floor.

'What's she like?'

'She sounded old enough to be my mother.'

Mark grimaced.

I laughed. 'You've just discounted Madonna.'

'Er, yeah.'

'All angles and humourless. Fair point,' I agreed. 'Hang on, I know who.' I got up again and returned to the phone.

'What? Who?' quizzed Mark.

I pressed the buttons and put the receiver to my ear, leaning against the wall. 'Rob, of course. He's always game on. For one thing, he could do with the cash.'

'Well, yeah,' shrugged Mark. 'He could always do with the cash. Isn't that his problem?'

Rob had never quite got the hang of money, especially since his bank seemed so keen to give him more of it whenever he wanted. Except they had now decided to call in the debt. The magic had fallen out of the plastic.

Come on, Rob, I prayed. *Pick up, pick up.*

He eventually picked up.

'Hey, Rob. It's Luke. How'd you like to make a fast

336

buck? We've had a client call for an escort and your name came up.'

Flatter the guy.

Across the room, one of Mark's eyebrows arched up. Rob was up for it too. I could sense his excitement down the line.

'I tell you what. As this is your first time, forget about the commission and just come back and tell me all about it and buy me a beer.'

I took a swig from my own can, and set it down on the seat of the chair beside me. I couldn't help noticing that, across the room, both of Mark's eyebrows were now up his forehead. The sense of that anger was a distraction even as I gave Rob the details. I ended the call, and confronted him.

'What?'

'How's the business supposed to survive if nobody puts any money in the pot?' he steamed as I sat back down.

'Aw, I know, but if you can't help out a mate, eh? Anyhow, it *is* our first ever call – not that Rob knows that. It won't happen again.'

We sat in silence and drank our beer. Then Mark grinned, his spirits obviously lifting.

'God, Luke, we're officially launched. Can you believe it?'

I smiled and nodded. We high-fived.

Rob called after I'd finished at the café the following evening and was putting together my dinner. I could hear pub clatter in the background and hoped he wasn't soaking up too much Dutch courage before his assignment.

'Luke, I'm not sure about this. I don't know if I can go through with it.'

Don't get cold feet on me, Rob.

'Don't worry about it. Think of it like any other date. You meet, have a drink, you go back to her place . . .'

I picked at the peeling wallpaper around the phone. A previous tenant had used the plaster to jot down numbers that I sometimes wondered if I should call just for the hell of it.

'Yeah, but I *fancy* my dates,' Rob flung back. 'What if I don't fancy her?'

'Well, that's where the dosh comes in. Just think about the money!'

I thought of nervous Jenny wanting someone who'd treat her well, who wouldn't ride roughshod over her. *No, it wasn't just about the money.*

'Look, Rob, everyone gets nervous their first time. Of course they do. She'll be just as anxious. Take it easy.'

A slither of wallpaper came away in my hand, and I let it fall to the floor.

'Did you get nervous, Luke? What was it like?'

I gulped. He had no idea he was the first of any of us to test out our escort scheme.

I evaded the question. On the carpet beneath the phone was a growing pile of peelings that needed a good vacuum. If we'd had a vacuum cleaner.

'It's different for everyone. You've got to go out there and make your own mark. Be every woman's dream!'

338

'Yeah, right,' said Rob, not sounding at all confident.

'You know what to do, of course you do. You're used to scoring, yeah? Just be a bit more of a gentleman when you go about it.' On second thoughts: 'Unless of course she requests otherwise.'

There was a chuckle on the other end of the line. That was better.

'Okay, okay.'

'Don't worry. You'll be fine,' I reassured him. 'Just be careful you don't drink too much beforehand. You want to make a good impression.'

'Will do.'

'And I want to hear all about it afterwards. Now, go forth and enjoy yourself.'

When he called back around ten thirty, Rob was clearly back in the pub. He sounded as if he'd won the Lottery.

'Easiest hundred and fifty quid I ever fucking made,' he shouted over the bar hubbub.

'Told you you'd be fine,' I laughed, caught up in his high spirits.

'Nah, you'll never believe it. She didn't want to go through with it.'

'No!' I was gobsmacked.

'You bet. We met at Dunkin Donuts, like you said. Off Piccadilly. And it lasted about forty minutes and we just had a cup of coffee. And that was it. We never even reached the hotel. And she still paid me!'

The jammy bastard.

'If it's that fucking easy, send me out to every woman you get,' he burbled.

'If it's that fucking easy, Rob, I'll keep them all to myself.'

Jenny called the following week. The only call we received. We weren't about to make a living out of this game just yet. Nor escape my shifts at the café and the pub anytime soon.

'Hello, Luke, it's Jenny.'

My mind went blank for a second. *Jenny?* I'd been so rushed off my feet with the waiting this week I'd almost forgotten about our advert. But then it all flooded back, and I went into receptionist mode straight away.

'Hello, Jenny, it's lovely to hear from you. Rob told me he enjoyed meeting you last week.'

Didn't he just.

'He was very nice.'

'See, I told you I'd give you a pleasant surprise,' I boasted.

'Yes, thank you. Um . . .'

There was an awkward silence. I jumped in feet first. This was a business we were running, after all.

'Is there anything we can do for you? Perhaps you'd like to see him again?'

When she spoke next, her voice was halting and quiet:

'The thing is, Luke, I'd like to meet you.'

You fucking bet. Rob's just made one hundred and fifty quid. Count me in.

'Is that allowed?'

This time I was ready. But first I had to cover myself

so Jenny didn't start wondering why the last time she called I was just the receptionist.

'Well, Jenny, as it happens, we do have a policy when there's a run on the boys.' *Like heck we do.* 'We'd hate to leave any of our clients waiting.'

'So we can meet?' There was a hopeful girlishness to her voice.

'Certainly, Jenny.'

I began mentally spending the money on some decent jeans, a couple of CDs, and putting something towards the phone bill. The calls back home cost a bomb. And she'd even be paying for the coffee!

'Oh, I'm so glad. Because this time I want to go through with it. I want you to make love to me, Luke.'

There was a screech of brakes in my head.

Just my fucking luck.

'When would you like me to visit? And if I could take your address,' I asked, through gritted teeth I hoped she couldn't detect.

I scribbled down her details, said goodbye and hung up.

Yep, we were officially launched, Mark. Well and truly fucking launched . . .

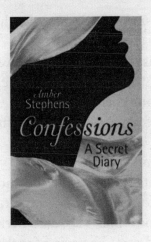

CONFESSIONS: A SECRET DIARY
AMBER STEPHENS

"My name is Shelley… and I'm a sex addict."

Shelley Matthews is married to her job. Which is just as well, as
she hasn't had sex for over a year. But when her editor decides
a re-vamp of the magazine is needed, Shelley is forced to go
undercover – as a sex addict.

Attending therapy sessions, Shelley hears the intimate
confessions of a whole host of extraordinary characters.
Including Cian, a pop band pin-up who is enjoying all the
trappings of fame.

Can Shelley keep her secret from the others as well as writing the
story of the year? And most importantly can she keep her cool –
and chastity – intact? And does she really want to?

Find out more at www.mischiefbooks.com

ISBN: 978-0-00747-971-9

GAME – JUSTINE ELYOT

The stakes are high, the game is on.

In this sequel to Justine Elyot's bestselling *On Demand*, Sophie discovers a whole new world of daring sexual exploits.

Sophie's sexual tastes have always been a bit on the wild side – something her boyfriend Lloyd has always loved about her.

But Sophie gives Lloyd every part of her body except her heart. To win all of her, Lloyd challenges Sophie to live out her secret fantasies.

As the game intensifies, she experiments with all kinds of kinks and fetishes in a bid to understand what she really wants. But Lloyd feature in her final decision? Or will the ultimate risk he takes drive her away from him?

Find out more at www.mischiefbooks.com

ISBN: 978-0-00-747775-3